# THE PROFESSIONAL NETWORKER'S PLAYBOOK

## JOE MILLER, JR.

Illustrations by Godfrey J. Ellis, PhD

Copyright © 2024 Joe Miller, Jr.

All rights reserved. No part of this book may be reproduced, stored, or transmitted by any means—whether auditory, graphic, mechanical, or electronic—without written permission of both publisher and author, except in the case of brief excerpts used in critical articles and reviews. Unauthorized reproduction of any part of this work is illegal and is punishable by law.

# CONTENTS

Preface . . . . . . . . . . . . . . . . . . . . . . . . . . . . . . . . . . . . . . . . . . . . ix
Why Networking: An Introduction. . . . . . . . . . . . . . . . . . . . . . . xiii

## PART 1: FOUNDATIONS FOR PROFESSIONAL NETWORKING

### Chapter 1: What is Professional Networking?. . . . . . . . . . . . . . . . . . . . . 1
Nets, Networks, and Networking. . . . . . . . . . . . . . . . . . . . . . . . . 1
Introducing the Power Formula. . . . . . . . . . . . . . . . . . . . . . . . . 3
    Breaking Down the Formula . . . . . . . . . . . . . . . . . . . . . . . 3
    The Multiplicative Power of Referrals. . . . . . . . . . . . . . . . . 4
    Applying the Formula. . . . . . . . . . . . . . . . . . . . . . . . . . . . 4
    Why This Formula Matters. . . . . . . . . . . . . . . . . . . . . . . . . 4
Sharing Referrals Through a Network . . . . . . . . . . . . . . . . . . . 4
Generating Referrals from Your Network. . . . . . . . . . . . . . . . . 7
Related but Different Activities . . . . . . . . . . . . . . . . . . . . . . . . 8
    Is Using Social Media Networking?. . . . . . . . . . . . . . . . . . . 9
    Difference Between Selling and Networking . . . . . . . . . . . .10

### Chapter 2: Mindsets for Networking Success . . . . . . . . . . . . . . . . . . . 13
Service Through Sales . . . . . . . . . . . . . . . . . . . . . . . . . . . . . . .15
Confidence That You Will Succeed. . . . . . . . . . . . . . . . . . . . .17
    Programming from the Past. . . . . . . . . . . . . . . . . . . . . . . .17
    Zap Collars and Pachyderm Strings. . . . . . . . . . . . . . . . . . .18
Networking 7-7-7. . . . . . . . . . . . . . . . . . . . . . . . . . . . . . . . . . 20
Abundance not Scarcity . . . . . . . . . . . . . . . . . . . . . . . . . . . . . 22

## Chapter 3: The Liberation of The Rule of 12 . . . . . . . . . . . . . . . . . . . 25
12% Love You; 12% Hate You . . . . . . . . . . . . . . . . . . . . . . . . . . . . . .25
The 76%ers in the Middle . . . . . . . . . . . . . . . . . . . . . . . . . . . . . . . . 29
    Work With, But Don't Focus on, 76%ers . . . . . . . . . . . . . . . . . . . 29
    The Miracle of the Ripple Effect . . . . . . . . . . . . . . . . . . . . . . . . .31
The Incredible Potential of the Rule of 12 . . . . . . . . . . . . . . . . . . . .33
    Fun Examples from Literature . . . . . . . . . . . . . . . . . . . . . . . . . .33
    Percentages and Numbers. . . . . . . . . . . . . . . . . . . . . . . . . . . . . 36

# PART 2: A FORMULA FOR POWER IN PROFESSIONAL NETWORKING

## Chapter 4: The Power of a Professional Network . . . . . . . . . . . . . . . . 41
Networking Power to Find Help . . . . . . . . . . . . . . . . . . . . . . . . . . .41
    Getting Help from the First Tier . . . . . . . . . . . . . . . . . . . . . . . . 42
    Getting Help from the Second Tier. . . . . . . . . . . . . . . . . . . . . . . 44
Gratitude as a Boost to Network Power. . . . . . . . . . . . . . . . . . . . . .45
Power of a Network: The Park-n-Ride Fiasco . . . . . . . . . . . . . . . . . .47

## Chapter 5: Creating Contacts for a Professional Network . . . . . . . . . 51
The Elevator Speech: A Power Play . . . . . . . . . . . . . . . . . . . . . . . . .52
    The Five Steps of an Elevator Speech . . . . . . . . . . . . . . . . . . . . . 54
    Possible Responses You May Receive . . . . . . . . . . . . . . . . . . . . . 56
Remember Your Contact's Name . . . . . . . . . . . . . . . . . . . . . . . . . . 58
    Get the Name Exactly Right . . . . . . . . . . . . . . . . . . . . . . . . . . .59
    Three Times to Practice; Four to Lock . . . . . . . . . . . . . . . . . . . . 60

## Chapter 6: Nurturing Your Professional Network . . . . . . . . . . . . . . . 63
Nurturing Through Service and Referrals . . . . . . . . . . . . . . . . . . . .63
    The Story of James Davidson . . . . . . . . . . . . . . . . . . . . . . . . . . 64
Nurturing Through PIQs. . . . . . . . . . . . . . . . . . . . . . . . . . . . . . . .67
    1. A PIQ as a Get Acquainted Session. . . . . . . . . . . . . . . . . . . . .67
    2. A PIQ to Provide Information . . . . . . . . . . . . . . . . . . . . . . .71

## Chapter 7: Smart and Relevant Referrals . . . . . . . . . . . . . . . . . . . . . 77
Three Characteristics of Relevant Referrals. . . . . . . . . . . . . . . . . . .78
    1. The RR is Clear and Specific. . . . . . . . . . . . . . . . . . . . . . . . .78

2. The RR is Direct and Bold. . . . . . . . . . . . . . . . . . . . . . . . . . . . . 79
3. The RR is Personal and Complete . . . . . . . . . . . . . . . . . . . . . . 79
Power by Connecting Through Referrals . . . . . . . . . . . . . . . . . . . . . 82
Tier One: Brianna's Story of Woe. . . . . . . . . . . . . . . . . . . . . . . . 82
Tier Two: Escalating to the Prez . . . . . . . . . . . . . . . . . . . . . . . . 84
The Story of Tanya Hanson. . . . . . . . . . . . . . . . . . . . . . . . . . . .85

# PART 3: CHOOSING A PROFESSIONAL NETWORKING GROUP

## Chapter 8: Four Types of Networking Groups . . . . . . . . . . . . . . . . . 91
One: Your First Network . . . . . . . . . . . . . . . . . . . . . . . . . . . . . . . . .91
    The Family: Your First and Best Network . . . . . . . . . . . . . . . . .91
    Extend Out to Your Extended Family. . . . . . . . . . . . . . . . . . . .93
Two: Casual Social Networking Groups . . . . . . . . . . . . . . . . . . . . . 94
    Types of Casual Social Networks . . . . . . . . . . . . . . . . . . . . . . 94
    Social Media Networks . . . . . . . . . . . . . . . . . . . . . . . . . . . . . 96
Three: Informal Networking Situations. . . . . . . . . . . . . . . . . . . . . . 96
Four: Formal Networking Groups . . . . . . . . . . . . . . . . . . . . . . . . . 97
    What's in a Name? . . . . . . . . . . . . . . . . . . . . . . . . . . . . . . . . 98
    The BRING! Philosophy . . . . . . . . . . . . . . . . . . . . . . . . . . . . 99
    The BRING! Prototype . . . . . . . . . . . . . . . . . . . . . . . . . . . . 99
    Understanding the Four Types of Networking Groups . . . . . . . 100

## Chapter 9: Consider the Logistics of a Networking Group . . . . . . . . . . . . . . . 101
Membership Policies of the Group . . . . . . . . . . . . . . . . . . . . . . . . 102
Assess the Costs of Membership . . . . . . . . . . . . . . . . . . . . . . . . . 104
    Do Cheap Fees = Cheap Quality?. . . . . . . . . . . . . . . . . . . . . . 104
    Non-Monetary Costs – Figure Profit/Loss . . . . . . . . . . . . . . . 105
Factor in the Numerical Size of the Group . . . . . . . . . . . . . . . . . . 106
Consider Geography and Scheduling . . . . . . . . . . . . . . . . . . . . . . 106
Member's Perceived Value as a Barometer. . . . . . . . . . . . . . . . . . 107

## Chapter 10: Assess the Tone of a Networking Group . . . . . . . . . . . . . . 109
The Personality Style of the Leaders . . . . . . . . . . . . . . . . . . . . . . 109
The Professionalism of the Group . . . . . . . . . . . . . . . . . . . . . . . . 110

    Put the Agenda on Your Agenda . . . . . . . . . . . . . . . . . . . . . . . . 111

    Dress and Speech Can Reveal a Lot. . . . . . . . . . . . . . . . . . . . . . . 112

    Are Members Self- or Other-Oriented? . . . . . . . . . . . . . . . . . . . . 113

Opportunities for Weekly Presentations . . . . . . . . . . . . . . . . . . . . . . 114

Education and Other Trainings. . . . . . . . . . . . . . . . . . . . . . . . . . . . 115

Putting it Together to Assess Fit . . . . . . . . . . . . . . . . . . . . . . . . . . 116

## Chapter 11: Joining a Group as a New "Brought" . . . . . . . . . . . . . . 119

Definition of a "Brought". . . . . . . . . . . . . . . . . . . . . . . . . . . . . . . . 119

Tip #1: Don't Forget Your Tools . . . . . . . . . . . . . . . . . . . . . . . . . . 120

Tip #2: Expect to Meet People . . . . . . . . . . . . . . . . . . . . . . . . . . 123

    Sell Through, Not to . . . . . . . . . . . . . . . . . . . . . . . . . . . . . . . 123

    Wait, There's a Professional Handshake? . . . . . . . . . . . . . . . . . . 124

    Wait, Where Do I Sit? . . . . . . . . . . . . . . . . . . . . . . . . . . . . . . 126

Tip #3: Dress with Impact . . . . . . . . . . . . . . . . . . . . . . . . . . . . . 127

Tip #4: Speak with Impact . . . . . . . . . . . . . . . . . . . . . . . . . . . . 130

    Five Speech Habits You Can Abandon . . . . . . . . . . . . . . . . . . . . 131

BRING! Members: Invite Broughts for Sociability & Credibility . . . . . . . . 136

# PART 4: THE POWER PLAY OF "STICKY" COMMERCIALS

## Chapter 12: Sticky Commercials: The Concept . . . . . . . . . . . . . . . 141

Just What is a "Sticky" Commercial? . . . . . . . . . . . . . . . . . . . . . . . 142

The Curse of Knowledge . . . . . . . . . . . . . . . . . . . . . . . . . . . . . . 144

    Type 1: Industry Jargon . . . . . . . . . . . . . . . . . . . . . . . . . . . . . 145

    Type 2: You Forget What You Didn't Know . . . . . . . . . . . . . . . . 146

Be Specifically Specific . . . . . . . . . . . . . . . . . . . . . . . . . . . . . . . 147

Sell Through... Not To. . . . . . . . . . . . . . . . . . . . . . . . . . . . . . . . 149

    The Power of Selling Through... Not To . . . . . . . . . . . . . . . . . . 149

    How to Distinguish Selling Through... from Selling To . . . . . . . . . . 150

## Chapter 13: Sticky Commercials: The Content . . . . . . . . . . . . . . . 153

The Power Play of a Good Story . . . . . . . . . . . . . . . . . . . . . . . . . 153

The Power Play of Catchy Taglines . . . . . . . . . . . . . . . . . . . . . . . 156

    Catch a Catchy Tagline . . . . . . . . . . . . . . . . . . . . . . . . . . . . . 157

    Get Creative – The Sky's the Limit . . . . . . . . . . . . . . . . . . . . . . 159

    The Power Play of Memory Hooks . . . . . . . . . . . . . . . . . . . . . . . . . . . . . . 160
        Verbal Memory Hooks . . . . . . . . . . . . . . . . . . . . . . . . . . . . . . . . 161
        Visual Memory Hooks . . . . . . . . . . . . . . . . . . . . . . . . . . . . . . . 161
        Give-Aways as Memory Hooks . . . . . . . . . . . . . . . . . . . . . . . . . 162
    Practice Plan A and Prepare Plan B . . . . . . . . . . . . . . . . . . . . . . . . . . 164

## Chapter 14: Sticky Commercials: Presentation Style . . . . . . . . . . . . . 167
Style Tips for a Sticky Commercial . . . . . . . . . . . . . . . . . . . . . . . . . . . . . . 167
    Cultivate Enthusiasm and Confidence . . . . . . . . . . . . . . . . . . . . . . . 167
    Stand, Smile, Speak with Boldness and Clarity . . . . . . . . . . . . . . . . 168
Tic Toc, Time Your Commercial . . . . . . . . . . . . . . . . . . . . . . . . . . . . . . 174
    Time Your Commercial to the Second . . . . . . . . . . . . . . . . . . . . . . 174
    Locate Your Commercial in the Agenda . . . . . . . . . . . . . . . . . . . . 175
The Power Play of Practice . . . . . . . . . . . . . . . . . . . . . . . . . . . . . . . . . . 177

# PART 5: STEPS FOR LEVERAGING NETWORKING EVENTS

## Chapter 15: Becoming a Member of a BRING!-type Meeting . . . . . . . . . . . . . . 183
Members Sell Through… Not To . . . . . . . . . . . . . . . . . . . . . . . . . . . . . . 183
Put Away Hand-held Distractions . . . . . . . . . . . . . . . . . . . . . . . . . . . . . 184
Members Build Others with Testimonials . . . . . . . . . . . . . . . . . . . . . . . . 185
Members Listen More – Talk Less . . . . . . . . . . . . . . . . . . . . . . . . . . . . . 186
    The Hunger to be Heard . . . . . . . . . . . . . . . . . . . . . . . . . . . . . . . 186
    Cultivating the Art of Listening. . . . . . . . . . . . . . . . . . . . . . . . . . . 188
Members Build Others with Humor . . . . . . . . . . . . . . . . . . . . . . . . . . . 189
    Quit Negative Humor; Embrace Positive Humor . . . . . . . . . . . . . . . 190
    The Best: Confidence-Enhancing Humor . . . . . . . . . . . . . . . . . . . . 193
Members Convey, They Don't Spray . . . . . . . . . . . . . . . . . . . . . . . . . . . 194
    Business Cards Can Help or Hurt . . . . . . . . . . . . . . . . . . . . . . . . . 195
    ABC Pockets for Business Cards . . . . . . . . . . . . . . . . . . . . . . . . . 198
    Rubber Duckie Follow-ups . . . . . . . . . . . . . . . . . . . . . . . . . . . . . 200
    Coup de Grâce Rejections . . . . . . . . . . . . . . . . . . . . . . . . . . . . . 202

## Chapter 16: Serving Others as a Compeer . . . . . . . . . . . . . . . . . . . . . . 205
Definition of a Compeer . . . . . . . . . . . . . . . . . . . . . . . . . . . . . . . . . . . 205
The Role and Responsibility of a Compeer . . . . . . . . . . . . . . . . . . . . . . .206

The Benefits of Serving as a Compeer . . . . . . . . . . . . . . . . . . . . . . . . . . . . . . 208
    1. Inspiring Broughts – Reinvigorating Compeers . . . . . . . . . . . . . . . 208
    2. Serving as a Compeer Enhances Relationships . . . . . . . . . . . . . . . . 209
    4. Serving Grows Professional Networks . . . . . . . . . . . . . . . . . . . . . . 213

## Chapter 17: To Be or Not to Be… in BRING! Leadership . . . . . . . . . . 215

The Pros and Cons of Visibility. . . . . . . . . . . . . . . . . . . . . . . . . . . . . . . . . . 215
    Pro: Visibility Brings Credibility and Referrals . . . . . . . . . . . . . . . . . 215
    Con: Visibility Can Also Bring Heat . . . . . . . . . . . . . . . . . . . . . . . . . 217
    Con: Becoming the Scapegoat and Fall-Guy . . . . . . . . . . . . . . . . . . . 218
The Pros and Cons of Expert Status . . . . . . . . . . . . . . . . . . . . . . . . . . . . . . 219
    Pro: Expert Status Opens Doors . . . . . . . . . . . . . . . . . . . . . . . . . . . . 219
    Con: Expert Status Feels Awkward . . . . . . . . . . . . . . . . . . . . . . . . . . 220
The Pros and Cons of Extra Involvement. . . . . . . . . . . . . . . . . . . . . . . . . . 221
    Con: The Lack of Monetary Compensation . . . . . . . . . . . . . . . . . . . 221
    Pro: The Many Non-Monetary Compensations. . . . . . . . . . . . . . . . . 222

## Chapter 18: A Few Final Thoughts. . . . . . . . . . . . . . . . . . . . . . . . . . . . . . 225

Beyond Networking – Investing in Yourself . . . . . . . . . . . . . . . . . . . . . . . 225
Networking as a Path to Personal Growth . . . . . . . . . . . . . . . . . . . . . . . . . 225
Investing in Yourself Through Lifelong Learning. . . . . . . . . . . . . . . . . . . . 225
Networking as a Lifestyle. . . . . . . . . . . . . . . . . . . . . . . . . . . . . . . . . . . . . . 226
THE Final Thought . . . . . . . . . . . . . . . . . . . . . . . . . . . . . . . . . . . . . . . . . . 226

Glossary . . . . . . . . . . . . . . . . . . . . . . . . . . . . . . . . . . . . . . . . . . . . . . . . . . . 227

Index . . . . . . . . . . . . . . . . . . . . . . . . . . . . . . . . . . . . . . . . . . . . . . . . . . . . . .231

# PREFACE

It was a hot Saturday afternoon in mid-summer. Although it happened several years ago, I remember it like it was yesterday. I was in my garage and I had the garage door fully open.

At that time, I ran a promotional products business. We put logos on t-shirts, pens, coffee mugs, calendars, baseball caps, and so on. I was engaged in the twin roles of both selling the service and producing its products.

That hot afternoon, I was printing an order of t-shirts. Suddenly, here came a young man up my driveway. He casually asked me, "What are you doing?"

Thinking his question was somewhat intrusive, I sharply replied, "So, what are you selling?"

He told me he represented a financial investment company and was interested in helping me invest for the future. Whoa! That was a tough sell, on a cold call, on a hot day. I listened to him but gave no commitment.

The young man showed some interest in the process of printing t-shirts. I thought, "Right, you're really interested...," but he was letting me work and wasn't slowing me down. Then he asked me for my contact information, which I shared with him for some reason. He left me some of his literature without trying to close the sale.

I was surprised a few days later when he phoned to ask if he could send me some information about lost funds that the State was holding from the past. I skeptically gave him my email, and he sent me the link. There was a fair amount of money there, and I was able to successfully claim it. No direct benefit to him.

He had certainly impressed me, but a retirement portfolio was very different than a few hundred dollars.

In a couple of weeks, he called back. He invited me to a networking meeting he regularly attended. I responded, "What's a networking meeting?" I had never heard of such a thing.

He briefly explained that I'd be able to meet with people who might have a need for the services and products that I offered. Well, that sounded interesting. It was worth an hour of my time.

Once there, I recognized immediately this was a great opportunity. All of these people could use my promotional products. They could all use pens, mugs, and shirts with their logos on them.

Here was a room full of people who I couldn't wait to talk to. I had my business cards, and I was all ready to go. I made the same mistakes that everyone makes when they first start out. I tried to tell them all how much they needed my services. They were polite and courteous and a couple of them were wise enough to ask if I'd like to meet with them on the side. Thinking these were sales, I readily agreed.

I was quickly educated that I was only pushing people away. They wanted to network; they didn't want to buy. At the time, I didn't understand the difference, but I became a part of that group. I made many of the typical mistakes, but I watched and learned. I also read as much as I could about networking, but there wasn't all that much out there at the time – still isn't. Little did I know that I would eventually write this book to plug that hole.

Several more years passed. I eventually became the group's leader. During my tenure, we merged the group into becoming a local chapter of a large international networking entity. In fact, I was later recruited by this national entity for some leadership roles above the local chapter. In that capacity, I attended groups all over the state. But the more I saw from the corporate side, rather than the networking side, the more I realized that it was good, but it could be better.

By this time, I had a cadré of people around me – what might be called a "mastermind group." One of those people was the young man who had first introduced me to networking. Over the next several years, our small group met regularly. We often had animated discussions.

After a lot of consideration, we decided to launch our own networking group independent of the international entity. I took the lead in that, and we hammered forward over many months. We emphasized the goal of helping our members, not padding the pockets of corporate big-wigs. From that, emerged a philosophy called "BRING!" (which will be discussed in depth later in this book you are holding in your hands).

I began teaching courses and giving presentations on the science and the art of professional business networking – all from a service model. Using the BRING! philosophy, I was privileged to see people move from struggling and spinning their wheels to achieving impactful results. I saw them leverage networking into reaching sales and profitability at levels they had not previously imagined.

Writing this book seemed a natural extension of my encouragement and teaching the BRING! philosophy of networking. I had something to share, and I needed to share it.

In doing so, I want to gratefully acknowledge the day-to-day support of my loving wife, Sheryl. Many have been the times she has staggered out into our home office in the wee hours of the morning to find me dictating text and ideas that I would then send to my writing associate, Godfrey Ellis. "Come to bed," my wife would say, and sometimes I would. I had much to share, and little time to share it given my many pulls from full-time work, my involvement as a church leader, and my active family of young adults.

Instrumental in helping me share my thoughts was the assistance of Dr. Godfrey Ellis. He spent over 800 hours helping me to smooth and polish my presentation of information for you. As a retired university professor, mental health counselor, and psychology chairman, he brought and shared a 45-year background. His expertise on the underlying psychology of relationships enhanced and supplemented my own expertise. He also contributed the drawings and illustrations that help support the text.

Thanks, also, to the young man who walked up my driveway, all those years ago. And thanks to Marc Evans, the referral partner who arranged that frantic flight home you will read about in the Introduction.

I would be remiss to not thank my loving parents who instilled in me an ability to meet the world with enthusiasm and optimism.

# WHY NETWORKING: AN INTRODUCTION

"He's gone! He's gone!" …and then just broken sobs.

"What? Who's gone…? Gone where…? Is it Dad? Did Dad die?"

"No, it's Doug…. Doug is gone."

That traumatic evening is etched forever in my mind. It was my sister on the phone slamming me with the shocking blow that our younger brother, Doug, had just passed away. I had been tempted to ignore the call, thinking it was just one more of those annoying robocalls that we all love to hate. But it wasn't a robocall. It was one of the worst calls of my life.

"It can't be!" I said. "He was only 31 years old!"

"Could you come right away?" was all she could say.

"Of course…."

I suddenly needed to get to where they were in that small town and in a different state. I had to drop everything and rush home. Lost in an instant daze, I somehow wrote down the basic information I needed for the incident. Then I hung up the phone and immediately started packing. But I was in a fog.

As I packed, my brain slowly started working again. I began thinking, "Okay, I need to get on a flight. When can I get on that flight? How do I go about this?" I knew I could get a flight at the last minute, but the cost would be extraordinary. I recalled there was a way to have a significant amount refunded later but would need some documentation and such. I wasn't sure what exactly the airline would require. Then I recalled that there was somebody in my professional network who worked for an airline. What was his name? Marc…. Marc Evans. Surely Marc would know how that process worked. I called him then and there. Phone in one hand, packing with the other.

He was wonderful. I talked to him and tried to express my thoughts while I packed. I told him about Pat's phone call, what little of it there was. Then I said, "Look, I know that there's a way that this can happen. I can get on a flight in an emergency. I know the cost is higher, but I also know that part of that can be refunded later. I'm just not sure how that works. What's the best way for me to handle this?"

He told me to wait a moment. Then, he started to ask a few questions about my situation. He asked me a few details, how I was doing – things like that. While he was asking me these questions, I packed furiously. I could faintly hear him clicking away on his computer. A few minutes later he said to me. "Okay…, there's a flight leaving at such-and-such a time. Can you be at the airport at that time and get on that flight?"

I told him, "Sure, yes."

He said, "Okay, you're on the flight. Go!"

I dashed to the airport. How I avoided a ticket or a collision, I'll never know. With the shock of the death and the stress of the situation, I was mainly coasting on autopilot. I parked and ran into the terminal with my carry-on and a small suitcase. When I arrived at the ticket counter, still feeling shell-shocked, they were all ready for me. I found that Marc had taken care of the whole thing. Matter of fact, he had arranged for the pricing in such a way that I had no cost. To this day, I'm not sure how that happened. I hadn't asked for that; it never crossed my mind. I just wanted a little information about procedures.

I was ushered through TSA security and directed toward the gate. It wasn't until I was in the air that I had time to contemplate what had just happened. I clearly could not have accomplished all of that on my own, not at that speed and certainly not at that price. It was only by reaching out to Marc that everything had fallen into place so perfectly and so unexpectedly.

When I talk about this at networking functions – in fact, any time that I think it – I am humbled and awed. My mind races back to that evening. Some of it is still a blur, yes, but some of it creates sharp images that burst back into my consciousness.

More than the memories, though, is the realization that there were no answers that I could find at the time. Everything was swirling around in my mind, out of control, on that horrible Tuesday night. Yet, the chaos that took place was resolved, and my house was set in order. And how?

Because of a professional relationship.

It was because of a contact in my network that an impossible issue was smoothed out – at least, as much as it possibly could be.

When I reflect back on those events, I feel something else, too – a returning rush of immense and eternal gratitude for this individual who helped me through such a stressful time. This man, Marc, this member of my network, was truly there for me when I needed him.

This story is not about a free plane ticket; it is about support. It is about friendship and service.

Now, years later, I travel around to business groups and provide in-service training for small businesses. From time to time I'm asked what the value of professional networking is? How do we monetize and put a value on it? How do we know that it's really worth it? I do not know. But this I do know. The value of networking on that one Tuesday night was priceless. Not just because I got a free airplane ticket, but because I had support that lifted me up and carried me through a crisis.

So, instead of my trying to answer those questions for you, I throw the ball back in your court. As you hear my story, I ask you to think about those questions:

What *was* the value of networking for me that night?

Can you put a price-tag on that?

In this book, *The Professional Networkers' Playbook*, we are going to talk a lot about networking and its incalculable value. We'll also discuss confidence, goals, and specific tips for success. We'll talk about making contacts and taking prospects to business events. We'll find some broad keys to motivation – as broad as the mindsets we hold and as narrow as the limitations that shackle us. But the main topic of this book will be professional networking: what a network is, how to build one, how to help others, how to leverage the network for your good and, above all else, for the good of your contacts, and much, much more.

You may well have attempted to harness the power of professional networking in the past. People try multiple ways to become networkers, but they often do not achieve the success they hope for. They may tell every member of their family and all of their friends about what they do. They spent lots of time at networking functions introducing themselves, shaking many hands, and handing out business cards. They often spent lots of money trying to get other people to understand what they offer, but it just doesn't seem to make a difference. They still have a problem making it all work. You may be in that position, too

If you are, it is important for you to understand that this is not your fault. Up to now, you've had enthusiasm and zeal. That's wonderful. But the knowledge to translate that enthusiasm into networking success may have been lacking. Both are needed. As one writer put it so well:

> *Zeal is the engine that drives the whole vehicle – without it we would get nowhere. But without clutch, throttle, brakes, and steering wheel, our mighty engine becomes an instrument of destruction, and the more powerful the motor, the more disastrous the inevitable crack-up if the proper knowledge is lacking. There is a natural tendency to let the mighty motor carry us along, to give it its head, open up and see what it can do. We see this in our society today.... We have the zeal, but not the knowledge, so to speak. This is a very dangerous situation.*

Now that you have this *Playbook* in your hand, you now hold the knowledge to advance in your career. With this *Playbook*, you will gain the opportunity, the right, and the knowledge to be successful in your professional networking. You will also take on the responsibility to serve others through your business.

Professional networking is never done in a vacuum. Networking is unlike other tools that you can develop. With most business tools, if you're the only person that has it, you are at a distinct advantage. Networking is not like that. Professional networking is about relationships.

Networks do best when multiple people have the same tool. The American novelist, Susan Elizabeth Phillips, expressed a truism when she wrote: "celebrate the success of others" for the rising tide of their successes will "float all ships. When the tide rushes in, all the ships are lifted, not just one."[1]

In our current business environment, there is too much emphasis on sales and competition. This book is somewhat unique in emphasizing cooperation, service, and relationships. When you remember that folks prefer to do business with people they like, you will see the importance of maintaining, building, and re-establishing personal relationships.

For an example, as you use this *Playbook, understand* that it presents tools that will benefit others as well. You might think about colleagues who could benefit from this information. Share what you learn from this *Playbook* with others in your network. In doing so, you will help them become stronger and more reliable professional networkers. In addition to this *Playbook* being a toolkit for you and an opportunity to learn or relearn important skills, use it to help strengthen your network.

Now that you have this *Playbook*, the results are completely and totally up to you.

---

[1] Quote taken from Phillips, Susan Elizabeth, 2001, in *Romance Writer's Report*; see: http://quotationsbywomen.com/authorq/52222/

# PART ONE

## FOUNDATIONS FOR PROFESSIONAL NETWORKING

# WHAT IS PROFESSIONAL NETWORKING?

We repeat that critical question from the Introduction: Just what *is* the value of networking? As I told you in that Introduction, the night my brother died, having a network was priceless to me. It continues to be today. Marc Evans was far more than a free plane ticket; he was a lifeline.

You likely have a "Marc" in your professional network.

In this chapter, we describe just what networking is all about. We will distinguish nets and networks and introduce a formula for power and success in professional networking. We will help you recognize several Marcs in your network, and show you how you may be a Marc for someone.

## NETS, NETWORKS, AND NETWORKING

At its simplest, **networking** starts with the concept of a **net**—a tool designed to gather and connect. Think of a net: whether it's used to catch fish, butterflies, or even ideas, the goal is the same—collection and cultivation. But there's more to this metaphor. A **network** isn't just a tool; it's the collection itself, the interconnected system that grows and strengthens as more pieces are added.

This distinction between a **net** and a **network** is critical in understanding professional networking. A net represents your efforts—attending meetings, reaching out to contacts, and making introductions. A network, however, is the web of relationships created through those efforts. It's not just a collection of people; it's a structure of interconnected relationships that support and amplify each other.

In professional networking, you are both the fisherman and the weaver.

To illustrate, let's consider a well-known story from the Bible.

*One morning, a few fishermen were busy cleaning up their nets after a fruitless night of fishing. Their teacher, Jesus, asked them to pull back away from the shore and cast out their nets once again. One of the men protested: "We have toiled all the night and have taken nothing; nevertheless, at thy word, I will let down the net."*

*They immediately caught so many fish, probably from a swarming school, that their net actually broke under the weight. They had to call for help from a nearby boat to save this enormous catch. In fact, it was so large that <u>both</u> boats then started to capsize. That's a lot of fish! Needless to say, everyone was astonished and dumbfounded. Then the teacher drew a metaphor of fish to people. "Come ye after me," he said, "and I will make you to become fishers of men."* [2]

The lesson wasn't just about abundance—it was about collaboration. One net wasn't enough, but by working together, they achieved more than they could have alone.

This story highlights a key principle: a network becomes exponentially more powerful when multiple nets are weaved together. Whether in fishing or professional networking, the value isn't just in what one person can gather but in what a collective effort can achieve.

Another example comes from an unlikely source: criminal organizations. Consider how organized crime syndicates, such as the Mafia, built expansive networks. Initially, they operated as small, localized groups. But through deliberate collaboration—combining their "nets" of influence—they expanded their reach and power. Eventually, these networks grew to national and even international levels, forming alliances like the infamous five families of New York. Similarly, law enforcement had to form its own "networks" to counteract these groups, pooling resources and working together across jurisdictions. The lesson here is clear: a network's strength lies in its reach and the quality of its connections.

In professional networking, the same principles apply. Your "net" represents your individual efforts to meet people and build relationships. But your **network**—the collection of those relationships—gains strength and influence when linked with others. By combining efforts, you expand the reach and impact of your network far beyond what you could achieve alone.

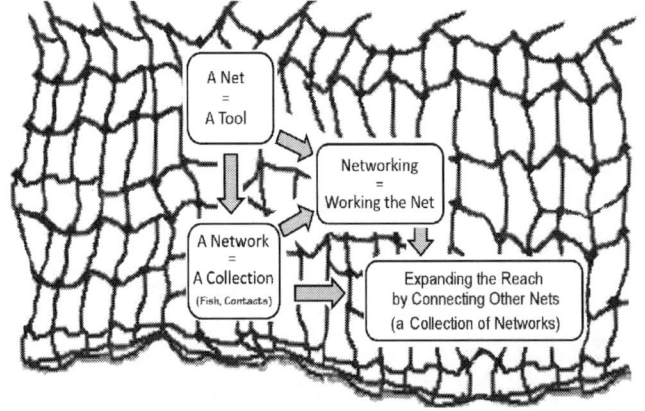

The power of networking lies not just in gathering contacts but in creating a system of mutual support. Think of each connection as a thread in a net. When woven

---

[2] The story is from Luke 5:5 and his invitation to them is from Mark 1:17; the quote is from John 15:13 KJV.

together with purpose and care, those threads form a strong, reliable network capable of catching opportunities and solving problems. This is why professional networking is so much more than collecting business cards—it's about building a structure that serves both you and those within it.

Whether you're inspired by the fishermen in the Bible or by the tactical strategies of law enforcement, the lesson remains the same: your network grows stronger when you collaborate, share, and support others. With each new connection, you're not just adding to your net—you're strengthening the entire network.

## INTRODUCING THE POWER FORMULA

In science, formulas provide clear frameworks for understanding how variables interact to create results. In networking, the same principle applies. Success doesn't come from random effort; it comes from focusing on the right components and how they work together. That's where the **Power Formula for Networking** comes in:

$$NP = (CC + NN) \times RR$$

- **NP** stands for **Network Power**—the ultimate measure of your networking success.
- **CC** represents **Creating Contacts**—the foundation of any network. Without contacts, there's no network to build on.
- **NN** is **Nurturing your Network**—the consistent effort to maintain and strengthen relationships.
- **RR** refers to **Relevant Referrals**—the connections and opportunities shared within your network, which multiply its power.

### BREAKING DOWN THE FORMULA

At first glance, this formula seems straightforward, but its power lies in its application:

1. **Creating Contacts (CC)**: Every network begins with connections. These are the people you meet and add to your professional circle. However, the goal isn't just to collect business cards or followers—it's to establish meaningful relationships that can grow over time.
2. **Nurturing Your Network (NN)**: Building a network doesn't stop at making contacts. Relationships must be maintained and nurtured through regular interaction, trust-building, and mutual support. Without this step, your contacts remain surface-level and lose their potential.

3. **Relevant Referrals (RR)**: Referrals are the most powerful element in the formula because they multiply your network's value. Unlike CC and NN, which are additive, referrals are multiplicative—they enhance every other aspect of your network. A well-timed, relevant referral can unlock opportunities that benefit everyone involved.

## THE MULTIPLICATIVE POWER OF REFERRALS

Why are referrals so important? Consider this: you could spend countless hours cold-calling or pitching your services to strangers, or you could leverage your network for warm introductions. A referral carries trust and credibility, saving time and increasing your chances of success.

## APPLYING THE FORMULA

To fully unlock the potential of this formula, all three components must work together. Simply creating contacts without nurturing them leaves your network shallow. Nurturing contacts without giving or receiving referrals reduces your network's ability to grow. The formula emphasizes balance: invest in building relationships, nurture those connections, and actively seek opportunities to share and receive referrals.

## WHY THIS FORMULA MATTERS

Networking is often misunderstood as a collection of random activities. The **Power Formula** gives it structure, showing you exactly where to focus your efforts. By understanding and applying this formula, you can amplify your results while building a network that benefits not just you, but everyone involved.

## SHARING REFERRALS THROUGH A NETWORK

Remember the definition of a referral:

*A relevant referral is an introduction to, or between, people in a professional network for the purpose of solving a problem.*

Notice that the formula states that the first essential elements (creating contacts (**CC**) and nurturing the network (**NN**)) are additive. However, the use of relevant referrals is multiplicative.

This means that the _sharing_ of relevant referrals (**RR**) through helpful introductions is, by far, the most important element in giving the networking its power. We will talk about this in more depth in a later chapter, but let us point out, here, it is essential to understand this sharing is a two-way process.

Often the mistake is made of thinking that _getting_ referrals is the largest and most important part of networking. This may seem to be intuitive, but that is an illusion. It is not correct. It belongs down to introductory 101-level thinking. The concept of 101-level networking is networking that is done by those who do not fully understand how powerful networking can be.

When you are truly networking at a high level, let's call it 212-level networking, you shift your focus to _giving_ referrals to those with whom you have established relationships. This elevates your orientation to a more seasoned and higher-level thinking. Placing the emphasis on giving, not getting, is a key component of professional networking. When you understand that fully, you will change the way you interact with other professionals, especially at networking functions.

The difference between getting referrals and giving referrals may seem simple but incorporating this is not easy. If it were a college class, the push _to get_ would be an introductory 101-level class. The push _to give_ would be a 212-level class, which would be taken by seasoned and successful networkers. Why? Because giving helps others and, at the same time, helps you.

As an application of this, consider how 101-level networkers often view others in a networking meeting. They may unconsciously think of the other group members as their own "sales force." They may try to send them out into the bleak and hostile world as their hands and ears with the vain expectation that referrals will then flow back to them. In a sense, they are attempting to build, not a network, but an unpaid sales force.

Would you be interested in being a part of that? Probably not. Neither are the other members in the networking group.

So, 101-level networkers will not succeed in getting free sales or even free referrals. By trying to get, not give, they will come up empty. By contrast, more seasoned 212-level networkers will recognize other 212-level networkers, and all will focus on giving _each other_ relevant referrals (**RR**). By giving, they will receive. One could say that 212 networkers are long-term thinkers in what is often a short-term situation. 101-level networkers haven't yet caught this long-term vision.

The truth is that the landing of new clients comes from either cold-contacts or referrals. If you want more relevant referrals, you will need to become a 212-level networker. That means creating contacts (**CC**), building and nurturing relationships in your network (**NN**) and seeking opportunities to _give_ relevant referrals (**RR**). When you develop this mindset, you will then be better equipped to help others to achieve network power (**NP**). There is no faking this. You must be in a position of strength (giving referrals) in order to effectively and consistently strengthen others and, through this, receive referrals given to you.

Imagine you're in the business of selling soap, and you need customers. One day, while getting your haircut at the local barbershop, you say to your barber, Phil, "Hey, Phil, I just started selling this incredible dishwashing liquid. It's guaranteed to make your dishes squeaky clean. Would you like to buy a bottle?"

This attempt at a direct sale doesn't land well. Phil feels cornered, not interested in switching roles from barber to customer. He's caught off guard and doesn't know how to respond. After an awkward pause, he mumbles, "Thanks, but I just bought a big jug of dish soap at the store yesterday. ...Uh, do you want your sideburns trimmed?"

Not great, right? Now, let's try a slightly better approach. You say, "Phil, I just started selling home care products, including this amazing dishwashing liquid. Here are a few brochures about it. Would you mind passing them along to a few of your friends who might be interested?"

This is a step up—it's networking, but at a beginner, 101-level. You're still asking Phil to do something for you, essentially recruiting him as a junior salesperson. While less awkward, it still doesn't foster a genuine connection or provide much value to Phil.

Now let's shift to professional, 212-level networking. Imagine saying instead, "Phil, this haircut is fantastic. I look 10 years younger! My friend Kyle was just saying he needs a great barber. Let me give him a call." You pick up your phone and dial Kyle. "Hey, Kyle, I'm at Hair Today, Gone Tomorrow, and Phil just gave me the best haircut I've ever had. You mentioned you're looking for a barber—let me put him on the phone for you." Then you hand the phone to Phil and watch as he connects with a potential new client.

Now that's professional networking. Notice how you've helped both Phil and Kyle without expecting anything in return. You didn't try to sell soap, recruit Phil, or ask for a favor. You simply strengthened your network by providing value to two people.

Will Phil rush to buy your soap? Probably not—and that's okay. By giving him a meaningful referral, you've demonstrated generosity and goodwill. You've strengthened your relationship with him and added value to Kyle's life. This is the essence of professional networking: focusing on serving others, not on what you might gain in return.

When you adopt this mindset consistently, you shift your focus from chasing personal gain to building a thriving network of people who trust and respect you. Over time, the benefits will come—whether through referrals, opportunities, or goodwill. Helping others isn't just a tool for profit; it's a way of life that enriches everyone involved.

## GENERATING REFERRALS FROM YOUR NETWORK

Professional networking is primarily about:

1) Increasing our contacts
2) Nurturing our networks
3) Giving referrals to help others

You're in business to generate an income and support yourself and your family. If referrals do end up being reciprocated, nobody is suggesting you turn those referrals down. Nobody is suggesting you overlook opportunities to ask your contacts (referral partners) for relevant referrals (**RR**). A good relationship is always a two-way relationship.

You likely do an excellent job in your vocation. Your clients are happy with your services and/or they are pleased with your products. They appreciate your friendship and are grateful for the service that you have provided with no strings attached. It is only normal and natural that some of your clients will be thrilled to mention you to their friends and their own contacts. Especially if your network is large, you will receive relevant referrals (**RR**) and introductions to people who will allow you to create contacts (**CC**). Humbly and gratefully accept those referrals and/or professional introductions. These clients, who have become your friends, represent opportunities to expand your network, obtain business referrals, and receive valuable testimonials and endorsements.

Madison Williams is an example of this. She is a hypnotherapist with a small but very successful private practice in Oregon. She tells a common story:

*I see most of my clients from 3 to 5 times, and I'm able to give them positive results. After the initial few sessions, though, they feel they have received a resolution to the presenting issue. They're very grateful but feel they no longer need me. Some-times it seems like picking up a hand-ful of pondwater and having it quickly slip right through my fingers. In a funny way, it's almost like I'm <u>too</u> success-ful for my own good! They come for a short-term resolution of a simple issue and, having received that, they thank me and then go back to their busy lives.*

Madison met with a seasoned and experienced professional networker who was able to help her to revise her business plan. She picks up the story:

> *Helen, the networker I met with, was wonderful. She suggested several ways to generate new referrals. Now, things are different. I call my satisfied clients about 30 days after their last session to confirm that their progress is solid. Then I use the call as an opportunity to ask them for a little help. I ask them to put my contact information into their phones and, if an occasion presents itself and a friend asks, to recommend me to their friends.*

Asking her clients to put her information into their electronic devices has made a huge difference. It is not intrusive. It is not asking her friends to recruit for her. It only suggests that her clients share their satisfaction with her work with others who may ask. Putting the contact information into their devices avoids them having to say, "She's really good but I don't remember her phone number." They have easy access to her information.

One of Madison's recent clients, a man by the name of Tom, had been a long-time smoker. Just like that, he quit. His friend, in amazement, asked the obvious question: "Tom, that's great! How did you do it?" Tom replied that he had gone to a hypnotherapist and seen great results.[3] His friend then asked Tom the question that is typically asked in this kind of a situation: "Who did you see?"

Having entered Madison William's contact information in his phone, Tom was able to quickly pull out the contact information. He had experienced great results and was only too pleased to give a little testimonial and pass on her information.

How many clients have you worked with? How many of them would be happy to endorse your business when asked? You, too, can encourage clients to have your information easily accessible. When you've completed your sales to a customer and given great service, the customer can then be encouraged to refer business your way. Ask for these relevant referrals (**RR**). Also ask for written testimonials that you can share.

## RELATED BUT DIFFERENT ACTIVITIES

We have now defined nets, networks, and networking and introduced the formula for networking power (NP). Before leaving the discussion of what networking *is*, it may be helpful to talk about what networking is *not*.

There are two closely-related activities that are both worthwhile and valuable but are not true business networking. The first is the use (and abuse) of social media and the second is confusing networking and salesmanship.

---

[3] The number of sessions varies from person to person. Most websites indicate that "people will need 3 to 4 sessions spread out over two weeks." This estimate is from: https://northernutahhypnosis.com/how-many-sessions-to-stop-smoking.

## IS USING SOCIAL MEDIA NETWORKING?

Social media has undeniably transformed how we connect, but is it true **networking**? The answer is both yes and no. While social platforms can enhance your professional relationships, they rarely replace the depth and authenticity of in-person connections.

Online, everyone presents a version of themselves, carefully curated to highlight their best qualities. These digital "masks" can make it hard to truly understand the person behind the profile. Written posts often lack the nuances of tone and body language, leaving room for misinterpretation. As playwright George Bernard Shaw observed,

> *The greatest enemy of communication*
> *is the illusion that it has taken place.*[4]

This is particularly true in the world of social media, where emojis, likes, and quick comments may create the illusion of meaningful interaction without the substance.

This limitation is especially apparent in professional networking. True relationships are built on trust and shared experiences, which are harder to achieve when communication is limited to posts, comments, and likes. While a social media connection may spark initial interest, it takes time, effort, and real interaction to develop it into a meaningful relationship.

That said, social media is not without value. When used wisely, it's an excellent tool for nurturing existing relationships. Platforms like LinkedIn or Facebook allow you to stay connected with contacts you've already met in person, share updates, and even showcase your expertise. Social media also helps bridge gaps in time and geography, enabling you to maintain relationships when face-to-face meetings aren't feasible.

For example, a quick message to congratulate a colleague on their recent promotion or a thoughtful comment on their post can keep you on their radar and reinforce your relationship. These small actions, while simple, can significantly strengthen your professional network over time.

However, relying solely on social media has its risks. The term "friend" in a digital context is often misleading. Many of your online connections may be more like acquaintances than true allies. Real networking requires more than sending a connection request; it involves meaningful conversations, shared goals, and mutual support.

In short, social media is a tool, not a substitute, for professional networking. It can amplify your efforts, but the foundation of your network should always rest on genuine, in-person connections.

---

[4] This saying has been attributed to the playwright, George Bernard Shaw, but it more likely came from William Whyte, 1950, "Is Anybody Listening?" *Fortune* magazine; see: https://quoteinvestigator.com/ 2014/08/31/illusion.

By combining the convenience of digital platforms with the authenticity of real-world interactions, you can build a network that is both broad and deep—a true asset to your professional success.

## DIFFERENCE BETWEEN SELLING AND NETWORKING

The second activity that is closely-related to networking but is different in nature, is selling products and services. Selling is _not_ synonymous with networking. There is a time and place for everything, and without question, there is a time and a place for sales. But selling is selling, and networking is networking. They are not the same activity. There are many appropriate occasions to sell and there are many appropriate occasions to network. Very seldom should these two activities happen at the same time. Often, it's just a case of knowing the difference between the two activities.

"Selling" is defined by the Cambridge Dictionary as "the job and skill of persuading people to buy things."[5] The Merriam-Webster dictionary is less kind. The first several entries under "sell" mention betrayal, foolishness, slavery, profit instead of conscience, persuading, influencing, inducing, and cheating.[6] While we mention this more in humor than anything else, it is true that selling is very different than networking. The American Heritage Dictionary defines "sell" as:

> To persuade (another) to recognize the worth or desirability of something
> (and then) …to exchange ownership for money or its equivalent.[7]

That is not networking. We define networking as:

> Creating and nurturing contacts and inter-relating
> with them in a social and serving context.

It is the _focus_ of the interaction that is so critically different. In the first definition (selling), the focus is on the merits of a product or of services offered, not on a relationship. The focus of the second definition (networking) is on the long-term relationship between two persons, or on referring to a third relationship. Both networking and selling are valid and, as long as all parties are fully aware of where the focus is, everything is fine. If the parties are not aware, problems erupt. If a networking exchange turns into a sales attempt, the result can destroy the relationship. Too many of us have experienced the surprise and unpleasantness of an attempted close when we didn't expect it.

---

[5] See: https://dictionary.cambridge.org/us/dictionary/english/selling
[6] See: www.merriam-webster.com/dictionary/sell
[7] See: https://ahdictionary.com/word/search.html?q=sell

# WHAT IS PROFESSIONAL NETWORKING?

As professionals we should be aware of the situations we are in and the expectations of all involved. Many times, we get caught up in the moment and forget to consider the long-range effects. Some situations are for sales, others for networking. Professional business net- workers know the difference and think long term.

Here is an admonition that you will see throughout this book:

> Sell *through*... (your network) not *to*... (your network)

Your network is a collection of people. This admonition ("sell through, not to") is based on the idea that those in your network are people who have contacts; they are not customers.

Now, to be fair, you may give them referrals of another person who will buy their product to solve a problem they have. That's absolutely fine. Likewise, they may give you a referral to a third person to whom you can sell your product. That's great, too! Either of you might make an introduction to a third person who has a product or service that would solve a problem. But all parties need to be equally aware that the relationship has temporarily become a transactional relationship.

If all this makes sense, and you have it firmly in your mind, temper with the following. The people in your network are friends. They are a contact. However, there may be times when they will take the *role* of a customer or a salesperson, which will put you in the *role* of selling or buying. All of that is just fine, as long as everyone in the exchange understands exactly what roles everyone is playing. The vast majority of the time, they are in the role of a friend, and you are selling through them, not to them.

So, this is what networking is – and is not. Networking really is not complicated. It is intensely engaging, not to mention fun and profitable. You can do this. In the next chapter, we will take a look at some worldviews and mindsets that will be a great help to you as you incorporate networking into your life and career.

# MINDSETS FOR NETWORKING SUCCESS

In Chapter One, we briefly presented a formula for how to generate networking power.

**NP = (CC + NN) x RR**

Network power comes as a result of decisive actions. Your personality is a powerful action tool. So is your energy. The quality of your handshake, the sincerity of your smile, your use of a person's name, are all actions you can use to apply the formula. But decisive actions, by themselves, are still not enough to bring networking success. The actions must flow out of correct and positive mindsets. Mindsets give direction so that actions can find their target. Both are needed.

A pair of scissors comes with two blades, not one. Decisive action and positive mindsets are the two blades that work <u>together</u> to give networking its power. Synergy.

Another metaphor for thinking about all of this is that mindsets provide direction for actions. Imagine climbing up a ladder to repair a hole in the wall. The ladder is the action – the "how." The hole is the motivation – the "why" of your actions. But when you reach the top of the ladder, you find it was leaning against the wrong wall. The mindset was the angle that held up the ladder. The mindset was what gave the action its direction.

Below are the four positive mindsets upon which you must lean your ladder in order to fix holes in your professional networking. If your mindsets are solid and correct, then your goals will be correct, your "why's" will be validated, and your "how's" will reveal themselves as your learning progresses. The four mindsets of this chapter are:

1. Service Through Sales
2. Confidence That You Will Succeed
3. Networking 7-7-7
4. Abundance, not Scarcity

It is critically important to strengthen the core values behind your mindsets on a frequent basis. Everyone operates from a base of values, whether they recognize it or not. A habit of visiting those values on a daily basis will provide a secure anchor for the ways in which you will govern your life. Just as an athlete can learn all the right plays for every situation, it doesn't matter if the athlete's physical conditioning is lacking. The book you hold in your hand isn't to teach theory; it is provided for your active success. Getting your mindset right requires continual conditioning. You must not just put the plays in place, you must retain and maintain them. Such a daily or near-daily touching of your core values may take a variety of forms: from meditation to yoga; from bubble baths to massages; and from reading autobiographies to prayer and scripture study.

1. For the first mindset, that of <u>Service Through Sales</u>, you might study the lives and teachings of great examples of service. These could include such figures as Mother Theresa, Mahatma Ghandi, Abraham Lincoln, or Jesus Christ.
2. For the mindset of <u>Confidence That You Will Succeed</u>, read the inspirational stories of bold heroes like Helen Keller, Martin Luther King, Rosa Parks, or even General George Patton.
3. For the mindset of <u>Networking 7-7-7</u>, reward yourself for getting up and getting going and keep a count of efforts you extend so that you can concretely see your efforts. It is a good idea to write down daily, monthly, yearly, and life goals and accomplishments.
4. For the mindset of <u>Abundance, not Scarcity</u>, reframe your view of the world from one of few resources to one of plenty. Give up an approach to business based on competition and embrace an approach based on cooperation. A good idea is to spend some daily study time reading about the lives and the generosity of business giants from Dale Carnegie to Warren Buffet.

Whatever form it takes, it's important to touch your values routinely and regularly. It doesn't have to be for long, but it is an important tool in your toolkit and an excellent daily practice.

Let's take a closer look at each of these mindsets that will bring you success and happiness.

## SERVICE THROUGH SALES

The first mindset may be the most important of all. It is the philosophy of service through sales. This mindset refers to doing business with the major motivation being to help others around you through your approach to life and/or your products. This might seem a strange approach for a book on business, but this value is the foundation for the entire book, as you will see.

In order to develop this mindset, you have to understand and believe that your product or services will significantly improve the lives or situations of others. If a person's one and only purpose in business is to make money, then this book might give you the tools and the how, but your life will not be as full and rich as it could be. By contrast, if your purpose is to use your products to help people solve their problems and fill their needs, you will produce revenue and experience success, but you will also fill your life with meaning and purpose. With this approach, networking becomes about service as much as about success.

Your day is filled with opportunities to talk about your career, your business, or the industry you represent. You may not always recognize those opportunities, but they are there. The question becomes, "For what purpose are you engaging in your professional activities and actions?" It may be helpful to think of people in sales as falling into three broad categories:

1. Those who trick and exploit others for profit and monetary gain.
2. Those for whom a career is nothing more than a vehicle for generating revenue.
3. Those who believe that their product or services are of great value and will truly benefit others in their lives.

The *first* group are those who manipulate others into purchasing products that are of little or no value. They are frauds who are out to separate the innocent from their money simply for financial profit. Examples of this are unfortunately all too common. They come in the form of appliances that will need replacing in a year or so, rather than lasting a lifetime. They come in websites that disable the back button so you can't close it. They come in the form of robocalls or emails that threaten bad outcomes or offer unearned windfalls. If your goal is to seduce others into buying products that are not beneficial, this book is not a book for you.

If you are in the *second* group, you have the mindset that your career is a vehicle to finance activities that you enjoy or to put food on the table and spend more time with your friends or family. That's not necessarily a negative thing. You will need to come to terms with the reality that your main motivation is money. If that's the case, learning skills that will enhance your networking ability will bring you professional success in the short-term, perhaps even in the long-term. It is unlikely, though, that your professional activities will bring you long-term satisfaction. It will be necessary to find opportunities to serve outside of your profession.

If you are in the _third_ group, even your professional activities have the goal of serving others. You are so committed to your products or services that you offer them as a means of truly benefiting people. While many of your professional activities will bring immediate revenue, some activities will have less of a monetary component. They will bring happiness or success to the people around you, whether clients, customers, fellow networkers, or just other human beings. If you are in this third group, you tell people what problems you solve in hopes of having them, or someone they know, benefit from what you are offering. Your goal is to sell as a way to serve.

Long-term success comes when you are in business to offer solutions to people's needs and problems. If that's truly how you feel about your career, then you have evolved past this being merely a job. Your career becomes something that you truly feel is a benefit to other people. At that point, you almost become an evangelist for what you represent.

For example, you may be helping others to invest for a secure retirement, or you may be maximizing people's appearance through a beauty product or service. You may build quality roofs with skylights that never leak or install air conditioners that will last for many years. Doing the best that you can do to provide the best for others is integrity. It will result in great satisfaction and success. It will also bring in revenue – often more than would come from merely doing a "job".

In the Introduction to this book, I told the story of Marc Evans, the fellow networker who got me on a plane to rush to my family's side at the time of my younger brother's death. Marc saw no financial gain from his actions. I didn't give him the equivalent of what my airfare would have been. I sent him no customers, no gifts – not even a loaf of home-baked bread (though I probably should have!) What Marc did, he did out of a love for his fellow humans. It is this kind of mindset – a mindset of service – that brings long-term personal happiness and long-term professional success.

It is for Marc, and for many men and women like him, this book was written. These pages are meant for enthusiastic professionals who represent companies or activities they wholeheartedly believe in. You are also in this third group of professional networkers if you have difficulty understanding why others don't see the greatness of the career field you represent. In fact, the failure of others to see the beauty in the product or services you offer can be discouraging to you – that's how much you believe in serving others.

Does this mindset produce personal growth and satisfaction? Yes, it does. If you are committed to your career at a personal level, then, yes, your professional actions can definitely bring meaning, not just money, to your life.

During the Second World War, a Jewish neurologist and psychiatrist by the name of Viktor Frankl was interred in several Nazi concentration camps, including the infamous horrors of Auschwitz. During that unthinkable ordeal, Frankl discovered "the importance of finding meaning in all forms of existence, even the most brutal ones, and thus, a reason to continue living."[8] Although death was an outcome over which most prisoners had absolutely no control, some who were not immediately killed found meaning and survived. After the war, he published a book about his observations called, *Man's Search for Meaning*.[9] The book has become a classic selling over 12 million copies. It has been called one of the most influential books in America. According to Frankl, it is the meaning that we find in life that determines the level of happiness and fulfillment we achieve.

These principles are true in one's professional life as well. Your mindset of Service Through Sales is incredibly important. But it is only the first of four mindsets that will help you find happiness and success.

## CONFIDENCE THAT YOU WILL SUCCEED

Throughout this book, we will recommend many actions and activities that may take you outside your comfort zone. It is our position that a comfort zone is a mental landscape bound with an imaginary line. More importantly, it is you who have put that line in place – or allowed others to so limit you. When you understand this, you will realize that you have the freedom to now move that boundary. To do so, it is vital that you develop confidence in your abilities and opportunities. So, the second mindset for you to adopt is that of confidence. To succeed, you must be bold and brave, especially in meeting people and adding them to your professional network. If you think about it, there is really nothing of any significance that could hold you back or limit you – other than a treatable lack of confidence.

### PROGRAMMING FROM THE PAST

We urge you to take steps to erase anxieties that limit you. If you were bullied as a child, realize that you are now an adult. If you have some physical abnormality, realize that the people who you would want to have in your network would look right past anything like that. There is nothing

---

[8] Quote from: https://en.wikipedia.org/wiki/Viktor_Frankl
[9] Viktor Frankl, 1946, 1959, 1992, *Man's Search for Meaning*, Beacon Press. The book was originally published under the title: *Trotzdem Ja Zum Leben Sagen: Ein Psychologe erlebt das Konzentrationslager* (*Nevertheless, Say "Yes" to Life: A Psychologist Experiences the Concentration Camp*). The 1959 version was called, *From Death-Camp to Existentialism*.

about being overweight, having a large nose, being hard of hearing, having a speech impediment, and so on that needs to limit you. For that reason, limiting yourself because of such irrelevancies is avoidable and conquerable.

Some people have real challenges, and so might you. Or, you may be limiting yourself because of a perceived flaw based on some insult that came from an equally flawed person and was probably made years ago. The point is that such challenges, real or imagined, do not have to limit you. They are learned; they can be unlearned. Find ways to stop limiting yourself based on old wounds. One author put this same idea well by writing:

> *I can give up all of my games, hypocrisies, and facades. I do not need them any more to protect my tender heart. I am willing to feel.... I know who I am because at heart, I am who I am.*[10]

Like a cocker spaniel coming out of a polluted pond, shake off the petty lies of the past. High-speed cameras show that dogs can spin themselves dry in less than 5 seconds. Be kind: give yourself 10 seconds to shake off. Vow to miss no more opportunities to meet others. This means no longer waiting in silence in grocery store lines. It means chatting with waiters and clerks. It means speaking in elevators and asking others for introductions to new people.

## ZAP COLLARS AND PACHYDERM STRINGS

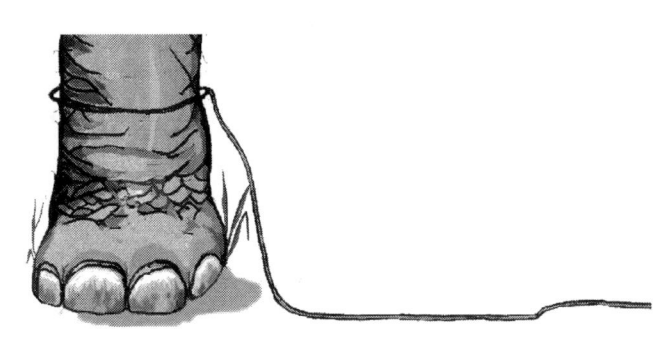

A friend who recently got a new puppy purchased a dog collar that was linked to a charged perimeter fence. When the dog came near the perimeter, the collar would shock the puppy lightly. Zap!

The biggest shock was not to the dog, but to the owner when, about a month later, she realized that the battery on the dog collar had totally run down and the collar no longer had any power at all. Yet, the dog still wasn't even approaching the fences. That puppy had no way of knowing that her limitations were all in her mind. There was literally nothing holding the dog back other than the dog's own belief system.

A similar story was told of a huge elephant that was used to help set up the Big Tent for a traveling circus. When it was little, the elephant was chained to a thick, heavy post that was staked deep into the ground. But as the elephant grew larger, the great chain was replaced by a

---

[10] Blake T. Ostler, 2013, *Fire on the Horizon*, Greg Kofford Books, p. 110.

rope, then by a thick string, no thicker than an ordinary boot lace. How does a great elephant get tied by a shoestring?

The reality was the elephant could break that string at any time. It could roam wherever it wanted to. The elephant's early belief system simply remained intact. There was really nothing stopping it or holding it back.

How true those stories are for all of us! Too often it's your own belief systems that hold you back. But you are not a puppy or a pachyderm; you're a highly intelligent human being. You can re-educate yourself to understand the belief system that was imposed upon you, even the addictions you fought and that bound you and your old wounds, are only limitations that you still entertain. More than that, they are the *only* limitations of your behavior today. Maintain the parameters that make you a good person but throw off the collars and strings that confine you to old comfort zones that no longer serve you well. The tethers of years past are no longer monster cable binding you in place. The batteries have all lost their power. Be bold and chart your own destiny.

In some cases, you may be imagining limitations that were truly never there. It is simply your mindset that is holding you back. You may have created an illusion of a limitation. What would it take to shatter that illusion? Does your whole world have to fall apart? No… you are the captain of your own ship. You get to decide when and where it sails.

As a child, you were told such safety-issue limitations as "don't play in the street" or "stay close to someone else." That was fine then. Now as adults, you need no longer be tethered by the programming you received as a child. It was appropriate for you then. However, it may no longer be appropriate. One of the advantages of being an adult is you now have the ability to think this through. Take the time to evaluate your limiting systems. Sometimes those things are still valid as limits. You should still not play in the street. You need to do those things that keep you safe. But other times your abilities as an adult allow you to cross the street safely without relying on someone else.

Sometimes it just comes down to giving yourself permission. Why do you need to rely on others to give their approval for you to step outside your comfort zones? You don't! Wouldn't you be more successful and happier if you expanded your comfort zones? Your comfort zones are merely obsolete tethers you place on yourself.

*If you feel you need permission to expand your comfort zone, you now have that permission!*

Better yet, give yourself permission to remove these collars and tethers if they are no longer helpful.

## NETWORKING 7-7-7

Internalize the principle of 7-7-7. This means that from 7 in the morning till 7 in the evening, 7 days a week, you encounter opportunities to network. Are you able to recognize them, appreciate them, and put them to work for yourself and for others?

Particularly in the area of creating contacts (**CC**), develop the third mindset of talking to most people in most situations 7-7-7. Meet people frequently and with confidence. Make it a habit. For these actions to become habits, professional networking must become a *lifestyle*, not a series of individual and haphazard events. People who say that networking does not work have usually tried it only once or twice. The key is consistency.

One who can see opportunities as gifts to explore is far different from one who is an "opportunist." Merriam-Webster defines an opportunist as one who is "a slick, shady, and a-moral" person who "has only one desire: to get through life without a day of labor."[11] Don't be an opportunist – but do recognize and utilize the opportunities with which you are surrounded and daily blessed.

When you fully develop a 7-7-7 mentality, you pivot from one who grasps and snatches at random opportunities for profit, to one who regularly and systematically develops opportunities into occasions to enrich and serve others. This may come through, as well as outside of, sales, but they are there, and they are frequent. By looking for them 7-7-7, you will not only find business success, you will find abundant satisfaction in life.

Let's translate this into concrete examples. Suppose you stop for a hot beverage on the way to work every morning. You interact with the staff and they may actually get to know who you are or what your name is. Do you take the time to get to know them and learn their names? Do you know who they are and what their skills are? Could you recall their names if you bumped into them in a different place and context? Do you know what makes them smile, or what they would like to do with their lives? Are you making their lives better because of their interaction with you?

Whether you take advantage of it or not, these otherwise incidental or invisible people are a part of your network just because you interact with them. You may not even know their names, but you interact, so they are in your network, at least in a superficial sense. If you learn their names beyond just ordering a hot beverage on a regular basis, you will see them as contacts.

The point is that all of these opportunities are around you all the time. When you interact with anybody, especially on a consistent basis, you have the opportunity to either create or strengthen a relationship. Simply smiling at people may help them remember who you are. It may also help them feel better about themselves. Everyone responds to smiles.

---

[11] See: www.merriam-webster.com/dictionary/opportunist

## MINDSETS FOR NETWORKING SUCCESS

If you remember nothing else about building and strengthening your professional network, remember the advice of Zig Ziglar, a well-known motivational speaker. He famously taught:

> *You can have everything in life you want, if you will just help other people get what they want.*[12]

That's not a one-time effort. Again, we are back to service. To the extent that you can, help other people to get what they want and need. But you need to recognize this consistently and constantly as a part of a mindset of 7-7-7.

You may ask, "Where are these 7-7-7 opportunities to move toward realizing what you want?" The answer is that they are all around you. You can make otherwise invisible people be more than mere strangers in your life who you don't notice or think about. How do you make them more than just another object in your environment? Find the answer to that question and do it. A story is told of a Charles Schwab CEO, Walter Bettinger, who failed to pay attention to such invisible people.

> *After spending hours studying formulas for calculations, young Bettinger showed up to find that the exam was nothing but a blank sheet of paper. The professor said, "I've taught you everything I can teach you about in business in the last 10 weeks," he recalled. "But the most important message, the most important question, is this: What's the name of the lady who cleans the building?" Bettinger had no idea. He failed the exam and got a B in the class. "That had a powerful impact," he said. "her name was Dottie, and I didn't know Dottie. I'd seen her, but I'd never taken the time to ask her name." Bettinger shared that, since then, he's "tried to know every Dottie I've worked with. It was a great reminder of what really matters in life."*

When you network with the mindset of 7-7-7, every person with whom you interact is potentially an opportunity to grow.[13] Those people may become contacts and perhaps friends. If you are helping people move along their paths to achieve their goals and ambitions, you are often helping yourself to do the same thing. You are also working on the **CC** element of the networking formula.

Summertime is a great opportunity to create new contacts when you didn't expect to. You're involved in your children's (or grandchildren's) sporting events, you go to concerts, have neighborhood activities, get involved in clean-up groups …the list is endless. These activities usually

---

[12] Hilary Hinton "Zig" Ziglar (November 6, 1926 – November 28, 2012) was an American author, salesman, and motivational speaker. See: https://en.wikipedia.org/wiki/Zig_Ziglar

[13] For an excellent sharing of the meaning of relationships see: Dalton-Brown, Melissa, 2016. "My Deceased Son's Answer to What it's all About" - melissadaltonbradford.wordpress.com/2016/05/28/my-deceased-sons-answer-to-what-its-all-about.

have folks you have not met previously attending also. Seize the networking opportunities while at these events. And, don't make the mistake of thinking that when you get out of your professional "uniform," you won't need business tools such as business cards. Think 7-7-7. Summer activities create wonderful chances for you to share your information, and the business card is the easiest way to follow-up those introductions with your contact information.

Some people may question if there are really enough contacts to go around, especially if more networkers begin to adopt this 7-7-7 value. Fearing that there are not enough, some approach business with a spirit of competition rather than cooperation. This leads to an unfortunate reluctance to help other business people, seeing them as competitors. Like puppies waiting for crumbs to fall from the table, they snap at others, protect any advantage they think they have, and growl if others approach. We are here to tell you that you don't need to be stingy. There is enough and to spare. That brings us to the fifth mindset: that of abundance.

## ABUNDANCE NOT SCARCITY

The most successful professional networkers operate with a mindset of abundance. This means they know there is plenty of work to go around and plenty of opportunity to grow their business. They know that there is room for everybody to engage in their own enterprise, especially if they are able to specialize, i.e., tighten their niche area.

Conceptualizing business as dogs fighting for scraps from the table rather than working together to grow, and then share, a vast pie of opportunity is a glass half-full, glass half-empty proposition. By contemplating the world through the eyes of truly successful and generous people, your own views can grow and mature.

The world out there is not a one-size pie where the bigger one person's piece is, the smaller the pieces available for competitors are. Instead of approaching networking from the point of view of competition, the best networkers approach with a spirit of cooperation. They understand that they truly can make everyone's pie bigger. In that way, they can all, cooperatively, enjoy a similar percentage of the pie. It is simply that the pie itself begins to grow. There is room at the table for everyone. Pie for all.

How, exactly, can you grow the pie?

There are several ways to accomplish this. Naturally, the best growth and the most successful networks that you have are built with the clientele that you relate to the best. That is the low-hanging fruit.

Look higher!

There is more fruit higher up and out on the branches. So, the first way to grow the pie is to grow the number of people with whom you relate well. Is that a small number or a large number? If you think about it, the answer to that question is in your control, not in the control of others. You are not a victim of the market; you are far from helpless. If you so choose, you can expand your appreciation of others just as you can eliminate criticism, judgment, and rejection of the people around you. Much has been written about doing this very thing beginning with Dale Carnegie's 1936 classic, *How to Win Friends and Influence People.* This is a must-read for those wishing to grow the pie by growing the number of people with whom they can relate. We will expand on many of Carnegie's ideas in this book.

A second way in which the pie grows is as the local market broadens and the industry itself expands. A good example of this is in the area of marriage counseling. Several decades ago, receiving marriage counseling brought with it a strong stigma. Counseling was thought to be a sign of marital misery and of impending divorce. At that time, many counselors became alarmed that the field of counseling was becoming saturated.

None of that fear-mongering was even worth stating. No flooding ever took place. Instead, having marriage counseling gradually became seen as a refining opportunity for couples to find greater joy in their relationships and achieve much deeper communication. The perceived stigma gradually transformed into a bragging point.

Soon, having 12 marriage counselors in a city became 100, and then 200. The field was not saturated. Instead, there was abundance to be discovered and developed. There is no reason to be narrow-thinking and fear-consumed like those counselors of the past. Cultivate a mindset of abundance. That is how the pie grows. Grow your pie.

A similar example comes from the career of Keith Woodcook, who sold polyester and nylon ropes and small cables. That is not as simple as it sounds. There are many gauges, types, tensile strengths, and stretch rates. Keith found that just the mere fact of understanding rope and talking about its uses and benefits lent itself to creating more purchasers of rope. That ripple effect ran from big boxes stores to tiny specialty hardware stores. He increased his presentations about ropes among his prospective contacts and soon, more and more people became interested (**CC**) and gave him relevant referrals (**RR**). His percentage of contacts stayed the same, around 8% of the market in his area, but the pie, itself, became much bigger. So, his percentage actually represented more people. The 8% of 20 became 8% of 200.

Focus on the clients who you want to work with. Don't focus on the perceived parameters and limitations of the field. It is white, all ready to harvest. Do the best you can with the opportunities all around you.

Those are the four essential mindsets that we recommend. However, there is one final approach to networking. It could be considered a fifth mindset, but it is also a principle that stands alone. It is called the Rule of 12. We will turn to that in the next chapter.

# CHAPTER 3

# THE LIBERATION OF THE RULE OF 12

In Chapter Two, we explored four essential and positive mindsets that lay the foundation for successful networking. Now, we're introducing a concept that builds on those ideas: The Rule of 12. Think of this as more than just a mindset—it's a lens through which you can view both networking and life. By adopting The Rule of 12, many have discovered a new sense of freedom, both personally and professionally. It's a perspective that challenges assumptions, shifts priorities, and can lead to transformative results.

## 12% LOVE YOU; 12% HATE YOU

The Rule of 12 states that there is a portion of people you meet, approximately 12%, who will love you immediately and unconditionally. As soon as they're introduced to you, they will want to be a part of what you are doing and will want to be around you. And there is almost nothing you can do to upset that. So, you don't need to break your arm patting yourself on the back for having won them over because they were going to love you anyway.

From a networking point of view, the Rule of 12 states that this proportion of the people want to associate with you – with _you_. No matter what, they want to be around you. They will connect with you on a personal level and be completely loyal to you. They are members, you might say, of your fan club. They want to help _you_ and, significantly, want to do business with _you_. These people will be repeat customers for as long as you offer something they need. As eager referral partners, they will move heaven and earth to give you relevant referrals, buy from you, and support you all the way. For these reasons, they will be your primary focus, just as you will be theirs. These are the people you are most going to serve and nurture. This is home; this is family.

The Rule of 12 also states another reality. Some people may find this one harsh, but it turns out to be extraordinarily liberating. The harsh reality is that:

1. Some people you meet will *never* become a contact.
2. Some you meet do not *want* to be your friend.

The first point is just a simple reality of any endeavor – there is always a percentage of success and a percentage of failure. That's fine; that's just a part of life. We are all used to that and accept it. There's no news here. It is the second point that is much more interesting. The Rule of 12 says that not everyone you meet will even *want* to be associated with you. In fact, some people will hate you unjustly and for no apparent reason. They will not like you, your voice, your waistline, or your face. They will reject your mannerisms, the way you part your hair, the way you write your name, or something. That will be particularly upsetting for you if you are a people-pleaser and an approval-seeker, but it is simply a cold fact of life. There are going to be people who will not now, nor ever, want to associate with you. No matter how fast you tap dance, no matter how much you smile and flirt, no matter how many jokes you tell, or how much mouthwash you gargle, they will *not like you*. And there is absolutely nothing that you can do about it.

If that sounds bleak and depressing, here comes the liberating part: Quit trying! Since there is absolutely nothing that you can do about this, give yourself permission to not care. Having people not like you is *not personal*. It is not about you; it's not your fault. If you present yourself warmly with a smile, a firm handshake and the funniest joke in the world, this proportion of the people you approach will think your approach is intrusive or arrogant; your smile is forced; and your jokes are cheesy, insulting, or just plain stupid. Let that go! Give up the frustrating and hopeless task of trying to get everyone you meet to love you. Ain't happening! And, it's not your fault! That's the great news! That's what's so liberating.

Recognize that this bottom 12% exist, but don't expend energy on trying to win them over to do business or exchange referrals. They are likely good people, they just don't see the world the way you do.

Are the bottom 12%ers really even in your network? Well, yes and no. They are in your network since you know their names and you know they exist. However, they are not really a part of your network in that you don't interact with them. Some of them, you may have not even met. Some have rejected you without knowing you or allowing you to know them. Let that go. Some folks are just too much effort to do business with.

Remember, your top and bottom 12% will be different from other people's. Let's say Kevin is in your top 12%. Kevin is a local real estate agent. Though you know several agents in the area, Kevin is the one you prefer to do business with. If there is something new in Kevin's professional life, you want to know about it and be a part of it. When Kevin has a new listing, you're interested in hearing more about it. When Kevin offers classes to the public about first-time home buying, you want to attend, and you want to tell all your friends about it. When Kevin is serving spaghetti at a local charity event, you want to be there and, by golly, you are going to buy some. If Kevin is involved in a networking group, you want to be involved, too. When you have a friend who is considering purchasing a home in the local market, it is Kevin who you connect your friend with.

Meanwhile, he is doing the same kinds of things with, and for, other people who are in his 12% who may or may not be in yours. In fact, you may not be in his top 12%. You don't necessarily even know or recognize that. Similarly, you may have 12%ers who don't particularly connect with Kevin. That is normal and expected.

One obvious analogy is to the essentially two-party system of American politics. Whether you are a Democrat or a Republican, each party has a base. In recent years the core base of each party is higher than 12% – more like 25% for each side.[14] This means that if you are a Democrat running for president, you can count on a core of Democrats who will vote for you anytime, anywhere, without fail and without hesitation, no matter what mud is thrown up against you by your opponents. Of course, the same would be true if you were running as the Republican candidate. There is a solid base of hardcore Republicans who would vote for you without regard to platform or scandal.

The Rule of 12 is abundantly obvious with all of the last several presidents, but there is nothing new in that; it was always so. Think way back to the time of Abraham Lincoln, the 16th President of these United States. In surveys of the success of US Presidents, he is usually ranked as one of the three greatest and most successful.[15] Yet, he had a similar pattern: a percentage who loved him and voted him into office, a percentage who were neutral or indifferent, and a percentage who hated him. Don't believe it? Below is a quote from 1861. It was published, not by a newspaper in the deep South, but from one in his own State of Illinois:

> *Honest Old Abe...is no more capable of becoming a statesman, nay, even a moderate one, than the braying ass can become a noble lion. People now marvel how it came to pass that Mr. Lincoln should have been selected as the representative man of any party. His weak, wishy-washy, namby-pamby efforts, imbecile in matter, disgusting in manner, have made us the laughing stock of the whole world.* [16]

---

[14] According to Gallup polling, the percent of states that are solidly Democrat is 26% and solidly Republican is 28%. The ratio is uncannily equal on both sides. - see: https://en.wikipedia.org/wiki/ Political_party_strength_in_U.S._ states.

[15] The other two are Franklin D. Roosevelt and George Washington. See: https://en.wikipedia.org/wiki/Historical_rankings_of_presidents_of_the_United_States

[16] This quote was cited in www.battlefields.org/learn/articles/evidence-un-popular-mr-lincoln

"Ahh," you say, "but that was before the Emancipation Proclamation made Lincoln the Great Emancipator, which made everyone love him." No, it didn't. Even after the Proclamation, he had his negative 12%. The *Chicago Times* called the Emancipation Proclamation "a criminal wrong and an act of national suicide" while *The Crisis* in Columbus Ohio warned: "We have no doubt that this Proclamation seals the fate of his Union as it was, and the Constitution as it is…." Lincoln's secretary told how the hate mail "heaped up in wastebaskets." Much of this hate mail hurled negatives. One bottom 12%er wrote, "They never, never told him that he might set the negroes free and, now that he has done so… he is a more unconstitutional tyrant and a more odious dictator than ever he was before."

And don't forget his most famous hater John Wilkes Booth who entered the presidential box of the Ford Theater in 1865 and shot Lincoln in the back of the head.

On the other side were the 12% who loved him completely and unconditionally. One of those was his closest friend, William Seward, who served as Abe Lincoln's Secretary of State. Another was Edwin Stanton, who was unable to control his weeping for weeks after the assassination. Another was Frederick Douglass, one of the many slaves liberated by Lincoln, who proclaimed in 1876 that:

> *There is little necessity on this occasion to speak at length and critically of this great and good man, and of his high mission in the world. That ground has been fully occupied….*[17]

Today, Lincoln has millions of what might be called top 12%ers; many of them are scholars who base their admiration on the military success of the Civil War and his abolition of slavery. One wrote of what she called his: "political genius revealed through his extraordinary array of personal qualities." Another author went so far as to build a case that:

> *…Abraham Lincoln was a man inspired by God to bring the nation closer to heaven and to healing. I know he invoked a covenant relationship between America and its Maker.* [18]

---

[17] Doris Kearns Goodwin, 2005, *Team of Rivals: The Political Genius of Abra- ham Lincoln*, Simon & Schuster, N.Y, "Introduction," p. xv.
[18] Timothy Ballard, 2014, *The Lincoln Hypothesis*, Deseret Book, Salt Lake City, UT, p. 265.

There will be a group of your contemporaries who will put you down – people who will seek to destroy you no matter what you do. There is nothing you can do about that. Happily, you may safely ignore the detractors since none will follow you to a movie theater with a loaded gun. Spend your time with the 12%ers who see you as a "noble lion" and not the 12% who see you as a "braying ass."

As a presidential candidate, you could not, nor would you want to, ignore your base. You would do that at your own peril. The same thing is true in business networking. Focus on your 12% base who love you. Lean on them for support and sustenance and referrals. Share relevant referrals (**RR**) with them, sell to them, nurture and care for them (**NN**). This is your base of operations.

On the other hand, you can let go of the 12% who will never want you. This is liberating good news. It is liberating because this awareness provides a structure for your efforts and frees you from blaming yourself. Revel in the 12% who love you, ignore the 12% who hate you.

## THE 76%ERS IN THE MIDDLE

An obvious next question is to ask, "Well... what about the undecideds – in this case the 76% who do not belong to either end. What about those people? That large group of people, who we might call 76%ers, can, of course, be added to your network, but they are not part of your 12% fan club. They fall on a continuum or spectrum that ranges from those closer to the fan club all the way to those closer to the 12% rejectors. Obviously, the greatest success will come from those nearest the top 12%, while the ones closest to the 12% haters will be harder to reach. But all of the 76% are potentially attainable.

### WORK WITH, BUT DON'T FOCUS ON, 76%ERS

In an election year, the politicians go after the undecided 76%. The question is: should you? For some, the answer to that question seems to be obvious and intuitive, yes. However, that answer is false. It is based on an assumption: You should spend most of your time working with your 76%ers, because that is the largest percentage of contacts.

This assumption is mistaken and incorrect. First, you are _not_ a politician, and it is _not_ an election year, anyway. Second, you will, and should, spend most of your working time and effort with your top 12%ers. Never ignore them as givens. It doesn't matter that the 76%ers are a larger percent of your network. Yes, they are wonderful as referrals and customers, but they are not your loyal and unconditional supporters. The assumption is false because it doesn't take into account the reach of the net. Although the percentage of 12% will not change, the number of people in that 12% can grow to be all that you can handle, and more. So emphasize them over the 76%ers.

Trying to win over your haters will not work. You cannot change how people think. Trying to do that will only make you a phony and an approval-seeker.

Here's a way to think of it. You associate with, play with, serve, and give referrals to your 12%ers. You sell to them and buy from *them*. Yes, you definitely accept referrals from your 76%ers as well. You also connect your 12%ers to them if that can benefit the 12%ers. You are cordial to the 76%ers. However, you don't particularly associate with them or look for opportunities to serve them. The trick, again, is to be able to distinguish between 12%ers and 76%ers – to be able to describe them to other 76%ers because some of the people who they know will become 12%ers for you. And that is what you want! The 76%ers need to know exactly who are the kinds of people you're looking for, so you need to be able to tell them.

It is a mistaken idea to spend the bulk of your time and energy on the 76%ers? Save it for the 12%ers who love you, and whom you love. Most of your engagements with 76%ers will take more effort than working with any of your top 12%ers. So, if they come to you, accept that. Use the relationship to sell to. Use the connection as a contact to meet the needs of your 12%ers. And definitely accept their referrals to you. But don't knock yourself out working with the 76%ers. That is a misplaced focus.

Another mistake is to think you must, or even can, convert 76%ers into 12%ers. No, don't try that. Don't put that on yourself. You can't do it anyway. You cannot control what people think and how they feel. Don't even try. If you try, you become an approval-seeker or a panderer, and you don't want to be either of those. Don't try to convert. People either plop automatically into your 12% fan club, or they don't. We are talking about networking, not proselyting.

Those in the middle (76%ers) are on a continuum and can shift. The top 12%ers and the bottom 12%ers are not. To understand this, think about a star entertainer – an actor or a singer. She seems to have the whole world wrapped around her little finger and following her on social media. They seem to adore her. Now, she still has her 12% haters and her 12% who love her. The 76%ers are all hovering on the high side of the middle. In other words, they are crowded near, but not altogether in, the top 12%. Now, let's say that a catastrophe hits. Maybe she puts out a series of box office bombs or boring songs. Or maybe she jumps on the soap box and starts making political statements that divide her fans. At that point, the folks on the 76% continuum begin to shift. However, the true 12%ers (top or bottom) don't even blink. They stay with her, or against her, through it all.

So, it is possible to shift 76%ers, but not to win over the bottom 12% (which you can't do) or recruit 12%ers. The goal is not to convert 76%ers, it is to find more 12%ers. They are out there; hundreds of them – just waiting to find out about you. Remember the mindset of Abundance.

So, don't ignore the 76%ers. They are people who are willing to listen to what you have to say, evaluate what you have to offer, and possibly purchase your product or services. As such, these are good people to network with and have as referral partners. But they are not your core and your base. Focus on the 12% who most want to associate with you, be a part of what you are doing and who you are, and want what you offer.

## THE MIRACLE OF THE RIPPLE EFFECT

We can hear you already: "But... I don't have that many people who I could consider as 12%ers!" Remember that each of these 12% of people who enjoy you the most, also know at least 100 other people who don't yet know you. That amounts to thousands of people. Your 12%ers will be only too happy to introduce them all to you because they feel so close to you. Some of them will become new 12%ers for you. Granted, every professional has a specific 12% and is the "sol" (or soul) of that network. Their network will never line up exactly the same as yours. The good news is that it doesn't need to. Most of your friends' 12%ers won't come over to you as 12%ers. That's just how it works. But most will at least come over as 76%ers for you. If for no other reason than their loyalty to their own "sol" who has recommended you, these new people will take a long look at what you have to offer. Many will buy from you or interact with you. This could potentially add a thousand or more quality 76%ers for you. Think of it! That means oceans of potential business as well as the creation of contacts (**CC**) and hundreds more relevant referrals (**RR**).

As amazing as that is, it's only the tip of the iceberg. The Rule of 12 states that the majority of those people will come over "only" as potential business. However, it also states that:

*12% of those thousands will immediately become new 12%ers for you.*

It will happen as soon as they meet you and see the type of person you are.

Do the math: 12% of 1,000+ new people equals 120+ new additional 12%ers who would swim the English Channel for you, move mountains for you, who want to be around you. You need to be introduced to these people. Think about it. Suppose you spent the next 3 to 6 months doing nothing other than meeting and creating contacts (**CC**) with some of these new 12%ers. They would, without hesitation, do business with you, give you referrals, and help you in any way they can. How radically different would your career become? How much would your income increase? How powerful would your network become (**NP**)? That's the target of top-level 212 professional networking.

Don't forget, too, that you are also trying to help others to find their own 12%ers. Again, everyone's network is unique. Some of your contacts will become 12%ers for someone else. That's part of the Rule of 12. This is where referrals become beneficial to everyone involved. That's why there is abundance and cooperation if you want to seize it. As you help your business friends to achieve their victories, they will help you achieve your goals. As we've pointed out, you don't help them in order to help yourself. You help them because it is your orientation and mindset to help others. It's who you are. By the way, they will reciprocate in a mutual win-win manner. This process is never-ending. This mindset becomes a lifestyle. This is another way in which the conceptualization of the Rule of 12 is liberating and beneficial.

Here's how it all works. What you want to do is to comb through the contacts who your 76%ers give you, or who find on your own. Also, search through your casual contacts. You are looking for people you have not yet met and don't really know. You are looking for either those who will naturally become a part of your 12% fan club, by themselves, as soon as they meet you, or you are looking for people who you can refer to as your friends.

If you find new contacts who become new 12%ers, that's wonderful, amazing! Deepen those relationships through interaction and loving service. Maintain and nurture those friendships. The 12%ers are your very best referral partners. Their value far exceeds anyone else.

On the other hand, If the new contacts become 76%ers, that's okay, too. Keep them safely in your network as possible future referrals or sources of new introductions and refer them to others in your network. In the 1990s, British anthropologist Robin Dunbar proposed that the human brain had a cognitive limit of 150 stable relationships. The so-called, "Dunbar's number" asserts that there is a…

> *…cognitive limit to the number of people with whom one can maintain stable <u>social</u> <u>relationships</u> – relationships in which an individual knows who each person is and how each person relates to every other person.*[19]

Even if your brain is larger than most peoples and you can maintain a 12% fan base of 200 people, that is far less than the 500 to 1,000 contacts we recommend you have in your network. That is the difference between social relationships and business contacts. Nobody can have more than 150 best friends; but you can have more than 150 12% business contacts who you nurture once or twice a year – far more. That is also the difference between 12%ers and 76%ers. That is why you need to develop some systems to manage your network.

---

[19] See: https://en.wikipedia.org/wiki/Dunbar%27s_number – emphasis added.

- *Nurture the 12% fan club,*
- *Maintain the 76%ers,*
- *Ignore the 12% haters.*

We are fully aware that most beginning networkers don't have 150 total contacts, let alone 150 12%ers. You likely have around 9 to 10 true 12% fans, so your job is to work 7-7-7 to cast out your net. You are seeking more 12%ers with whom you can interact, refer, buy, and sell, and otherwise enjoy and serve.

Given all of this, how ridiculous is it that a surprisingly large number of networkers spend the majority of their time going after the bottom 12% who don't like them and won't ever like them? They expend their resources and their energy in a vain pursuit of the unattainable. That 12% will never appreciate what they have to offer. The 12% haters will never buy their products or pay for their services. That is crazy! The good news is that you do not need to make that same mistake. Quit wasting your time trying to reach the unreachable.

Having failed to reach the 12% haters, those same few networkers – who have zeal without knowledge (see Introduction) – then make mistake #2. They then turn their time, their energy, and their money over to trying to reach the sometimes valuable, sometimes inert, and sometimes fickle 76%ers. No! Don't make that same mistake. Value your 76%ers, but don't fuss over them. Instead, search for more 12%ers.

## THE INCREDIBLE POTENTIAL OF THE RULE OF 12

The Rule of 12 is quite simple, but it is also profound. This three-way split is a fact of life that people don't talk about all that much. Yet, it occurs for all people, and at all times. It can make a major difference in your networking activities.

### FUN EXAMPLES FROM LITERATURE

While we could list many examples of the Rule of 12 at work in the lives of people, it is also reflected in pop culture and in classic literature. Below are just three great books that might help make this point clear in a fun way. These widely-known books are all fiction, of course, however writers reflect real life in their stories. For that reason, we can see the Rule of 12 in their works.

1. *Moby Dick* by Herman Melville. Captain Ahab, the tragic captain of the ship, the *Pequod*, had his own top 12%ers. One was Fedallah, the captain's highly-regarded Persian servant and private seer who had a vision of the Captain's imminent death. There were also his chief mate, *Moby Dick*

THE PROFESSIONAL NETWORKER'S PLAYBOOK

also describes, Starbuck, the second mate, and Stubb, both of whom could, and did, look past the possessed captain's mad obsession and helped him to hunt and kill the great white sperm whale.

Captain Ahab's 76%ers included Pip, the young cabin boy, and Captain Boomer, who had lost his own arm to Moby Dick. The mysterious Queequeg from the fictional island of Rokovoko was a 76%er, as was Ishmael, the narrator and observer of Melville's classic. Poor Ishmael could never understand the captain and looked on in amazement as Ahab pursued his destructive addiction.

But who was in Ahab's bottom 12%?

Why ...Moby Dick, of course

Captain Ahab simply could not let that 12% go, as we have advised you to do. Captain Ahab could not ignore the white sperm whale. Interestingly, although Ahab believed Moby Dick hated him as much as he hated the whale, that wasn't the case. Another whale hunter, a Captain Boomer, recognized that and tried to warn Ahab:

"What you take for the White Whale's malice is only his awkwardness, for he never meant to swallow a single limb." But Captain Ahab just couldn't hear that.

Instead, he expended all his time and all of his resources in chasing his "nemesis," the great whale who he could never defeat. He could not accept that there was nothing he could do about that bottom 12%.

"Thar she blows! Thar she blows!"

Captain Ahab's total refusal to give up that obsession about the bottom 12% finally resulted in Ahab's death and the total destruction of his ship. Don't you make that same mistake with your own bottom 12%! Let those 12%ers go!

2. *The Lion, the Witch, and the Wardrobe* by C.S. Lewis. This famous fable and allegory centers on Lucy Pevensie, one of the children sent to the country to avoid the Nazi bombing of London during WWII. Lucy would be able to count among her top 12%, her brother Peter, her sister Susan, and Mr. Tumnas, the faun. Then there was Mr. and Mrs. Beaver and, of course, Aslan, Narnia's majestic ruler.

What about Edmund, Lucy's other brother? Although he likely had an underlying familial loyalty, he betrayed his family for a mess of pottage in the form of Turkish Delight, an English candy. And the more he consumed, the more he fed his addiction. His actions put him among the 76%ers.

In the bottom 12% of those who wanted to destroy Lucy (and the others) was the White Witch, the self-proclaimed Queen of Narnia. Lucy did not succumb to her subtle temptations and hatred as Edmund had done for a tin of Turkish Delight candy.

Out of his unconditional and majestic love for Lucy and Edmund, Aslan, the Great Lion, sacrificed his own life to the White Queen to redeem Edmund. C.S. Lewis then has Aslan miraculously come back to life for a final battle in which he defeats the Enemy.

But the focus of *The Lion, the Witch, and the Wardrobe* is Lucy, who proves to be the exact opposite of Captain Ahab. By ignoring the White Witch (her bottom 12%) and putting all her energy, focus, and faith on Aslan (the top of her positive 12%), Lucy was able to achieve her goals and help to save Narnia.

<u>3. *Pride and Prejudice* by Jane Austen</u>. Elizabeth Bennett also had a fan club who loved her always and unconditionally. In addition to her family was Mr. Bingley and Darcy's sister, Georgiana, who entered the picture later but immediately became an enthusiastic top 12%er.

Among her 76%ers would be the out-of-touch Sir William Lucas, the pleasant Colonel Fitzwilliam, and the comedically awkward Mr. Collins, who was only looking for a wife, not someone to love.

In the bottom 12% were the hypocritical Caroline Bingley and Louisa Hurst, who pretended to be Elizabeth's friends but in fact were not. But central to that bottom 12% had to be Lady Catherine de Bourgh. After one especially in-her-face attack from Lady de Bourgh, Elizabeth exercised the perfect attitude toward that bottom 12%, telling her ladyship, "You may ask questions, which I shall <u>not</u> choose to answer.… [You] will have no effect on me." Austen then dismisses de Bourgh outright when Jane adds, "You have insulted me in every possible method. I must …return to the house. …Lady Catherine, I have nothing further to say." Then she pointedly added …[Your resentment] will not give me one moment's concern." Go Elizabeth! What an example to us!

So far, we have not mentioned Mr. Darcy, another interesting study in *Pride and Prejudice*. Mr. Darcy loved Elizabeth instantly and totally but denied his feelings because of the pride of a rich man and his prejudice against anyone who was in a lower social class. But he could not help himself. He finally confessed, "My feelings will not be repressed. You must allow me to tell you how ardently I admire and love you." This wonderfully illustrated two things.

First, it is not always obvious how people feel about you. You must learn to correctly recognize 12%ers in your search for them. Elizabeth thought that Mr. Darcy was a hater when he was really a lover. And, she thought Mr. Wickham was in her top 12% until she recognized that he was only an opportunist pretending to love her in order to secure money. Some of your business colleagues are like that. Be sure to recognize a true 12%er.

Second, there is nothing you can do to affect the feelings and opinions of 12%ers. It is what it is. There is also nothing you can do to court 76%ers and convert them into top 12%ers. They may migrate somewhat closer to either a hater or a fan but, if it happens, it comes from them; not from you. So, do not try. Sell, refer, and provide service among your 76%ers as the occasion may arise, but do not try to win them over. And certainly, realize that there is nothing you can do to win over anyone in your bottom 12%. Instead, spend your time trying to nurture 12%ers.

## PERCENTAGES AND NUMBERS

Realize that your own network can expand. It may be as short as 50 contacts, or as long as 500, or even 5,000. While the numbers can grow astronomically, the percentages of 12, 76, and 12 do not change. This means that the size of your 12% fan club is only limited by the number you can contact, nurture, and serve. So, concentrate on expanding your total contacts. According to the Rule of 12, roughly 12% of everyone you contact will naturally emerge as your fans. Then spend the vast majority of your time and energy nurturing this 12% who love you, want what you have, and want to help you as much as you want to help and serve them.

Changing your behavior in order to win over people is futile anyway. It is a grave error. It can turn you into someone who panders. What does that word really mean? Pandering is "expressing one's views in accordance with the likes of a group to which one is attempting to appeal…"[20]

Worse, perhaps, are approval seekers. These people are externally oriented out of a fear of not being accepted. They sacrifice their wishes and even their personhood, turning those over to the will of someone else to win love. This is an affront to personal agency and personal identity and an abandonment of individual autonomy. In the extreme, it becomes a diagnosable mental disorder known as "Dependent Personality Disorder." When you try to win someone's approval at any cost, you are either pandering or approval-seeking. Don't do that, especially in a vain attempt to win over a bottom 76%er. You give that person power by prostituting yourself. Worse, it will not work.

What you really want is respect, which is very different. Pandering and approval is based on actions you perform to please others. Respect is something that comes to you unbidden and unsought. Respect is an incidental reaction that comes as a result of actions that you perform in the interest of integrity. You do not seek respect, you seek to do what is right. If respect comes, that's fine. If it does not, that doesn't matter. You weren't doing it to seek respect anyway. Abraham Lincoln did not emancipate American slaves to win voters' approval or enhance his legacy; he did it because he believed it was the right thing to do. Incidentally, it happened to win the respect of many, which has now blossomed into the respect of tens of millions. But he would have done it anyway.

---

[20] See https://en.wikipedia.org/wiki/Pandering_(politics).

Vernon Howard, an American author and philosopher, wrote:

*A truly strong person does not need the approval of others any more than a lion needs the approval of sheep.*[21]

Do not seek the approval of anyone in your network, least of all a bottom 12%er. Do what is right and serve with love. Respect will inevitably come on its own and in its own time. So will success, for that matter.

Now, you may ask, "Where do the 12% come from? It is 12% of what?"

It is 12% of everyone.

That means that the potential is limitless. Look at it this way. If you know 25 people, then the Rule of 12 states that you will have …three 12%ers. That's not a very big fan club for you to operate within. Let's say you know 250 people. Now you have 30 in your fan club. That's good, but not good enough. Let's go for 500 people, which the Rule of 12 says would give you 60 or so 12%ers. Very nice! That's manageable, but there's still room to grow. If Dunbar's number is correct, you need a network of 1,250 to max out your fan club at 150.

We aren't talking about a thousand close friends. Nobody has that, even with social media. That is an illusion and a mistaken goal. In fact, Facebook's maximum number of contacts is capped at 5,000, a number which at least one web poster called "frustrating" and "silly."[22] It's not silly; nobody can manage 5,000 contacts. But 1,000 quality contacts in a network and 100 or so 12%ers is not an unreasonable goal. Can *you* have 1,000 contacts in *your* network? That depends on you – not on others, not on luck, not on fate – on you.

Remember that you are not alone in any of this. With some thought and skill, you can use your initial 12%ers to find more 12% contacts. By doing that, the 12% will grow and the pie will also grow. The 12% will still be 12%, but it will be 12% of a larger pool. That is called, leveraging your assets.

All that the 12% who care about you and your product need in order to help you find other contacts is to understand who you are and what you need. They don't know this intuitively; you must tell them. The point is that people in your network can help you find similar people from the same pool.

---

[21] Quoted and attributed to Vernon Howard in Larry Chang, 2006, "*Wisdom for the Soul: Five Millennia of Prescriptions for Spiritual Healing*, Gnosophia Pub, Washington DC.

[22] See: http://authoritypublishing.com/social-media/what-to-do-when-your-facebook-profile-is-maxed-out-on-friends/

You can do this. There's a great hunger in the United States. It is not a hunger for food. It is a hunger for connection and contact. There are people who are waiting to join your fan club; they just don't know it yet. So, growing your 12% is not that difficult. It's not like growing demanding vegetables like cauliflower and artichoke. It's more like growing vegetables that are easy to grow like summer squash or carrots. Sure, you need good soil, regular watering, and pest control, but anyone can have success with a little learning and a little effort.

Having now discussed four helpful mindsets to adopt in Chapter 2 and the Rule of 12 in Chapter 3, we turn in the next chapter to the power formula for professional networking and begin with the **NP** (networking power) part of the formula.

# PART TWO

## A FORMULA FOR POWER IN PROFESSIONAL NETWORKING

# CHAPTER 4

# THE POWER OF A PROFESSIONAL NETWORK

Do you fully understand the potential power of your professional network? It is enormous. Your network is a powerhouse waiting to serve you in several important ways. We hope that this chapter will enlarge your perspective and open your vision to some of the abundant opportunities and potential of your professional network.

In Chapter One, we introduced a formula for professional networking. According to this formula, Network Power (**NP**) is achieved by the interworking of several elements including Creating Contacts (**CC**) plus Nurturing a Network (**NN**) multiplied by Relevant Referrals (**RR**). Let's begin by talking about what **NP** really is, and what it can do for you and others:

$$NP = (CC + NN) \times RR$$

So far, we've talked about the mindsets that will help you to put this formula to work and we've presented the Rule of 12. With all that in mind, let's take a look at what this formula can do for you and how you can harness its power. We'll show you how to leverage the network that you already have in place to meet your own needs. Then we'll discuss what you can do for others in your network.

## NETWORKING POWER TO FIND HELP

The referral opportunities that are available to you through your network are nothing short of astounding. Your network is a storehouse – a wealth beyond anything that you can imagine.

## GETTING HELP FROM THE FIRST TIER

Think of it this way. Let's say that your network consists of a modest 500 names – and, ideally, it has many more than that. Around 60 of those may be from your 12% fan club and another 440 are 76%ers. You've met them all and worked with them to some degree. Those 500 people represent a diversity of skills, a wide range of abilities, and an abundance of resources they can share with you. And, not only that, every single one of those 500 people knows many more people, each with their own additional skills, abilities, and resources. If each of those 500 know just 100 people who you don't know, that is indirect access to 50,000 potential contacts and referral partners.

*You don't even know who
the people you know, know.*

Translated, that means that you have no idea who your contacts happen to know and who can be added to your professional network. In other words, it is the case of the old adage:

*You can count the number of seeds in an apple;
but you can't count the number of apples in a seed.*[23]

Uncountable it may be …but it is a boatload of people and a football field of 12% fans. They cannot be counted because that number is (or potentially could be) ever-increasing since the people who you want to meet are really just an introduction away.

This means that many of the issues you have and the needs you experience can be solved by simply tapping into your network as I described in the *Introduction* to this book. There really are people who would love to assist you along your way and with no strings attached. When you know what you want and you can describe it and define it in such a way that people remember what it is, they will help you willingly and enthusiastically.

Oftentimes that solution comes in a way that is hard to describe. Words like accidentally, subconsciously, automatically, transparently, organically still fail to capture the smooth and seamless way that solutions can come. When you get your head fully wrapped around that concept, you will understand a little bit better the power that lies in the networking formula.

For those times when you are tapping your network to find your own solutions, it is a good idea to be as specific and clear as you can be. Get right to the point. You need to know specifically what your goals are and, even more specifically, how you want to achieve them. Now, we aren't talking about your five-year goals or your lifetime dreams. We're talking about your immediate

---

[23] This quote, a chiasm, has been attributed to, and used by, several people. Its true origins go back too far to determine the original source of this truism.

## THE POWER OF A PROFESSIONAL NETWORK

goals. What problems do you need solved right away? For example, if you want an introduction to a specific person at a company, know that person's name, the company name, and what position that person has in the company. Be specific.

Then, when you are clear on what it is you need, don't be afraid to ask for that specific introduction. "Hey, do you know JoAnn Nutter who works at Pierce College? I'd really like an introduction to her." Others will help you and make that professional referral for you.

Remember Marc Evans from the *Introduction* to this book? He was the one who was so kind and loving in that hour of great need. He was a first-tier contact, meaning a person who was already a known contact in the network. Since we presented his story earlier, let's try a new example to make this even more clear.

Let's say that your tired old homemade business cards have run out. It's time for new ones. This time, though, you decide to replace them with professionally-designed cards that present you and your company effectively and with a certain "Wow!" factor. You know that it is worth spending a few dollars to have them done professionally. Now you can find any number of print shops, but you want a graphics designer you can truly trust. You want someone who will take the time to do it right.

In thinking about it, Dylan Brown comes to mind. Dylan stood up in your last networking meeting and presented a funny and enthusiastic commercial where he gave a short history of how he loved art as a boy and grew up to become a graphic designer. He had samples of his work out on the tables. Afterwards, you met him and shook his hand. "Of course! ...Dylan!" you say to yourself after thumping your forehead. "He would be perfect."

Like Marc from the *Introduction*, Dylan is a first tier contact, meaning he is already in your network. You call Dylan, and he says he would be delighted to help. You've given Dylan a referral, and that is always appreciated.

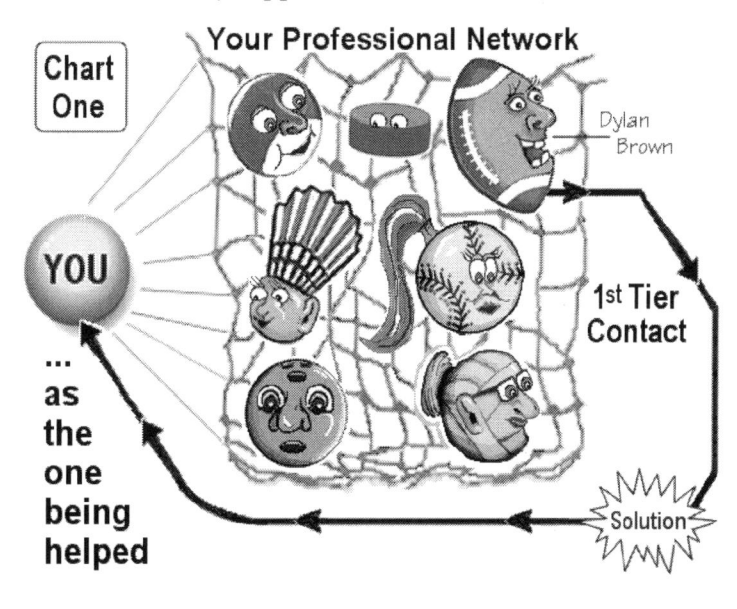

**Chart One** — Your Professional Network

In this case, the person you have referred to Dylan is ...*you*! And in return, you have found someone you trust to take extra care and do a bang-up job of designing the business card. First of all, you know him already and trust him to do a good job, but, second, you also know he would never do a sloppy job for a fellow member of a business group that he attends every week. That's double assurance that you will get great business cards.

— 43 —

We could say that Dylan accepted your burden (need, or problem) to carry (Latin, *ferre*) and returned it back to you (Latin, *re*) in the form of a great solution. You leverage your professional network to solve a problem using an established relationship at the first tier.

## GETTING HELP FROM THE SECOND TIER

Let's say that you've approved the art Dylan has proposed. You are so impressed that you want polo shirts with the same company logo. You want to give them out to all your staff and a few regular customers. You ask Dylan how that art gets to an embroiderer. Dylan tells you, "I know someone who does that. Her name is Sheryl Smith and she does a super job. She did some shirts for our big family reunion last summer, and people couldn't stop raving about them. She is a true artist. Here, just a second, I have her number on my phone list. Let me call her and get you two together." That is what is called, a second-tier contact.

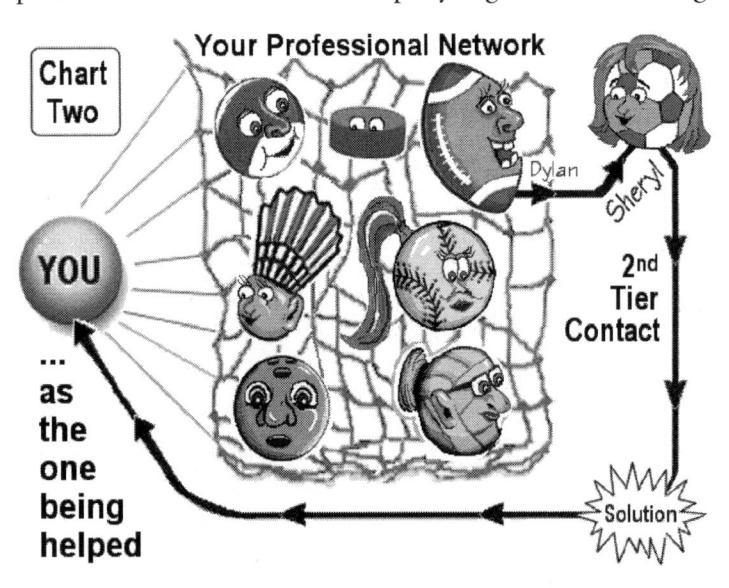

Dylan calls up Sheryl then-and-there. "Hello... Sheryl? So good to hear your voice again. Say, I'm here with a good friend, and he's looking for someone who can embroider a few dozen polo shirts. I told him how terrific you are. I know you're swamped, but I was wondering if you have a moment to speak to her. Here, let me put him on the phone." Dylan hands you the phone.

Notice that there have been two referrals made:

1. <u>The referral you made of yourself to Dylan</u>. Your sincere expression of gratitude, the effort he made on your behalf, and the solution to your problem all solidify and strengthen the bond you have with Dylan.
2. <u>The referral Dylan made of you to Sheryl</u>. The referral solidifies Dylan's bond with Sheryl and provides always-welcome business for her.

Notice, also, that you have now met Sheryl Smith who is a new contact for you – that's why she is called, "2$^{nd}$ Tier." You have shaken her hand and handed her one of your snazzy new business cards that Dylan made for you. Most importantly, you have added Sheryl into your professional network. That moves her from Second Tier to First Tier. That moves her from a stranger to an acquaintance.

Over the course of time, that same process is repeated 10 times, then 50 times, and then 100 times. That's the **NP,** or Networking Power, of the formula. But we're not finished. You are far from the only one who has needs and problems to solve.

## GRATITUDE AS A BOOST TO NETWORK POWER

To add one final boost of power to your professional network, make sure to recognize and express gratitude. When people to whom you send your contacts provide solutions and otherwise assist you in meaningful ways, don't forget to thank them. All too often, we forget to do this. There is a national bestseller entitled, *The Lost Art of Gratitude*.[24] Whether it really is a lost art or not, offering sincere thanks for services rendered is always appreciated. William James, a 19th century American psychologist who was often considered the "Father of American psychology,"[25] believed that gratitude is more than appreciated – it is a psychological need. James once wrote:

*The deepest principle in human nature is the craving to be appreciated.*[26]

It is not difficult to satisfy this craving. Yet, we often forget to do so. It has also been said that:

*Gratitude is the shortest-lived emotion.*[27]

We encourage you to elongate that emotion. As long as that gratitude is genuine, and we express it sincerely, three lives are blessed. Your contact who has received the solution to the problem, your second contact who has provided the solution, and you, yourself. All three relationships are strengthened.

There are three excellent ways to express your gratitude:

1. Express it Personally in a One-on-One Setting. It will make all the difference. Don't worry about it being well-worded – spirit will communicate with spirit if the feeling is sincere. In research

---

[24] Alexander McCall Smith, 2010, *The Lost Art of Gratitude*, Anchor Books.
[25] See: https://en.wikipedia.org/wiki/William_James
[26] Quote from: www.brainyquote.com/quotes/william_james_125466. It has also been expressed as "The deepest craving of human nature is the need to be appreciated"; for example: www.passiton.com/inspirational-quotes/4460-the-deepest-craving-of-human-nature-is-the-need
[27] This quote was cited by Jodi B. Katzman, 2016, "The Power of Gratitude," *Huffington Post*, but she mentions it as a 'saying' and does not claim this as her words. The origin is likely unknown. See: www.huffingtonpost.com/jodi-b-katzman/the-power-of-gratitude_1_b_7905614.html.

studies, social scientists have found that, "While the writers worried about choosing the right words, the recipients were happy simply by the warmth of the gesture."[28]

2. Express it Publicly and Specifically. That way, the helper will be acknowledged and recognized for the quality assistance provided. It won't be just a "thanks to all those involved" but a specific shout-out for a specific act. This is simple to do on social media, and there is nothing wrong with expressing gratitude on the numerous sites in common use. It would be more meaningful and impactful, however, if the recognition and gratitude were offered in a public setting such as a networking function.

Imagine the impact it would make to hear someone say something like, "I would like to offer a shout-out to JoAnn Nutter. I introduced her to a young woman in need, and she lovingly and effectively helped that woman solve her difficulties. I am extremely grateful for what JoAnn did for my young friend. Thank you, JoAnne!" That comment would likely increase your appreciation for JoAnn Nutter, for the young friend, and also for the person offering that thoughtful recognition.

Think, also, of what impact that would have on JoAnn. She would probably blush and discount what she had done but, deep down, it would satisfy that craving that William James mentioned and likely be a highlight of her day and week.

3. Express it in Written Form. Another way to express gratitude is by using a thank you note. Some people believe that thank you notes in the digital age are as old-fashioned as a Remington typewriter. They are not. Most people deeply appreciate a hand-delivered thank you card. In fact, in addition to a professional business card and well-designed letterhead, a stack of thank you notes and stamped envelopes is among the most important paperwork that you can have on your desk. They increase networking power (**NP**).

One person wrote that: "When I find a handwritten letter or card in the pile of bills and junk mail, I'm overjoyed! It's exciting to get something in the mail that is fun and interesting, instead of stressful and boring. …[It] is simply the right thing to do." She then listed five reasons to mail or deliver handwritten thank you notes:[29]

- Improves Mood – Gratitude can have a positive effect on overall well-being both by increasing happiness and by decreasing depression.

---

[28] Quote from Chicago Booth School of Business, 2018, "Expressing Your Gratitude is More Powerful Than You Think" in https://newschicagobooth. uchicago.edu/newsroom/expressing-your-gratitude-more-powerful-you-think.

[29] Katie Wells, 2019, *The Importance of Writing Thank You Notes,* **in** wellness mama.com/326494/thank-you-notes.

- <u>Good for Physical Health</u> – Those who express gratitude were found to be less likely to experience aches & pains and reported feeling healthier overall.
- <u>Helps You Stand Out</u> – Handwritten thank you notes are so infrequent in our digital age that when one of them is received, it makes a statement.
- <u>Fosters Connection</u> – It's so easy to send a quick text or Facebook message to show your appreciation (and that's much better than not expressing gratitude at all) but a handwritten note says so much more. It says, "thank you" of course, but it also says, "I spent the extra time to write this note by hand because your generosity is so appreciated."
- <u>Revives a Lost Art</u> – Emails are often deleted right after being read but thank you cards can be displayed and enjoyed for weeks, months …or even a lifetime.

## POWER OF A NETWORK: THE PARK-N-RIDE FIASCO

Most of us remember a time when flying meant luxury and respectful treatment of all passengers. Those days seem long gone. Ground transportation to the airport is increasingly becoming an issue. Air travel now seems more like a chaotic cattle-call than a leisurely voyage through the friendly skies.

At least, it seemed that way to Steve Mitchell who was trying to attend a business convention in Chicago. Normally, he'd have driven to the parking garage and taken his own bags across the breezeway to the check-in for his airline. This time, though, he thought he would save 50 dollars or so by parking for the week-long meeting at a park-n-ride about 5 miles from the crowded airport. He figured he could take one of the shuttle services from the park-n-ride to the airport.

The problems started when Steve did what he should not have done. He tried going online to gather the information he thought he needed. He searched through the complicated parking website and browsed through the internet for several shuttle services. He looked at the ads, the rates and the various schedules, and tried to determine which company would best facilitate his ground transportation for the lowest price.

Unfortunately, he made the rookie mistakes of believing everything he read. He picked the shuttle with the flashiest photographs and the best catch-lines.

The irony was that Steve knew several people who traveled more often than he did. Some also used the park-n-ride and took a shuttle to get them and their luggage to the terminal. At one of the recent business networking meetings, a colleague had actually mentioned that he, himself, had just switched to a different shuttle service because of problems encountered with scheduling and reliability.

What a fiasco!

Steve Mitchell's idea had been to catch an early morning flight to avoid the hectic holiday crowd trying to get out of town. Well, Steve got to the park-n-ride okay, but he hadn't expected so many cars already there. The traffic flow was not well marked, and it wasn't clear where he was supposed to park or how he was supposed to pay for the long-term parking. It was already a hassle to find where to get to where the shuttle service departed.

The website had promised to have an attendant at the site to help take care of all of that, but he didn't see anyone. He was already feeling mildly frustrated and pressured to find the shuttle by the time it was scheduled to pull out. After some hassle, he finally found the right area. The "attendant" turned out to also be the driver, and he was already loading people and luggage into the van. Steve passed the driver his several bags of sales and display materials.

Soon, the departure time passed. Steve asked the driver about it, and the driver replied, "Don't worry about it. It's only a 20-minute trip."

Okay. Steve still had plenty of time to get to the airport and catch his flight. But, then, some more people walked up late, and the driver allowed them to get on board and find seats in the van. Steve could understand that from the driver's perspective, but it was all taking time. An older couple, who were sitting behind Steve in the van, were starting to panic. Their flight was scheduled to leave, and very soon. The driver finally got the last of the luggage crammed into the van, and they were off – but another 15 minutes or so had passed.

It got even worse. Though the advertising and the driver had promised a 20-minute drive, the streets were icy, and the traffic was heavier and slower than normal. Steve could see that it was getting crunch time by the time the van finally pulled into the terminal, by now crowded with honking cars.

Steve realized that he was now running seriously behind. He was beginning to feel a degree of panic and the problems seemed to be having a cascading effect. Because it was later than Steve had expected, he found that he was running into the beginnings of the holiday crowd heading home. And the lines to get through airport security were getting longer and longer as people were piling in the doors. Voices were being raised; children were crying.

It just so happened that the line that Steve had chosen to pass through the TSA screening had to be closed for some reason. Steve and several others had to go to the back of another security line, which seemed to serpentine back and forth with what seemed a hundred people ahead of him. With the crowds that were pouring through the doors, any early advantage he had hoped for was long gone, and the security ordeal took much longer than he had expected.

Steve finally got through the TSA security but, by now, he was perspiring heavily. He got his shoes back on and had them all laced up before realizing that his gate was #D12 at the far end of Concourse D across the huge terminal. He didn't have time for all this!

# THE POWER OF A PROFESSIONAL NETWORK

With carry-ons in hand and coats falling out of his arms, he hustled down the concourse. Weaving through the crowd, he heard the final announcement. It was for his flight. They were saying he had five minutes before they closed the door.

Steve made one wrong turn. That's all it took. By the time Steve realized his error and made the correction he was two minutes late arriving at Gate #D12. They had closed the door!

The airline that Steve was flying with was very good about it all. They set Steve up with a connecting flight that worked out and he got to Chicago just fine. Of course, he had to make a few calls to arrange for the activities he had planned on the other end to be delayed by a couple of hours. It all worked out okay in the end, but when Steve got into Chicago, he was what people refer to as a hot mess!

The takeaway from this little story is the hard lesson that Steve had not used the power of his network resources. He hadn't stopped to ask for somebody else's opinion – somebody more experienced than him – somebody in his professional network. As a result, what could have been a nice business trip to Chicago turned into a horrible experience.

It was bad enough missing a fight but what really rubbed it in for Steve was when he met with the people who were waiting for him in Chicago and had more-or-less given up on him. They had known him for years. They told Steve that, of all the people they knew, "you, as the one missing a flight, would have been at the bottom of my list."

Now, _that_ was embarrassing!

To drive the point home a little more, if there's nothing else that you learn from Steve Mitchell's little tale, remember that there are people who have had the experiences that you are preparing to have for the first time. Don't be Steve! Reach out to those people in your professional network. It can really save you a lot of headache and problems – yes, and embarrassment. Tap your professional network by asking a few simple questions. Those people in Steve's network would have been happy to share their experiences with him and give him a few recommendations.

Do you see the tremendous power of your professional network (**NP**)? You have woven your net into a living mesh of closely linked friends, referral partners, and solid business contacts. That's how your network becomes incredibly powerful and is strengthened on a daily basis. It is a formula for success. It is _the_ formula for success in professional networking. How do you get there? For that, we must turn to the elements in our professional formula that produce the network power (**NP**). We will begin that in the next chapter.

# CHAPTER 5

# CREATING CONTACTS FOR A PROFESSIONAL NETWORK

The people you meet through introductions connected with business, at networking functions, and even in casual encounters are all potentially new contacts and referral partners. Many, if not most, of them can be added to your professional network. However, this requires action on your part. It is one of the elements of the formula that produces network power (**NP**). In this chapter, we will talk about this first element in the professional networking formula: that of creating contacts (**CC**).

$$\mathbf{NP = (CC + NN) \times RR}$$

It is important that you constantly seek to meet new people (7-7-7). Make it an ingrained habit. And when you find new people, lock them down in your network. The best way to do this is to add them to a written list of people that is accessible on your phone from the cloud. You can start by writing down who you already know and whom you anticipate interacting with in the future. If you haven't started such an organizing list, do that as step number one. It starts as simply as reviewing your phone list but understanding the phone list isn't sufficient by itself. You also need to write down notes and essential details as well. You may think you'll remember the basic information about each contact, but you won't. You need what are often called memory tags, and it is essential that all tags be computer searchable.

This level of organization takes time, but it will pay off many times over. It can even be fun. Think of it as collecting objects, much like coin and stamp collecting. Some people collect dolls that fill up their living rooms. Others collect license plates from every state and decorate walls with them. One man even collects wood planes from the year he was born; he has dozens of them. But what you are collecting is much more valuable than any of those. And, remember, you don't want just 10 names, or even 100; you want 1,000 or even more. That's why building a network is not an activity for a week or a month. This will be a collection that will continue for your entire career.

Don't be overwhelmed by this; just take it one name at a time. The creation, collection, and compiling of contacts needs to become a lifestyle, not a one-time activity. This is the first element in your formula for success (**CC**).

Not all contacts are created equal. The human brain can only track a limited number of acquaintances, let alone true friends. In Chapter 2, we introduced the so-called Dunbar's number, which states that "humans can comfortably maintain only 150 stable relationships."[30] That's fine. But what about the 1,000+ 76%ers who you can't possibly track using only your memory. Given the limitations of the human brain, rely on the computer's brain. This is why searchable identification tags are so important in your database. You need the computer to pull up names you can't remember by using such tags as hobbies, interests, social groups, business types, products used, family size, and so on. If you need a contact who is a hair colorist, or who grows beets and cucumbers, or who does wedding photography, or belongs to a Chamber of Commerce, you can pull up that name using a computer search.

Let's assume that you already have a good start on such a networking list. How do you create new contacts to expand the catch of your net and swell your network? An excellent way is to develop an ingrained habit of seizing every opportunity to talk with almost every person whom you even casually encounter and to do that on a 7-7-7 schedule. Opportunities pop up everywhere.

## THE ELEVATOR SPEECH: A POWER PLAY

As we seize these opportunities, it is essential for us to be able to answer the questions we are commonly asked about our profession. We should be able to be engaging, informative, even entertaining with our answers. The play in our playbook for doing this is called an "elevator speech". An elevator speech is simply a way to share your expertise and credentials quickly and effectively with people who don't know you. It is named an elevator speech to remind you that the length of your speech must be no longer than the time it takes to ride an elevator a few floors."

Creating and delivering an elevator speech is not difficult. How many times have you been asked, "What do you do?" I'd guess this has happened to you many times – it has happened to all of us. When people ask this question, and they universally do, the setting is usually an informal

---

[30] See: https://en.wikipedia.org/wiki/Dunbar%27s_number

occasion. Anytime that strangers are stuck in close proximity for 30 seconds to a few minutes and don't want to sit or ride in awkward silence. This could be when you are on vacation, bumping along in public transportation, standing in line for a movie ticket, nervously drumming fingers in a dentist's outer office and, of course, riding an elevator. People want to be friendly, so they ask, "So, what do you do?"

Why is that question asked so often? Because it is safe. In the age in which we live, many questions are not. You can't ask what country people are from based on their speech or, heaven forbid, their skin shade. You can't ask about their ethnic heritage. There's a saying, "Never ask a woman her age" – and you certainly would never ask about weight or a physical condition. It would be iffy to ask others about spiritual beliefs. And politics? It would open a can of worms to ask people about their political leaning.

So, what is safe to ask? People can ask about the weather. That's okay. It's safe. However, it is also trite small talk that is trivial unless there has just been a heat surge or a heavy snow. That brings us back to asking about what they do for a living. That's okay – that's safe – and it has significance. So, people ask "the question."

This can work to your advantage. But you need to be fully prepared, 7-7-7, to turn a casual conversation into creating a contact (**CC**).

Picture yourself attending a small collegiate basketball game. There you are, sitting in the stands in the stadium, surrounded by hundreds of your closest friends – who you've never met. Meet them! Does that seem a little awkward? How about if you took that awkwardness and turned it into a positive right away? How about something as simple as turning to the people around you, looking them in the eye, and saying, "Howdy, neighbor!"?

And don't forget summertime. At many outdoor activities, you will be asked what you do in your professional life. Be ready with your elevator speech.

No matter when and where you make it happen, when you are asked "the question" you immediately and smoothly reply with your prepared elevator speech. Notice clearly the word, "prepared." Your elevator speech must be well rehearsed. By repeated recitation, we become more natural at delivering the wording, smoother with the cadence, and more in command of the timing of the speech. The wording does not need to be intended to impress, but rather to be easy to say and impactful to receive. If the elevator speech invokes humor, concern, or any emotion, it will be impactful. Humans identify quickly when emotionally engaged. When we see others have any physical reaction, even a simple chuckle, an expression of compassion, or even sadness (if appropriate), we will have the attention of our audience.

## THE FIVE STEPS OF AN ELEVATOR SPEECH

There are five simple steps to constructing and delivering a perfect elevator-length response to "the question."

<u>Step One: Smile</u>. Look the person right in the eye and smile. That's all. You need a smile that says, "I'm really glad you asked that question." However, you do <u>not</u> want to say those words out loud. Those words can suggest that a sales pitch is about to be dropped on them, and you do not want to, nor will you, deliver any kind of sales pitch. You just want to communicate that with a smile. That smile sets the stage for everything else.

<u>Step Two: "Do You Know How…?"</u> When you're asked the question, "What do you do?" you're going to follow the smile with a return question. The return question is "Do you know how…?" You complete the second part of your question with whatever issue you enjoy solving and that you solve the best.

Most people have a desire to learn more about things …as long as they don't perceive that they are about to be pressured for some sale. That means that you want your question to sound vaguely philosophical and interest-oriented and not at all like a sales pitch.

Take a moment and define the problem(s) you solve. This may require careful thought and planning. Contemplate how you can frame your question in the fewest words possible. Refine it. Get it nailed down. Then become very familiar with that sentence. In the four examples below, none of them should sound like a sales pitch.

1. If you sell real estate, you might say, "Do you know how developers are looking for ways to sell the homes that they've just built, or how some people want to find a new home…?"
2. If you operate a roofing company, you might say, "Do you know how a roof only lasts 15 to 20 years before a strong wind starts lifting shingles, or a heavy rain leaks through a skylight…?"
3. If you're a plumber, you might say, "Do you know how some people's pipes freeze and crack in the winter or they lose a wedding ring down the shower drain and can't get it out…?"
4. If you run a bakery that specializes in decorative cakes, you might say, "Do you know how people want anniversary or wedding cakes like the works of art that they see on TV…?"

That's step two: "Do you know how…" That means you have already prepared a very concise story that you have in your back pocket.

Step Three: Solve That Problem. What you're doing here is completing your first teaser question by stating, more specifically, exactly what it is that you do to resolve the problem. You're not going into the _how_ – this is the _what_. What is the solution that you offer? Here are the same four examples:

1. Real Estate: "Well, that's what I do. I help find buyers for those developers and homes for people."
2. Roofing Company: "Well, that's what I do. I replace those old shingles and seal their skylights up tight."
3. Plumber: "Well, that's what I do. I fix their frozen pipes and recover lost wedding rings."
4. Specialty Cake Bakery: "Well, that's what I do. I design and decorate those kinds of artistic cakes."

Notice that, up to this point you have not specifically announced your profession. Instead, you have made a declaration of how you solve a problem. And it sounds …interesting. Most of the time, the listeners are intrigued. They are thinking, if not saying, "Really? That sounds fascinating!" They don't feel as if they are about to be broadsided by a sales pitch. They feel safe to be interested.

Step Four: State Your Profession. This is the time for you to declare your profession in one brief label. In the examples, it would be simply:

1. Real Estate: "I'm a real estate broker."
2. Roofing Company: "I'm a roofer."
3. Plumber: "I am a plumber."
4. Specialty Cake Bakery: "I am a baker."

Do you see the point? If you had started off with your profession's title, the conversation would have slammed shut instantly. Nobody wants to talk to a real estate broker, a beautician, a roofer, a plumber, or a baker. It's not that they dislike those professions or those workers. It's that they don't want to have a sales pitch thrown at them and have to retreat. Instead, you have focused on how to overcome a problem. People already know what a plumber does, but retrieving a lost ring is …a story.

Step Five: Now, Zip it and …Listen! In other language: Be quiet! Stifle it! Stop talking! Silence! More coarsely: Shut up! Muzzle it!

As strange as it may seem, Step Five is usually the most difficult step for people to master. You've served the tennis ball into that tiny square on the other side of the net and the ball in the other player's court. You'd never try to run around and hit it back to yourself. That obviously won't work. Even professional tennis players can't do that.

Make no mistake: People don't like silence. Psychologist Piero Ferrucci even speculates that: "We may have a terror of silence, because silence reminds us of solitude and death." Whether he is right about that or not, the fear of silence is very real.[31]

Let silence work for you. The other person will fear the silence more than you do. Trust the silence to work for you. Knowing about the psychology of silence should give you the courage to remain silent. In a very real way, this is a "battle of silence." It is like the game of chicken. Who will blink first? Don't let it be you. Maintain eye contact and maintain the silence. If it helps, you might think of it this way: The first one to speak loses. You might even have to silently chant in your mind: "If I speak, I lose! If I speak, I lose! Shut up! Shut up! Silence!"

## POSSIBLE RESPONSES YOU MAY RECEIVE

Notice that nobody is selling anything here. The goal of your elevator speech is to create a contact, never to sell a product. Don't try to make a social encounter into a quick sale. It won't work in 99% of all attempts. Selling to someone who you don't know – who didn't come to you – Is almost always the kiss of death and an instant turn-off. It just won't work.

Even if pitching your product or services to someone in an elevator (or on a bus, café, etc.) worked for that last 1%, it would only be a one-time purchase. And, very likely you will have alienated the potential contact. It isn't worth it. Instead, use these precious moments to gain a contact who you can nurture. The point is to not let a chance meeting go to waste. It's truly just to make a contact and be friendly. Creating a contact for life could become a multi-time success down the road.

So how does this end? That is determined by the silence. Any of three things will happen:

<u>Possibility 1: The Conversation Just Ends</u>: The person might say, "Oh, ...okay," and that will end the conversation. Now it's your turn to ask the other person, "What do you do?" If they are over-eager to tell you, it may be that they have only asked you "the question" as a means of telling

---

[31] Piero Ferrucci, 2015, "Who's Afraid of Silence? A crucial Need We Easily Forget," *Psychology Today*, emphasis in original; *see*: www.psychologytoday.com/us/blog/your-inner-will/201509/whos-afraid-silence.

what they do. They were waiting for you to finish; then it was their turn. If that happens, fine. You can still exchange information and reach out in a week or two.

Worst case scenario, you continue on in an awkward silence until one of you reaches the desired floor and steps out of the elevator. And that will be that. Nothing was lost, but nothing was gained. Better luck next time.

Possibility 2: The Other Fills the Silence: Sometimes, the other person will change the subject and say, "Did you see the big game on TV last night?" or "Did you survive the big snowfall we had?" That is not recoverable. Don't even try. To try to bring the conversation back to you and your product or services is futile at best, rude at worst. Just let it go and move on. You might reply, "I was out last night. Who won?" or "Yeah, wish I had a snowblower. My back almost gave out shoveling the driveway."

Possibility 3: The Other Asks a Question: Great! That's exactly what you wanted them to do. That's what these five steps are designed for. The steps should create the comfort and safety for people to ask follow-up questions. You don't have enough time then-and-there to answer the follow-up questions. That's okay. Show interest. Exchange contact information. Your business card is the tool for that. When you have their contact information, make detailed notes as to where you met and what was asked.

Most people who break the silence with a follow-up question will ask something like, "What does that entail, exactly?" or "That sounds fascinating!" Or they may say, "Oh, I've got a sister who does that." Those kinds of responses are just what you want. This is really good. It has opened up the possibility for a much longer conversation – then or later. Now you can talk about the sister or talk about how fortunate it is to have a career that's fascinating. Relate it back to you but, remember, you are not after a quick sale – that won't happen anyway. You are merely creating a contact. The person knows right away that you are not going to fulfill a need that they, themselves, have. That's fine. You have not given a sales pitch or asked for an appointment; you have just started an interesting conversation.

Again, having your business card _available_ and _with you_ at all times is essential. That is the right tool to use at that point. But try to get the other person's name and contact information as well. If you don't walk away with the name and number, you haven't created a contact, you have just given out a card that will likely be recycled.

Now you know all there is to creating and delivering an effective elevator speech. Although it might sound simple, don't be fooled. It is a very powerful tool, if done correctly. A great idea is to literally and physically rehearse these five steps. Sounds corny, but it works. You really will need to practice them a few times. If you do, you'll find that this is a very powerful tool.

A byproduct is that it can also be a lot of fun to do. What have you got to lose? You might even develop two different elevator speeches. That way, you can trade them off. But don't worry about that until you have the first one down and polished.

Here are two final notes to keep in mind.

1) Don't Apologize or Discount What You Do. When asked about their profession, many people refer to themselves as "just a ____" (fill in the blank). Why do that? You are damaging your potential each time you use this four-letter word in that way. Here are four negative ways this little word could be translated by your listener. They are all "D" words, meaning that using the term "just" gives you a D average. The words are Dismissing, Disdaining, Desperate, and Disingenuous. Do you really mean to communicate your career as something that is only, or merely, something? Your listeners might well hear you saying:

- "What I do is not important"
- "You'd be better spending your time elsewhere"
- "I'm wasting your time"
- "My opinion and ideas don't matter and have no merit"
- "Please help little me"
- "I'm not sincere. I want to appear humble, but I'm not"

You would respond assertively if you heard a peer refer to you as "just a …." And you would never refer to a colleague that way. So, why refer to yourself like that? No, if you use the "just" word, it's time to change your terminology. If you catch yourself using this four-letter word, stop and repeat the sentence without it. The difference will be noticeable.

2) Accept Your New Contact at Any Level. Most people who hear your elevator speech will not immediately become a 12%er. They barely know you. Even with instant rapport, they will likely just be intrigued and interested. And most won't even be 76%ers yet. Don't worry about that; it's still too early. Just plan to call them back in a day or two for a longer time to talk and get to know them. It will be during that longer get-together that the contact will become a 12%er or a 76%er. And it will be quite obvious which direction they are heading.

## REMEMBER YOUR CONTACT'S NAME

Whether you got your contact's name from an elevator speech, a referral, or an introduction, be sure to remember that name and pronounce it correctly. Remembering people's names is incredibly important in our attempt to gain network expansion as well as in refortifying and strengthening the networks that we have.

When we first meet somebody, there's a couple of things to do. The first one is to learn the name.

## GET THE NAME EXACTLY RIGHT

Be sure to get your contact's name right. If you think about it, a person's name is really one of the most significant gifts they've ever been given. After the obvious gift of life, the second gift that they were given was their name. If you garble their name, you garble them. Remember, this is a person's identity. Unfair though it may be, we simply do not expect the same behavior from a Bartholomew as we do from a Bud, from a Suzie as we do from a Bertha, from a Jack as we do from a Jeremiah. To an extent, names do not merely identify us, they partly make us.

What does it say if you get that name wrong? Well, it's not good! So, don't do that. Get the name right. Make sure that the name is pronounced clearly for you, and that you are pronouncing it correctly. Ask for clarification. Make sure that you understand the right way to say it. Verify how they want it said. "So, your name is _Keziah Mays_. Was that Ke*z*iah with a 'z' or with an 's'?"

Many people who have an unusual given name like Keziah will pretend that it doesn't matter whether you pronounce their name correctly. The same holds true for a tricky surname like Huntamer and Huntimer or Johnson and Johnston. "Don't worry about it," they will graciously say. "I get that all the time. Keziah or Kesiah. Either is fine. That's close enough. It doesn't matter." But it does matter! It's the same as very politely saying to visitors walking into your house on a wet day, "No, no, you don't need to take your shoes off. You're fine," and then watching them track their muddy shoes across your cream-colored carpet. It does matter.

So, when people say, "Oh, that's close enough," stop right there. Back up. Ask where you went wrong. Show them that their name is as important to you as it is to them. Make sure you care enough to get it right.

# THE PROFESSIONAL NETWORKER'S PLAYBOOK

## THREE TIMES TO PRACTICE; FOUR TO LOCK

The second thing to do is to remember that name. When you meet new people, you have an opportunity to hear them say it. Don't be afraid to stop them and slow them down. People are often so familiar with their own name that they say it rapidly and, often, not clearly. This is your best time to get an unusual name right.

Following the name, there will usually be at least a short conversation lasting a minute or two. Here's an amazing memory aid that you can begin in that one minute.

<u>Step One: Three's the Charm.</u> The first step is to say the name of that new acquaintance at least three times. Make it part of the conversation at the Introduction, Middle, and Ending. That's a minimum.

The initial use of the name almost occurs automatically, usually as a part of an introduction. The other person will give the name. Repeat it! Don't just hear it, HEAR it. Don't just hear it, SAY it! If someone else introduces the name ("I'd like to introduce you to Keziah"), say it. Repeat it. Pronounce it correctly. "So, your name is *Keziah? Keziah Mays?* That's the first use at the beginning.

Then, somewhere during the conversation, say the name again. Make it a natural part of the flow. Drop it in seamlessly. "So, *Keziah*, you said that you're from Tucson. When did you come here?" She will have no idea you are practicing the name to embed it deeper into your memory. Reinforce the name. The more you say it and the more you hear it, the more likely you will be to remember it.

There are any number of techniques for remembering names by creating image links. For example, you might think that she is memorable "cuz of her eye and her ear" (Kez-eye-ear). That's fine. We aren't getting into all of that. Many books on memory are available if you want to do a search.[32] All we are suggesting is to repeat the name orally at least three times during the exchange.

The final repetition of the name comes at the end of the chat. Regardless of the length, when that conversation ends, make sure you say the name one more time in parting. This is an easy one to do. Just say, "See you later, *Keziah*. Hope to see you again."

<u>Step Two: Some TIme Later, Say the Name Again.</u> The second step is to repeat the name again to someone around you – but only do this later. If the introduction was during the day, repeat it to a loved one that night. "I met a promising new contact at the lunchtime mixer. Her name was *Keziah Mays*."

When you see Keziah's face the next time, you will usually recall her name. It's amazing how often that will work. If you try this two-step device, you will be amazed at how much it will

---

[32] For example, see Kristi Hedges, 2013, "The Five Best Tricks to Remember Names," *Forbes Magazine*; www.forbes.com/sites/work-in-progress/2013/ 08/21/the-best-five-tricks-to-remember-names/#12cd7b5a501f

increase your ability to remember people's names. It's also amazing how many times people are embarrassed because they know they know you, but they can't remember your name. You can smile as you reflect on how you no longer have that problem. This is the number one practice that you can do in order to learn and remember people's names.

After that, and every time you see them, call them by name. We get into the habit of covering our tracks sometimes. "Hey, girl! How's it going? (What was that name again?)" Hey, man, whaz-up! (Whoever you are….)" This is a cop-out. You are covering your relational laziness. Don't let yourself get away with that. Force yourself to back up, even if it's embarrassing to admit you don't quite remember that unusual name. "I'm sorry…. You gave me your name but I'm struggling to pull it up. Was it Kesha? Casius? Kylie? …Oh, yes, *Keziah*, right! Thanks. That's really a pretty name; I should have remembered that one."

Better to try and use the name than to blow it off. Use the name, especially for someone you don't see regularly. People want recognition. They want to feel as if they are known and remembered. Just by using their name, you lift them up. You raise their status. When they feel important, they feel as if you're the one making them important. At an unconscious level, they want to be around you more. They want to be a contact in your network. And you want them there.

In this chapter, we've talked about creating contacts (**CC**) on a consistent schedule of 7-7-7. We introduced the idea of using an elevator speech to create the contacts, and we talked about the tremendous importance of learning their name as a sincere expression of regard and respect.

In the next chapter, we turn to the second element on the working side of the formula: that of nurturing those contacts in our network.

# CHAPTER 6

# NURTURING YOUR PROFESSIONAL NETWORK

The formula for power in professional networking continues with the second element. That element is the nurturing and maintaining of the contacts you've created, especially the 12%ers. In this chapter, we take a look at how, exactly and specifically, this can be accomplished.

$$NP = (CC + NN) \times RR$$

Once you've met new people and added them as newly created contacts (**CC**), then you must nurture that network (**NN**). You would never pay $40,000 for a brand-new car and then drive it into the ground. You would change the oil and filters regularly, rotate the tires, change the wiper blades, and so on.

Why would you do any less with your professional network?

The analogy to maintaining a new car is a helpful one, but it lacks one essential characteristic: that of the heart. To fully tap the incredible power of your network, you must do more than simply maintain them. In a word, you must nurture them.

## NURTURING THROUGH SERVICE AND REFERRALS

Nurturing one's network is one of those things that sounds simple to do. In fact, it is easy, but it requires attention and energy. It does not take care of itself any more than your new car does. But it _can_ be done, not just talked about. Below are two stories that may make this goal come alive and give you some specific ways to pull it off.

## THE STORY OF JAMES DAVIDSON

James Davidson is a phenomenon. He is a young man who excels in keeping in touch with old networking contacts. He truly understands the importance of maintaining, servicing, and nurturing his referral partners. He keeps those people warmly wrapped around him within his wheelhouse of contacts. James understands professional networking. He has a high **NN** score.

It is a skillset that you can learn and emulate. It is one of the most important plays in this playbook. But the play is available to you, just as it is for James. You just have to add the play to your own playbook and then run it. This means learning how to use the play.

It is most impressive to see exactly how James uses his tools to nurture his referral partners. On a regular basis, he reaches out to make contact with everyone in the 12% portion of his large professional network. His efforts can take many forms:

- Rendering simple favors or some service
- Dictating and sending quick texts
- Sending his referral partners interesting articles that relate to their business or personal life
- Forwarding a funny or helpful email with a personal note (but never sending unwanted spam)
- Using social media to share funny stories, anecdotes, and personal victories
- Making a brief phone call or two
- Sitting down for a social or business lunch
- Sending a card on a special occasion (yes, they still make paper cards)

No matter how he does it, James doesn't let any professional contact among the 12%ers in his network go stale. Even though that's a lot of people in his case, he doesn't allow more than a year to pass without some contact from him.

James has a high **NN** score, but so can you. This is a skill that all of us, as networkers, can develop. It's not easy, but it's easier with the technology that is now available than it ever has been in the history of the world. You have an unprecedented opportunity to keep your network strong, viable, and vibrant. It is a living document of contacts.

One of his best tools is his phone. Not only does he keep their contact information, he also keeps simple notes about them. That way, he can pull up the names of his contacts' family and friends and can ask about them as part of a reconnection. He knows the dates of special events such as birthdays and graduations. He has brief notes on where the last conversation left off and can pick it back up as if it occurred yesterday. In this way, he makes them feel warm and comfortable. They are all friends to him. And he is a friend to them.

James is a great example of how opportunities can be seized and internalized. He is a model of how to utilize a few tools of friendship and leverage them. Significantly, his act of reaching out is never forced and is never insincere. When James contacts a person, it never feels as if he's just checking a box or fulfilling an obligation. As you will see from the examples below, it's never about James; it's always about the other person:

> *"Hello, Frank, we haven't talked in a while. Thought I'd just give you a call to find out how things are going in your life? How's Julie? How's your business? Did you get that raise you were hoping for?"*

> *"Hey, Lorraine! I was just sitting here wondering if that banner that you ordered last summer turned out right?"*

> *"We were decorating the Christmas tree and putting up a few lights. It reminded me of how much you and your family always love the Christmas season."*

> *"I see that Junior is about to finish high school. That's great! How time flies."*

> *"I was just talking to a mutual friend of ours and that got me thinking about you and I started wondering how you're doing. I thought I'd give you a call."*

> *"Saw the most inspiring list of New Year's Resolutions made by kids and thought you'd also get a chuckle"*

James keeps unusually detailed notes about what is going on in the lives of other people. Unusual, but not impossible. Seldomly does he ever ask anybody for anything. James is a giver, not a taker. And this is probably the most important aspect of all: it is 100% sincere. When he asks others what he can do to help them, he really wants to help them. Then ...he does it! And he doesn't just pay lip service. He'll go out of his way to help people fix issues in their lives.

Once, he helped an older man repair his cell phone. Another time, he went to an auto dealership with a widow to help her purchase a new car. He has helped people to select just the right products for them – from wines and clothing all the way to homes to purchase. He connected a young couple with the right financial advisor so they could make the right investment for their future.

As remarkable as James is at putting it all together, and as second-nature as it has become for him, he is not doing anything that you can't do just as well. James has a genuine interest in what's going on in their lives, but you can cultivate that, too. You, too, can grow an attitude that is other-oriented. This can become a part of your lifestyle.

Now, here comes a paradox. If you truly nurture your network, it will also nurture you. It will absolutely pay back many times over in contacts and relevant referrals (**RR**). But that is only fully true if you do not nurture your network primarily for the purpose of creating contacts (**CC**) and making relevant referrals (**RR**). It simply will not work in the long run if that is your only motivation. Nurturing your network (**NN**) will only work, at least at the level where James operates, if your primary purpose is based on genuine and sincere caring for others. That is the paradox.

For James, if referrals and pay-back follow, that's well and good. They are appreciated side-effects. Again, this is about **NN** (nurturing your network) – not SM (sales made). It needs to be, and can be, the same for you. If your interest in others is returned (and it usually will be), so much the better. If it is not (and that will happen, too), you have lost nothing and gained a friend. That is the philosophy that James carries into his life.

There are people in your life who feel that you're a hero. It's that top 12% that we talked about earlier who want an excuse to be in contact with you. Seize the initiative every six months to a year to reach out to these people, so they can reach out to you. This is not to sell anything; just to renew a contact. This is not about a holiday mailing list or forwarding spam. You might use a text once in a while but, to really renew that connection, make it an individual phone call or an in-person meeting. It doesn't have to take a lot of their time, but just to let those people know you care – that you're thinking about them.

Sometimes we forget how important it is to people to know they count for something. Humans yearn for connection. And your contacts specifically yearn for connection with *you*. Most of the time, they don't know how to make that reconnection themselves, so when it comes from you it means the world. It may seem to you that the effort is minor, but to them, it is a big deal. It may be exactly the ticket they need to reactivate their commitment to you.

Ask yourself this: When was the last time you reviewed your contacts – both 12%ers and 76%ers? If you were to open your phone, email, or business contact list, would there be those you have not contacted in a very long time? Take the time to find three people you have not had contact with in at least 6 months. Scroll to the bottom of your texts and phone calls. The folks at the bottom of these lists have had the longest period of no-contact with you. Make a plan to contact them. Commit to contact them. Then, contact them. Use the medium that is best for you. If phone calls are best for you, call them. If text is your preferred method, text them. Now repeat this exercise every week.

Don't get discouraged if you do not receive an immediate reply. You made the re-connection, and that's good enough at this stage. Wait six months before you repeat the process.

When you reach out to a contact, don't talk business. Make it as personal (though appropriate). If they like golf, talk golf. If they were expecting an addition to the family, ask about the new baby. If there's been a recent snowstorm, ask if they lost power and if they still have any needs. Make sure they know the contact is about the relationship.

In the current business environment, there is too much emphasis on sales and not enough on relationships. When you remember that folks prefer to do business with people they like, you will see the importance of maintaining, building, and re-establishing personal relationships.

## NURTURING THROUGH PIQS

The best way to maintain, build, and strengthen personal relationships in your network is to get to know those people very well. This is abundantly clear in the story of James. But how, exactly, does he do that? The answer is he knows his contacts at a deep and personal level, and so can you.

One tool to accomplish this is called the Personal Information and Question session, also known as a PIQ (pronounced as, pick). A PIQ gives you a marvelous forum to get to know a person. It's similar to what some networkers call just a simple one-on-one. Done correctly a PIQ is a one-on-one on steroids.

Why? Because it is so much deeper and more intimate than a typical one-on-one. We are not talking about a 5-minute chat in a corner of the room. We are talking about dedicating an hour in a quiet place without interruptions. We have in mind you sitting down with somebody to strengthen your business relationship. PIQs can vary but they tend to focus on either of two forms:

1. To hold a deep get acquainted session with a contact
2. To nurture an already established referral partner.

### 1. A PIQ AS A GET ACQUAINTED SESSION

To have the kind of business relationship that James Davidson has with his referral partners, you need to know your contacts well. You need to become friends with a new contact or reacquaint and strengthen an established friendship. One of the reasons that James is so good at nurturing (**NN**) is he has conducted many PIQs. Let's look at how he handles a PIQ.

<u>Concentrate on Listening, Not Talking</u>. Focusing on oneself is a part of human nature, while focusing on others is an acquired skill. Although difficult to do, a focus on others can be learned and applied. It will pay off many times over.

This recommendation is not new. As far back as 300 BC, the Greek, Zeno of Citium, wrote: "The reason why we have two ears and only one mouth is so that we may listen the more and talk the less."[33] Similarly, around 60 AD, James wrote in an epistle: "Let every man be swift to hear, slow to speak."[34]

What a worthwhile goal this is! What a difference this will make in your personal and professional life. It is well worth cultivating the art of listening. At your next opportunity, stifle your natural inclination to tell others about the most fascinating person you know – you. Instead, make it about the other person. This may feel clumsy at first, even awkward. It will pay off. As others feel heard and validated, they will want to be around you. There will be plenty of opportunity for you to tell your stories and give your opinions later. For right now, listen and learn. Love others by listening intently to them. Feed them. More often than not, you will find what you learn to be fascinating.

So, the first guideline to deepen your relationship with a contact is:

*Listen 80% of the time and
talk only 20% of the time.*

This is critically important. The PIQ is not about *your* life and *your* stories; it is about the stories and experiences of the *other* person. Never top your referral partner's stories with more dramatic stories of your own – no matter how much you may be tempted to do so.

<u>Concentrate on the Person, not the Company</u>. Be sure you get to know the people, not just the company. When discussing the PIQ's you have given, you never want to say, "I had a PIQ with a representative of XYZ Company." Far more important is to be able to say, "I had a PIQ with (the person's name)." Companies are boring, people are interesting. During your PIQ, keep this in mind. Ask any of the following and more that you can think of:

- How did you get into your current position?
- What would you say are your personal strengths?
- What part of your job brings a smile to your face?
- What do you like to do in your leisure?
- If I were to introduce you as a speaker, what would I say?
- What achievement are you most proud of?
- And anything else you can think to ask….

---

[33] This is often translated as, "We have two ears and one mouth, so we should listen more than we say."

[34] James 1: 19, KJV. The New Century Version renders this verse as "always be *willing* to listen and slow to speak," which seem to have a slightly different meaning.

Concentrate on the Person, not the Product. James typically spends 45 of the 60 minutes hearing about the *person* and not hearing about that person's products or services offered. A PIQ is normally about relationships, not objects. You want to get to know the people and who they are – not what they do and what they sell. Be sure to understand that distinction. Also, be clear that you are *not* selling. Again, a PIQ is never a sales opportunity.

Yes, James is an outstanding example of strengthening a relationship with a contact, a peer, or a potential client. But you can do this, too. You can build relationships. Remember that you are engaged in a PIQ so you can know your referral partners well enough to provide better and more relevant referrals for them.

Here's an example to clarify. Let's say that you have a client named Keith MacDonald in your network, but you don't really know him that well. He owns a chain of 12 car-wash locations throughout Oregon and Washington called, "Old MacDonald Has a Car Wash." You arrange to have lunch with him. Keith picks a local Korean restaurant. Over an order of Galbi (marinated short ribs), you find out Keith has a passion for snow skiing. He goes out on the slopes almost every single weekend. He not only has racing skis and powder skis, he's at home on snowboards, too. Since you are listening 80% of the time, you hear all about his equipment. You ask about Keith's wildest experiences. He tells you about the time he was almost caught in a small avalanche and the time he saw Mikaela Shiffrin in Vail, Colorado. You ask what he enjoys about skiing and he tells you all about the thrill of speed and the freedom he feels going down an expert slope.

Notice that you didn't sell Keith anything at all, and he didn't sell you anything. Networkers never try to make a PIQ into a sales call. They use it as a way to strengthen a relationship. Now, it is possible that, as a result of getting to know the other person, one person in the PIQ could become genuinely interested in the product or services of the other.

For example, one could say, "You have a 50% clearance sale that ends today? Can I order a set of stainless-steel pans?" or "Your counseling program offers all of that? How do I enroll?" That would be unusual but just fine – as long as both parties are fully aware of what has happened, and nobody is springing a sales pitch or trying to close an unwanted deal.

Now that you know that Keith loves to ski, that information allows you to strengthen your relationship with him. Let's say you see an article about snow skiing. You think, "Oh, that's right, Keith enjoys skiing. I'll forward a copy to him." Your relationship with him grows stronger and stronger.

Anyway, a couple of months later you hear that Frank O. Phon, another person in your network and the owner of a local car dealership, wants his dealership to give up on washing their own cars. It's not cost-effective and his workers get pulled away from sales or car maintenance. He is looking to outsource to a specialist. As it turns out, Frank is also a snow skier. Ahhh! You immediately think of Keith MacDonald. Frank needs to outsource car washing; Keith has a carwash in that city. That's a good (i.e., relevant) referral.

But you can also join their hobbies of skiing together. Their possible connection is magnified tenfold by the coincidence that they both love to ski. It's as if Keith's credibility is increased for Frank. Keith seems more of a regular person, not just the owner of a chain of car washes. True, at the level of a business referral, the skiing is irrelevant, but at the level of connecting two human beings, the shared skiing addiction is huge. The referral and the introduction of the two is easier, faster, and more binding because of that connection.

What's in it for you? Keith wanted more cars to wash and Frank needed a company to wash cars that were out on the lot. It was a win-win for them – a highly relevant referral (**RR**) – and it has strengthened your relationships with both of them. Even if they never work out a deal between them, they both deeply appreciate your efforts. This is imbuing your network with power (**NP**).

Here's a more tangible benefit. Sometime later, you're trying to close a big sale with a third customer who, you learned, is planning a big ski trip up to Whistler Mountain Ski Resort in British Columbia, Canada. You have never even put on a pair of skis, but it would help with your big sale if you could do something with that information your customer is planning a skiing trip.

Quick as can be, you pull the contact information for Keith and Frank out of your network list. You call them and catch both of them in. They are only too pleased to answer a few questions about ski trips. They share some insights and recommendations about where to stay, good times of day to visit various venues, where to eat, and so on. That gives you information to share with your client. It helps you establish more rapport and increases the chances of more referral benefits.

A deep, get-acquainted PIQ with a contact or client is an enjoyable and enriching experience. You will not only know your contacts better, you will feel much closer to them, and they to you. Active and deep listening will be an amazing play in your playbook.

The PIQ doesn't have to be in the same type of place every time. If you're having a PIQ with a network partner who you already know pretty well, perhaps have already met with, try meeting somewhere and doing something that is a unique experience. Go to a ball game. Take in a boat show. Go skydiving. The ideas are endless. When your PIQ generates emotions not usually thought of in business environments, the bonds can be significantly stronger as a result.

Below is a table that gives a few examples. The first column gives the referral partner's comments. The second column shows sample responses that either top the contact's sharing or have little power. They may even discourage the referral partner and stop the conversation in its tracks. Notice that the third column is very brief. This illustrates the "80% listening and only 20% talking" at work. Most of what you say is to encourage the other person to share with, not to overshadow them or tell them about yourself.

| Information from a Contact/Client **PIQ** | **PIQ** Talking Responses Lacking Power | **PIQ** Listening Responses with Impact/Power |
|---|---|---|
| "I had a gall bladder operation that got infected, and I had to stay there in the hospital for another whole week." | Topping the Story: "Goofs happen. My doctor once switched files by mistake and told me that I needed open-heart surgery!" | Listening to Story: "Oh, I'm sorry! Is there anything that I can do for you?" |
| "I'm happily married with a wife and 3 sons who are all still teens attending the local high school." | Topping the Story: "That's a lot! I've been married 2 times, and we now have 5 active children between us!" | Listening to Story: "Are they active in sports?" |
| "I used to own my own kitchen cabinet shop. Now I install cabinets for one of the big box stores." | Shallow Listening: "Yeah, the little guy is forced out! What's the name of the store so I can boycott them?" | Deep Listening: "Why did you make that switch?" |
| "My husband and I are into vegetable gardening. We love growing our own beefsteak and cherry tomatoes – better than store-bought." | Unintended Put-down: "Yes, tomatoes are pretty easy to grow. We prefer to challenge ourselves by growing broccoli, artichokes, and even cauliflower." | Encouraging: "Really? How do you preserve them?" |

## 2. A PIQ TO PROVIDE INFORMATION

Most of your PIQs will be of the first kind: get-further-acquainted sessions that will help you become closer friends with your contacts. However, from time to time, referral partners will need information and will turn to you for help. They will sense that you have answers and will approach you for guidance or mentoring.

One of the best ways to strengthen relationships with new networkers is to answer such requests for information. This type of PIQ is not designed to get to know a contact better; it is more designed to respond to their requests for help. You *will get* such requests, especially after you give a particularly good business commercial or if you volunteer for leadership or committee work in your business group.

Although that will mostly involve just one other person, there may even be times when you might offer an informational PIQ to 2 or even 3 newbies if they have the same questions. Typically, these informational PIQs are network-oriented to share on topics such as:

- Oral skills or memory hooks to make commercials sticky
- What it's like to serve in leadership of networking group
- What it means to "Sell Through, Not To"
- Elements of an effective elevator speech, and the like.

However, PIQs don't have to be about business. There is no reason that it couldn't involve topics with no monetary value. Those could be on topics you happen to know something about such as skiing, breaking a brick wall in genealogy, or raising teenagers. (Wait, does anyone know anything about raising teenagers?)

Take young Brenda Lamont, for example. Several years ago, she was stuck in a go-nowhere job as a grocery checker. Her youth minister suggested that she would probably make a good financial planner. Brenda loved the idea, took some training, and started out as the assistant to an investment agent. She now has a small practice of her own with a limited clientele. She loves the work but has very few clients. She is now earning a better income.. This still will not do. Not at all.

You know Brenda from a bowling league and can see that she is just spinning her wheels searching for clients. She even tried to sell to you. You sit down with her and say, "Brenda, if I weren't already fully invested, I'd love to have you as my financial planner. Your BA was in business and you obviously have a natural understanding of investing and the stock market. You get on with everyone. Seems like your business ought to be booming. I'm guessing, though, you're spending all your time trying to sell to people who aren't interested rather than using professional networking."

After briefly explaining what professional networking is, you say, "I tell you what. I'm a member of a small networking group. We get together on Friday mornings at 8:00. Come with me as my guest. Hot chocolate and a croissant, on me. I'll introduce you to some other people who are also building careers. You can see what you think."

With much trepidation, and your support, she attends the next meeting …and a life is changed.

There is no immediate or direct advantage in this for you. You have merely been working 7-7-7 looking for ways to serve and help others. You've moved her from your casual network (the bowling league) to your professional network. Brenda is now flourishing in her business, and you have added to your network. Perhaps that will eventually come back to you in some manner. But that doesn't matter. You have served another human being because of your mindset of service. You have mentored her, but you can do even more.

We can hear you protesting already:

- *"Wait! What do I know? I'm not qualified."*
- *"I'm fairly new to networking myself. I'm not ready for that!"*
- *"That is something better left to others – to experts."*

You do <u>not</u> need to be an expert to do this. All it takes is a willingness to help in an area where you have some experience and knowledge. Not only is it acceptable for you to serve as a mentor and teacher of new networkers, it is a responsibility. While nobody wants you to be arrogant and full of yourself, the fact is you *are* an expert. That bears repeating: <u>You</u> are an expert. Make no mistake about it.

It's perspective; when you are three or more steps ahead of someone you're an expert to them.

Haven't you "been tested"? Haven't you overcome trials to get where you are? Of course you have. Haven't you "had experience"? How about "mastery of your particular subject" (business and sales)? That's an easy one, too. So, that definition takes us back to knowledge and skill and understanding. We've already seen that you have all of that. You have "special skills" that new networkers do not. You also have "knowledge" of sales and "knowledge" of how to relate to people.

Nothing calls for you to have the *most* knowledge or to have the *best* skills. All that is required is your knowledge and skills that your referral partner needs, which you do. Do you have complete knowledge? Of course not. Don't put that on yourself. But you have considerable knowledge and you have good skills. Remember, expertise is relative. Are there others with more expertise than you? Yes. But, compared to a novice, you *are* an expert.

So, don't start with an apology. Just start.

Share what you know for the benefit and growth of new networkers. It's about service with no expectation of reward or pay-back – at least, no pay-back in any financial sense. Remember that, as we quoted earlier, a rising tide raises all ships.[35] To help one is to help all. Plus, there is plenty of pay-back in the satisfaction of helping others and in deepening your relationships with those around you.

A training or tutoring PIQ typically involves a status difference between a beginner and a

---

[35] Quote taken from Phillips, Susan Elizabeth, 2001, in *Romance Writer's Report*; see: http://quotationsbywomen.com/authorq/52222/

seasoned networker (expert). However, a PIQ could also take place between two networkers at the same level. For example, two financial advising agents could have a PIQ to compare notes on changes in government regulations, investing strategies, and the like. Similarly, two roofers could have a PIQ to discuss each other's niche in roofing, deal with changes in city codes, or how to handle roofing in bad weather conditions.

On the next page is a table giving a few examples of requests for information. The second column gives responses that lack power or are actually dismissive of the referral partner's request for that information. The last column shows a high degree of PIQ effectiveness. Notice, again, that the third column is brief. Simply offer to help.

We'll start off with a repeat of Brianna's request and two possible responses – one helpful, one not so much. Then we'll give three more examples.

| *Question/Needs from a Newbie* **PIQ** | *PIQ ...Mentoring Lacking Power* | *PIQ ...Mentoring with Power* |
|---|---|---|
| Brianna: "Would you please help me to create and write a quality business resumé?" | Dismissive: "They aren't that difficult. If you Google that term, you'll find several very helpful websites." | Bonding: "I'd be pleased help you to write one." |
| "I've tried what some people are calling, 'elevator speeches' but I just don't get anywhere with them." | Superficial Training: "Let's hear yours right now, and I'll tell you if it's a good or a bad one. Go ahead…." | Valuable Training: "Let's practice some elements of one together." |
| "I can't seem to write commercials that other people care about and that they will remember." | Dismissive: "Yeah, those take time. Keep at it, though. It'll start to come after you give 30 or 40 of them." | Valuable Training: "Let me share 2 or 3 ideas that have worked for me." |
| "Some networkers talk about 'selling through, not to,' but I don't really get what that means." | Dismissive: "Talk to Bob Smith about that. He uses that phrase a lot, he can explain it to you." | Bonding: "Let's talk about that. I bet I can help." |

## NURTURING YOUR PROFESSIONAL NETWORK

The use of an informational PIQ, like a get-acquainted PIQ session, is not only a useful play to go into your playbook, it is also a great way to strengthen your network, serve others, and comfort those who may be feeling lost, alone, and confused. That is your privilege and your duty.

In the next chapter, we will look at the last element in the formula: how to give and receive relevant business referrals.

# CHAPTER 7

# SMART AND RELEVANT REFERRALS

The most significant part of the networking formula, by far, is the relevant referral (**RR**). This kind of referral usually includes a professional introduction, which is more than socially meeting someone who you would potentially like to know. Such an introduction is professional because it connects a specific contact, who has a specific problem, to others in your network who have specific solutions. That's why we call this kind of contact a professionally *relevant* referral.

In this chapter, we will talk about this most powerful element of the formula for power in professional networking, that of a truly relevant referral (**RR**). This is the element of power in the formula. It is the multiplying element that gives the network its power.

$$NP = (CC + NN) \times RR$$

In this formula, we first create contacts (**CC**) and maintain or nurture our network (**NN**). We then take the result and multiply it many times over using relevant referrals (**RR**). If you aren't making these referrals to other people within and among the members of your network, then your network is not being used to its full extent. Your net has become detached from its moorings. It is becoming porous. Solutions are slipping through the holes back into the ocean. The network is no longer strong; it does not have power. Relevant Referrals are what make a net of thread become a net of cords.

In Chapter 1, we mentioned that the word, "referral" comes from the Latin *re* or "back" and *ferre*, meaning "to carry." When you introduce your friends to others who can return powerful solutions to their problems, you create a relevant referral (**RR**). We defined a relevant referral as follows:

*A relevant referral is an introduction to, or between, people
for the purpose of solving a problem.*

In order for relevant referrals to become the multiplying factor in the formula, you must be able to match people up with each other. This requires that you become aware of both the needs and the strengths of those in your network. Those are action verbs. Without this knowledge and your connecting of people through the referrals, your network will deteriorate until there is nothing left. At that point, you won't really have a professional network. But if you use them well, they will multiply your successes many times over.

## THREE CHARACTERISTICS OF RELEVANT REFERRALS

Relevant referrals (**RR**) return solutions in areas related to your business when and if they share at least three essential elements.

### 1. THE RR IS CLEAR AND SPECIFIC

When you are connecting one contact in your network with a second contact, be very sure what your first contact really wants and needs. That's what makes it relevant. To do this, be as specific as possible when learning about the problem. That allows you to be certain who it is that needs to be connected to that first contact.

There is nothing like trying to introduce a contact with a financial investor only to learn that the contact is really needing help with writing a will and paying for burial expenses. A financial planner and an estate specialist are two entirely different animals. It is both embarrassing and an unfair timewaster to misunderstand who the person you are helping truly needs to be introduced. That would be a 101-level networking error.

Similarly, if you are arranging a Szechuan dinner for a visiting business delegation from Beijing, connect them with a restaurant that features cuisine from mainland China. They don't want a place that specializes in Cantonese cuisine from Hong Kong. If you want to refer a contact who is trying to brush up on her Spanish, she doesn't want a tutor who speaks Portuguese. Send a friend who wants to buy a Honda Civic to a Honda salesman, not to a Toyota dealership.

When you are a 212-level networker, you will not make these kinds of mistakes. You will know exactly what it is that your network member wants and needs. You will be crystal clear and specific.

## 2. THE RR IS DIRECT AND BOLD

Once you are certain what the needs are, then be bold in making the introductions needed to complete the referrals. You need not fear. Do anything it takes for you to be direct in speaking up and in seeking the introductions others need. There are ways to do that:

- Try pretending that you already *are* bold. Athletes mentally visualize themselves at the finish line before they even leave the starting gate. You can do something similar.
- The stereotypical advice for stage-fright is to imagine the audience in their underwear. Most media experts pooh-pooh that one. However, if that works for you and doesn't distract you, go for it. Gordon Lightfoot, a popular Canadian folk singer of the 1960s and 70s dealt with his fears by imaging that his audience could see *him* in *his* underwear.
- Try planning out what to say in advance. Some people practice or role-play in front of a mirror. Others carry notes or read from a mental cue card.
- Some people are fortified by imagining how someone they admire would make the contact and ask for an introduction that leads to a referral. How would the leaders of your networking group make introductions? Would they be direct and bold? Think of fictitious people or public figures. How would John Wayne ask for help? How about Rosa Parks who resisted bus segregation in Montgomery, Alabama in 1955?[36]

Above all, remember it isn't about you. Recognize that those you are helping or those from whom you are seeking help (on behalf of another) are almost definitely not judging *you*. You can feel free to ask people in your network to help with the goals and issues of your contacts. Many professionals in your group are happy to help others, especially people who are just starting out in their careers.

## 3. THE RR IS PERSONAL AND COMPLETE

Although introductions are also a part of creating contacts (**CC**), the introductions in **RR** are being made as a part of a full referral. In an **RR**, you're introducing a contact with needs to a contact with solutions. That's why we use the term, *relevant* referrals. Above all else, these referrals need to be personal (one-on-one) and complete.

Your business card, alone, is neither personal nor complete. Even accompanied with a handshake and a one-to-one contact, it is not a full introduction. Your business card is just a piece of paper with summary information. Yes, a well-designed professional business card will

---
[36] See: https://en.wikipedia.org/wiki/Rosa_Parks

help to establish your credibility. That's fine. But when you get right down to it, business cards are nothing more than a convenient conveyance of basic contact information. Don't get that confused with being a professional introduction. It is not. It is not even the lowest level of a 101 introduction, especially if you "spray" your cards all around without first making personal one-on-one contacts.

So, what exactly is a relevant referral? You can consider an **RR** in ascending levels of power – from a dud to dynamite. Let's say that you've just enjoyed a great lunch with friends. One of them, Laura-Leigh, enjoys her hobby of turning beautiful clay pots in her private studio. You've seen her ceramic works; they are truly objects of art and they're often a point of conversation. Relaxing around the table after dessert, Laura-Leigh happens to mention to everyone that she hasn't been able to spend much time in her studio recently because there is a leak in the studio roof. Several people laugh it off or tell their own stories about leaky roofs. You don't. You take Laura-Leigh's problem very seriously. In this case, you have several options:

The Dud: During World War Two, when Ray Hewell was a little boy in England, a Nazi bomb fell through a basement window where he slept, bounced across the concrete floor, and knocked over a water heater; but the bomb did not explode – true story! The house was spared, and Ray's life was saved. In fact, he didn't even wake up! The bomb was a dud. It had lots of potential, but no boom!

With a powerless dud referral, you empathize with Laura-Leigh, but offer no solutions and no referrals. There are no new introductions to someone who can help. At best, you offer a weak expression of sympathy, at worst you tell about a time your own roof leaked. This is not to say that sincere sympathy is not a wonderful gift to give. It is. But it is not an introduction and it is not a relevant referral (**RR**). Sympathy may comfort, but it does not solve problems.

The Sparkler: A sparkler is a fairly benign firework. It sends out tiny sprays of light, but it soon spurts and splutters and goes out. Even a child can be taught to safely hold a sparkler.

Let's say you tell Laura-Leigh about Scott Pike, a roofer you know. He's part of your professional network. You tell her that Scott does excellent work, is very fast, and charges a reasonable rate. You give her Scott's contact information. That's great. You've offered a weak referral at the first and lowest level. It sparkles, but not very much. Why is it weak? Because there is no introduction. You have not made the connection yourself; you have merely provided a phone number. Laura-Leigh has to make her own connection. We don't even consider this a serious referral, certainly not an **RR**, because it merely _suggests_ a connection, it does not _make_ that connection. It may be a bright sparkler in your hand, but it does not have explosive power.

Fireworks: Rockets and other pyrotechnics are another story. They can be dangerous to handle. People have lost eyes and limbs handling them carelessly. It is not appropriate for children to be setting off bottle rockets and Roman candles. They are for seasoned adults.

In networking, referrals can have a great impact. If you give Laura-Leigh Scott Pike's contact information and then give her contact information (with her permission) to Scott, actions will be set in motion. This is a much stronger and more relevant referral because you have taken much of the work out of creating the connection. You let Scott know that Laura-Leigh will be expecting a phone call. Scott will likely make that call because you've done the work for him; he would be lazy or incompetent to not follow up on what you have given him. Laura-Leigh knows you called the roofer on her behalf. She will anticipate Scott's call and accept him as her roofer. She more-or-less implicitly agreed to do so when she gave you permission to give Scott her phone number. It is only when you take it to this next level that the meeting becomes what we're calling, a professional introduction or a relevant referral (**RR**).

However, the link has not quite closed; there is still a gap. It still might not happen. Like most fireworks, it looks bright and flashy, but it quickly fizzles out.

Dynamite: Although dynamite has now been surpassed by other more powerful explosives, the introduction of dynamite revolutionized construction, demolition, and warfare. It represents the full deal.

The full deal in networking is not merely facilitating the connection between two people but actually completing that connection – and then getting out of the way. In our example, you confirm that Laura-Leigh would like to be connected to the roofer you recommended. You don't just give phone numbers, you and Laura-Leigh excuse yourselves from the lunch table, leaving the other guests to mingle. You walk into the living room and phone Scott immediately. You make sure he has a moment to answer a question about a leaky roof. Briefly, you tell him about Laura-Leigh's situation. Then you hand the phone to Laura-Leigh, telling her the roofer's name. "Laura-Leigh, this is Scott Pike. He's the roofer I told you about. Here, I have him on the line." You have closed the loop and filled in the gap. The power move at that point is to excuse yourself from the situation and let them talk alone on the phone. That is dynamite!

Can you see how powerful this referral is? When you are connecting two (or more) of your contacts for their benefit, then you are making introductory business referrals. This highest and most powerful level of **RR** is complete, respectful, and immediate. That is what it means to infuse your referrals with power. It will bolster your credibility in the eyes of both parties while nurturing and strengthening your bond with each of them. It will bring to your contact solutions that work. This is explosive power.

Notice it didn't result in any financial benefit to you. That's okay. It doesn't have to. You did it because you are a professional networker and you have a mindset of service to others. If it comes back to you in some way, you'll appreciate that. If not …well, that's fine, too.

Only the last of these levels ("fireworks" and "dynamite") have true explosive power. Only they are truly relevant, at least as we define the term. They include introductions for the purpose of solving Laura-Leigh's need (she wants to spend more time in her studio) and Scott's need (he wants more customers to generate income). They are relevant. They included professional introductions to others who will bear their problems and return solutions that work. They are personal, they are one-on-one, and they fill in all gaps in the connections.

## POWER BY CONNECTING THROUGH REFERRALS

Using relevant referrals of one contact in your network to another contact in your network is incredibly powerful. We have called relevant referrals the multiplying agent in the formula. This power multiplies like rabbits when you start interconnecting your referral partners.

Remember, a net is made up of <u>*intertwined*</u> mesh. It is not a collection of individual stamps in a stamp album. It is not a collection of separate coins in a safety deposit vault, or baseball cards in a cigar box under your bed. In fact, you're not collecting stamps, coins, or baseball cards at all. You are connecting living, breathing human beings. A professional network is alive and vibrant because it joins many individuals together into a mutually beneficial and living whole. A net is made strong by thousands of connected string squares. Your network is made strong by hundreds of connections of referral partners who you have carefully nurtured.

### TIER ONE: BRIANNA'S STORY OF WOE

Remember Brianna Wall, the 20-year-old from Chapter 4 who wanted to land that job in a mental health clinic? You helped her and her boyfriend create power resumés. Well, at the conclusion of one of the weekly networking functions, you ask her how she's doing and how her new resumé worked out. She has a new problem. She tells you that she has just graduated with her BA in psychology. Her plan was to work daytimes in a mental health clinic and work on a master's degree during the evenings. She has just found out the requirements of the job. She must have a master's degree in hand or be enrolled and working toward that degree – no exceptions. That part was okay but has just learned that the deadline for applying for the counseling program at the nearby community college has passed. "I just saw that in the College Application Packet. I can't wait an entire year. I don't know what I'm going to do now!"

Of course, there is absolutely nothing you, personally, can do for her in her sad situation. You can't help her this time. But you happen to know JoAnn Nutter. JoAnn is a close contact

SMART AND RELEVANT REFERRALS

in your professional network. She happens to be (are you ready for this?) – the Registrar for that particular College!

You call JoAnn Nutter up then-and-there. "Hello, JoAnn? It's me. How are you doing? I'm phoning with a sob-story for you. I know this wonderful and talented young woman, Brianna Wall. She is desperately needing to get into your counseling program for a job she's trying to land in the mental health field. She has apparently missed the application deadline. The clinic expects her to be actively taking classes. I was wondering if there was anything at all that you might be able to do for her? There might be…? That's great. Can I send her right over to you?"

In this example, the help needed for one contact in your network was provided by another contact in your network through a power referral. That makes it a first tier referral. Your job was to hook them up – to connect them. JoAnn bore the burden (Latin, *ferre*) of Brianna's need. Then she returned (Latin, *re*) the solution that solved Brianna's fears. Your role was also to facilitate that relevant referral and make those professional introductions. Brianna Wall wasn't up to going to the Registration Office by herself and getting into the spring semester. You provided a valuable referral for her.

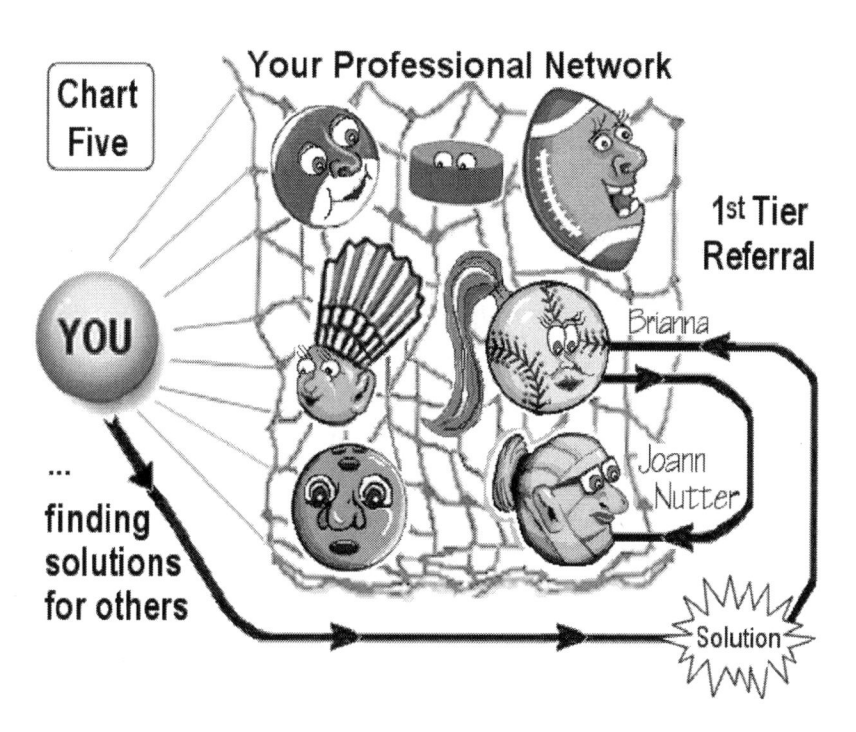

**Chart Five** — Your Professional Network — 1st Tier Referral — YOU … finding solutions for others — Brianna — Joann Nutter — Solution

What do you think your kindness means to Brianna?

What does your kindness mean to you?

Do you see the power in this? And this kind of knitting together of the problems of one member of your network with the resources of another member (meaning, first tier), can be multiplied many times:

- You hear of an older senior who needs someone to regularly drive her to medical appointments and you know a stay-at-home person who lives right near her. Make the connection.
- A business friend of yours wants to join the local Country Club and doesn't have any idea how to proceed. The Treasurer of that club happens to be in your professional network. Make the connection.
- A month ago, that same Club Treasurer was putting in a sprinkler system and was getting estimates that ranged an incredible $13,000 difference among them. You are able to connect him with a contact you have who specializes in pipe flow and sprinklers. Make the connection.
- A 40-year old you know is getting serious about her financial future and you have not one, but three, financial advisors in your contact list. Make the connection.
- A close friend is facing an intimidating legal deposition and you know a legal aid who can throw rapid questions at her so she can practice answering under pressure and calm her nerves. Make the connection.

The list could go on and on. If, by some chance, you introduce two people and find that they already know each other, that's completely okay. If anything, it validates your effort. It may be just what the first contact needs in order to have more confidence in the second contact you recommended. The unexpected coincidence that they already know each other might well enhance your credibility with both contacts. It will also give you a great feeling of worth and satisfaction.

As we've said, you're not serving others for what they will bring to you. However, it is a frequent side-effect that a lifestyle and mindset of helping others will come back to you many times over in happiness as well as in relevant referrals (**RR**) given to you. These will come in unexpected ways, but they will come as a result of a practice of service to others.

## TIER TWO: ESCALATING TO THE PREZ

Let's tweak this example of Brianna Wall. Let's say that JoAnn Nutter can't do anything. She says, "I would love to help. I just don't have that level of authority. A waiver of that deadline can only be made by the president of the college, President Lopez. I can't make any promises, but he is super nice. He's totally focused on student needs. If he can justify granting an exception, I know he will. I'll set up a meeting with President Lopez and Brianna. We'll see what he can do."

This is an example of a _second-tier_ introduction for a referral. You know Brianna and JoAnn. They are both in the first tier of your network. However, you don't know Dr. Lopez. So, he is a second tier for you. He was one person removed and not a part of your network.

This is diagrammed below.

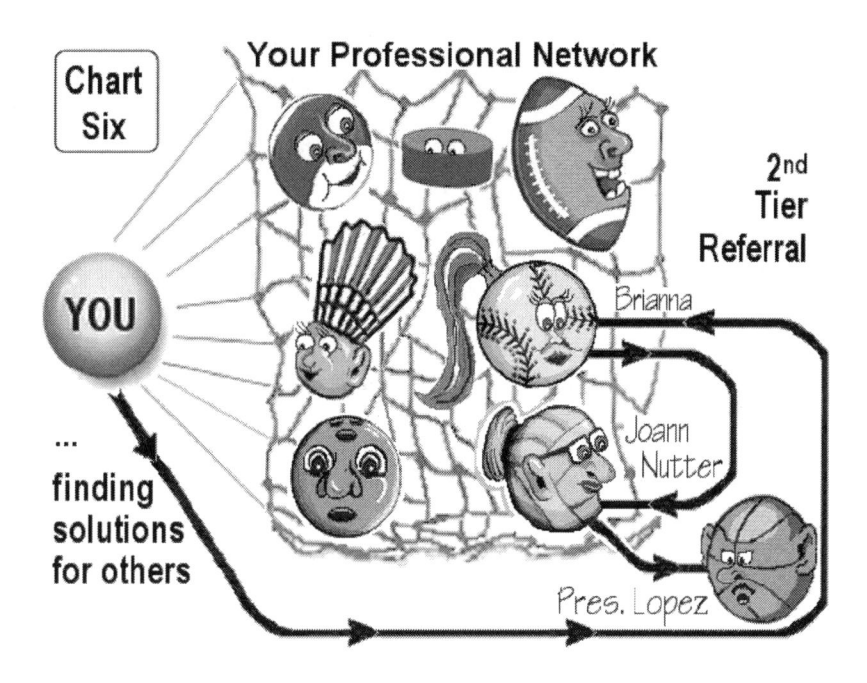

**Chart Six** — Your Professional Network / 2nd Tier Referral / YOU ... finding solutions for others

Even though you don't know President Lopez, there has been a professional referral from JoAnn. She has referred Brianna to President Lopez. You might think of that as a type of "vicarious" referral.

At this point, your power play is to stay out of the way. But once finished, you are at a decision point.

You can let it stand as is. Brianna met with JoAnn and President Lopez alone. It either got resolved or it didn't. But there is a second option. It would be good to follow-up with Briana to confirm that she got the results she wanted.

All of these relevant referral activities are the **RR**: the multiplicative factor in the networking formula. In fact, we might have written the formula so as to make **RR** be squared. It's that important. It's that much of a multiplying factor in this networking process.

## THE STORY OF TANYA HANSON

Consider another outstanding networker. It is the story of a woman named Tanya Hanson. She is an insurance professional whose networking skills and tactics are truly amazing. While James Davidson's networking work focuses on social connections, Tanya's work is more structured and focuses on generating referrals.

Tanya is one of those people who has a leadership air about her. When she walks into a room, people take notice of what she's doing, what she's about, and where she sits. They watch her actions and her interactions. It's no accident that her behaviors are frequently duplicated by others in networking groups. People are drawn to leadership.

What makes Tanya Hanson a great networker with a high network nurturing (**NN**) score is that she specifically targets people in order to help them grow their business. She might decide on her target for any number of reasons. Sometimes it is because she feels a rapport with that person and wants to help. Maybe she knows it's an off time in the season for that business. Other times, it's because she has just been introduced to one or two new people and wants to build up those relationships. Maybe because their fledgling businesses are trying to get established.

Regardless of the reason, the process is always similar. She blocks out a set amount of time in a specific day, every week, for this activity. She doesn't spend an enormous amount of time on this project – it's far from 20 hours a week, more like a couple of hours. She decides who in her network she's going to actively pursue in order to create relevant business referrals – and then she carries that out. She never betrays any trust or violates any confidentiality. Her mindfulness and ability to perceive the needs of others is highly specific and, because it is, it becomes a powerful referral. It is the kind of relevant referral that needs to be acted on immediately.

An example of this is Ken, the owner of a local roofing company. It was now his turn to experience the effect of Tanya's networking skills. Typically, she starts out by creating, in writing, a quick-and-dirty outline of:

1. what she likes about Ken,
2. what she knows about his company,
3. what she knows about his industry,
4. and what she wants to talk about.

After that, she does what she always does: She leans back in her chair and thinks about other people in her network, those who might benefit from an introduction to Ken. It might be a contractor, somebody who she knows has just had some wind damage to a home, or somebody planning a major remodel or adding a shed – something like that. She writes down what benefit a relevant business referral might be for each one of them.

Then she spends some time reaching out to each of those people. With some of them, that takes the form of a phone call. With some, an email. With others, it's a quick text message to follow up a phone call. It is always just a light and social call. She's friendly with them and says that she was just thinking about their situation and wondering if a referral could help them out. With their permission, she then provides that information to Ken.

The number of referral partners she contacts to help someone like Ken might vary from two or three people to as many as a dozen. The number depends on the time that she has available. Because she has this habit – this routine – she can be quick with people who she wants to assist.

What an example to keep in mind! Tanya sincerely wants others to succeed. This is a person whose networking is deliberate. Tanya is a skilled and creative professional whose networking skills and tactics are inspirational.

If you are inspired by her story, take note of two things.

<u>First</u>, this attention to others is a deliberate tactic; it is not an occasional activity. Because it is a routine, and she does it 7-7-7, it has become a part of who she is, a part of her professional lifestyle and mindset. She strives to do this, and she does it very well.

<u>Second</u>, in nurturing her network (**NN**) like this, the intent is always for *their* benefit and growth, not hers. Of course, there are secondary benefits for her, too. This commitment of time and energy has made her a leader in just about anything she does. It undoubtedly comes back, also, in relevant referrals to her. But the intent and motivation is to serve others among her network.

Others have expressed this philosophy of service much better. The original statement comes from the Bible:

*Whoever <u>finds</u> their life will <u>lose</u> it, and whoever <u>loses</u> their life for my sake will <u>find</u> it.*[37]

Mahatma Gandhi, and several 19th century writers, applied this idea specifically to serving other people:

*The best way to find yourself is to lose yourself in the service of others.*[38]

Similarly, American theologian, Thomas Monson, advised,

*Unless we lose ourselves in service to others, there is little purpose to our own lives ... [and] those who lose themselves in service to others, grow and flourish.*[39]

As impressive a referral partner as Tanya Hanson may be, she is merely putting into practice ideas that have been around for a very long time. She has made a relatively simple process into a valuable habit, as you can do. Start small and build toward the kind of referral action that Tanya routinely performs. She is a wonderful example to keep in mind. And, it will pay off for you as it has for her.

Having now talked about networks – what they are, what the formula for networking consists of, and how to do professional 212-level networking – we end this first part of the book. The next part of the book will deal with choosing network groups that will help you to put the networking formula to work in your life and career.

---

[37] New International Version of Matthew 10:39.

[38] This quote was attributed to Gandhi in Stone, 2001, *The Full Spectrum Synthesis Bible,* iUniverse. Similar quotes were used by others; this is according to: https://en.wikiquote.org/wiki/ Mahatma_Gandhi.

[39] See: https://www.mormonchannel.org/ blog/post/ daily-quote-lose-yourself-in-service

# PART THREE

## CHOOSING A PROFESSIONAL NETWORKING GROUP

# CHAPTER 8

# FOUR TYPES OF NETWORKING GROUPS

In any discussion of networking, and especially in this part of the book that deals with choosing the perfect networking group for you, it is important to understand that there are different types of networking groups and there are different kinds of networking functions. If you do not understand this, you can miss thousands of opportunities to network and hundreds of contacts that can be added to your professional network. In the long run, this means missing out on many, many business referrals. The four categories of networks are very different:

1. Immediate and Extended Family Networks
2. Casual Social Networking Groups
3. Informal Networking Situations
4. Formal Professional Networking Functions

## ONE: YOUR FIRST NETWORK

Your immediate family is an essential part of both your overall network and your core identity. In fact, it is probably the most important part. Please, please, please remember that the most important part of your professional network is your family.

### THE FAMILY: YOUR FIRST AND BEST NETWORK

The quality of this first network (although we wouldn't usually call it a network) is the foundation and the model for the quality of your professional networks. In other words, when you do things

THE PROFESSIONAL NETWORKER'S PLAYBOOK

as a family and you spend time with your family, you are networking. It may not be specifically for the purpose of business, but it is an important part of nurturing your network (**NN**).

Truly, the best networking always begins at home.

When you fully understand the 7-7-7 mindset that we discussed earlier (see page zzz), you will know that it applies first and foremost in the home. Seize the chances that you have to interact with your family members as often as possible. It will be uplifting for you as well as for any other person with whom you are fortunate enough to interact. Networking at home gives you opportunities to practice caring for others. You have more opportunities to practice the principle of 7-7-7 with your family than anywhere else in your life. Your interactions with your loved ones become habits that will be seamlessly and organically transferred to your interaction with all others in your professional networks.

In April of 1935, American theologian, David McKay, read an excerpt from a book by J. McCullough in a conference address.

It has tremendous value for us to consider and to apply in any discussion of networking:

> *The loss of fortune is nothing compared with the loss of home. When the club becomes more attractive to any man than his home, it is time for him to confess in bitter shame that he has failed to measure up to the supreme opportunity of his life.... No other success can compensate for failure in the home.*[40]

No matter how much success you have in your professional life outside the home, it is far more important to keep the relationships in your home strong. You must do everything you can, and take every opportunity that presents itself to you, to strengthen those relationships. This is the beginning of 212-level professional networking.

---

[40] This quote was part of a larger excerpt that McKay read in 1935. The excerpt came from *Home, The Savior of Civilization*. McKay read this title but, given his forum, did not read the publication date (1924), publisher, or the name of the author, J. E. McCullough, (*Conference Report*, 1935, pp. 115-116 in archive.org/stream/conferencereport1935a#page/ n115/mode/ 2up/search/ compensate.) The last sentence has incorrectly been attributed to McKay. Ironically, the phrase was not McCullough's either. Benjamin Disraeli (1804-1881) said, "No success in public life can compensate for failure in the home" (see: http://famousquotefrom.com/benjamin-disraeli).

– 92 –

## EXTEND OUT TO YOUR EXTENDED FAMILY

These same ideas hold true for your extended family. Don't overlook them anymore than your nuclear family. Parents and grandparents do not cease to be your parents any more than you cease to be their child or grandchild. The attitudes of society in general seem to be increasingly moving in the direction of exalting youth and ignoring seniors. Advertisers seem quick to present the young as inheriting the world, while seniors are shown as out of date fuddy-duddies. In *Forbes* magazine, an expert in personal finance asked and answered an important question:

> *What do respect and honor mean? Well, here is what they do not mean: In self-help books and blogs, you may come across the phrase, "parenting your parents," or even worse, "You have become your parents, and they have become your children." No, they have not.*[41]

Researchers have noted the trend for advertisers to portray seniors as "having undesirable personality traits (e.g. nosey, despondent, overly sentimental, and grouchy), or as comic foils for the purpose of attracting younger buyers."[42] They have warned:

> *Product and service marketers should note that both older people and students are aware that advertising stereotypes often portray old people inappropriately. …If the industry fails to address their use of older negative stereotypes, they risk alienating the rapidly growing older market.…*[43]

These societal changes in attitude toward aging need not be *your* attitude. Not only are your parents and grandparents to be respected, they are also important sources of networking contacts. Remember, those extended family members also all have their own networks. With some encouragement and direction, they can share with you many of their own contacts, friends, and work colleagues. Those are referrals. That will allow you to create contacts (**CC**) for your business network. Can you imagine the potential of adding, not just your parents and siblings, but your uncles, aunts, and your many cousins to your professional network?

---

[41] Gleckman, Howard, 2018, "It is About Respecting Aging Parents, But How Do You Do It? *Forbes Magazine* in www.forbes.com/sites/howardgleckman/ 2018/04/25/it-is-about-respecting-aging-parents-but-how-do-you-do-it/#71ffc6cb72e5.

[42] Robinson, T., Popovich M., Gustafson R., and Fraser, C., 2008, "Perceptions of negative stereotypes of older people in magazine advertisements: Comparing the perceptions of older adults and college students," *Aging & Society, 28*, p. 236.

[43] Robinson, 2008, p. 248-249.

## TWO: CASUAL SOCIAL NETWORKING GROUPS

Casual networks are a second category. These are groups of people who weren't collected for business networking. We have dozens of them. Now, we don't typically think of these sorts of casual groups as part of your professional network, but they can be. They fit in the category of casual social networking groups.

Each of us belong to many casual social networks that fit this description. They all require different ways for us to conduct ourselves and involve different activities for which we need to be available. Each one offers different networks of peers and associates. Examples seem endless.

### TYPES OF CASUAL SOCIAL NETWORKS

Below are 3 smaller categories within the casual social networks. We are including at least some examples of each of the smaller categories. We also list the typical networks they contain and that are, therefore, accessible to you:

- 1) Hobby and Interest Groups: Bringing people together, creating opportunities to connect with others who share your passions. The possibilities are nearly endless. Perhaps you're involved in genealogy or family history, stamp or coin collecting, mushroom hunting, or gardening. Maybe you enjoy birdwatching, woodworking, or exploring the arts. You might attend quilting bees, Bingo nights, or even dirt-track races.

  Groups centered around these interests are filled with people who already have something in common with you—an excellent starting point for building relationships. Whether you're playing cards at a Bridge or Canasta club, performing in a community theater production, jamming with a local band, or discussing your latest read at a book club, these shared experiences foster camaraderie and trust. These environments create a natural, low-pressure way to connect with others while pursuing something you genuinely enjoy.

  By engaging in these groups, you surround yourself with fellow hobbyists, collectors, book lovers, or enthusiasts who can become part of your broader network—not just as acquaintances but as people who already understand your interests and values.

# FOUR TYPES OF NETWORKING GROUPS

- <u>2) Faith-Based Groups</u>: You may be a member of a congregation of fellow believers who form a part of your religious organization. That may add hundreds, possibly thousands, of potential contacts (**CC**). Perhaps you minister with them in hospitals and for youth groups. You may attend Scripture study groups. You may go on missions to struggling countries to build places of worship or help provide clean water or wheelchairs. No matter the activity, network contacts from Faith-Based Group are plentiful. They include the parishioners, service volunteers, scripture study students, clergy and pastors, youth members, fellow visitors to the sick or aged, and lay leaders, and so on.

- <u>3) Community Service Groups</u>: Organizations provide incredible opportunities to connect with like-minded individuals while making a meaningful difference. Whether you're giving back to your community or supporting the development of children and teens, these groups naturally bring together people who value service, dedication, and collaboration.

    You might find yourself involved in organizations like the Shriners, Freemasons, Lions, Rotarians, or Kiwanis, all of which blend business-oriented networking with service. Perhaps you volunteer at a soup kitchen, collect goods for a food bank, or build homes with Habitat for Humanity. You might sew quilts for the homeless, participate in Special Olympics events, or serve as a PTA or HOA officer. Each of these roles allows you to work alongside others who share your passion for giving back.

    Likewise, organizations dedicated to supporting children and teens—such as Big Brothers Big Sisters, Boys and Girls Clubs, or the YMCA—offer rewarding ways to connect. Whether you're coaching a little league team, mentoring through scouting programs, or volunteering at your local hospital's NICU, these groups foster relationships with fellow mentors, coaches, families, and supporters.

    From creating safe spaces for children to thrive, to building stronger communities for everyone, these groups are united by their focus on service and connection. Engaging in these activities allows you to meet a diverse range of people, share meaningful experiences, and expand your network in deeply fulfilling ways.

You can probably add to the list above based on your own interests and affiliations. The point is that the category of Casual Networks consists of any group of people who share activities and involvements that aren't specifically related to business.

Are you starting to get the picture and see the vision? The others involved in all of these groups to which you already belong also form a part of your professional network. That means hundreds and hundreds of contacts for you.

Although you are not primarily seeking a return on your involvement and service, think about what it would mean if 20 to 30%, or even just 2 to 3%, provided you with relevant referrals. What would that do for your career?

For example, in Chapter 5 we talked about giving an elevator speech to strangers. That's essential. But opportunities to tell others what profession you're involved in are many times more frequent in casual settings. Those opportunities will crop up on the bleachers of the baseball field, waiting among other parents for a child to finish at dance club, walking out of a dull city council meeting, between hymns in the church choir, and while milling around on the platform of the subway. Don't overlook those opportunities to talk to people. Usually, you won't initially know those people but don't let that slow you down. If you handle it well, you *will* know them, and they are a part of your network.

Understanding how to conduct yourself, how to recognize opportunities to talk about your profession, to explain what you do and who you represent, are skills that will reward you time and again. Remember the old saying, "find a penny, pick it up." Well, these aren't pennies. These are hundred-dollar bills. And they are scattered all over the places that you frequent and where you have non-committed and confined moments.

The networking is happening between either just the two of you, or maybe a small cluster of people, but make no mistake – this is casual networking. You will find this invaluable. Knowing how to engage with others can supercharge your network growth.

## SOCIAL MEDIA NETWORKS

Earlier, in Chapter One, we talked about the role of social media in professional networking. We noted that social media can help you keep up with your contacts. But networks can actually offer more than simply nurturing your existing business network (**NN**). Social media can be a seedbed for creating new contacts as well (**CC**). It's true that networks created only online and as a part of social media are not "good business contacts for the reasons we gave earlier. However, they are casual social contacts all the same. Even if they are nothing more than names and phone numbers, they are an unexplored source for a professional network. These casual online personas can be changed into serious business contacts – the **CC** in the formula. By doing so, you will enhance and grow your formal professional networks immeasurably.

## THREE: INFORMAL NETWORKING SITUATIONS

Informal networking sounds a lot like casual networking, but they are actually different. Casual networks are made up of those with whom you interact in a non-business and non-career setting. Informal networking involves business or collegial contacts – but with whom you are relaxing or recreating. Such events are often presented as, "mixers" or "getting to know you" lunches.

Many informal networking functions involve meals, socializing over a cool glass of lemonade on a hot day, or even at business conventions between presentations and business sessions. They are simply opportunities for people to get together for the primary purpose of meeting other business people in a more relaxed and social setting. There is usually very little formality, it's primarily an open and social gathering.

Although business cards are a part of these informal networking events, they should follow-up one-on-one introductions, not replace them. Business people who want to make sure that every person in attendance has their business card are more likely to spray them carelessly. We will strongly caution against this practice.

There is one curious thing to note about both casual and informal networking. There is the potential for more business and relevant referrals to come out of those situations than in formal networking functions. As strange as it may seem, many more introductions take place in those relaxed settings. People are more relaxed and have their guards down. There is simply more time to talk than in a business meeting where time to mingle may be restricted.

## FOUR: FORMAL NETWORKING GROUPS

While informal opportunities to meet new people and grow your network are abundant, formal networking meetings play a critical role in serious professional networking. They're not optional—they're essential tools for the professional who is committed to building meaningful connections.

In the next two chapters, we'll dive deeper into this topic. Chapter 9 will focus on the logistical considerations for selecting a formal networking group, such as policies, size, location, and price. Chapter 10 will explore the intangible aspects, like the tone and professionalism of a group. Choosing the right formal networking group is one of the most important decisions you'll make. It determines not only where you'll place a significant amount of your networking focus, but also where you'll invest much of your emotional and intellectual energy.

Formal networking groups—what we'll refer to as BRING!-type meetings—come in all shapes and sizes. These groups share certain defining characteristics: they have structured meetings, minutes, dues, policies, and rules for their members. The names they choose can vary widely, but the name alone isn't what determines their value. Instead, it's their alignment with the BRING! philosophy that matters.

## WHAT'S IN A NAME?

Formal groups use a variety of naming conventions. Some reflect their membership or professional focus, such as:

- Groups for blue-collar professionals and service providers
- Small business owner or CEO networking groups
- Coffee shop meetups with less formal structures

Others are tied to larger organizations, like Rotary, Kiwanis, or Optimists, and include the parent organization's name. Groups connected to Chambers of Commerce often incorporate their chamber affiliation into their name. Still, others use geographic identifiers or creative, catchy titles. Here are a few examples:

**Geographically Oriented Names:**

- Manhattan Meetup
- Oak Park Area Business Leaders
- Salt Lake City Business Mastermind
- City Club of Chicago
- Catchy or Fun Names:
- Munch & Mingle
- Bagels & Business
- Power Hour
- Gals that Brunch

**Theme or Topic-Oriented Names:**

- Seattle Latino Networking Professionals
- Black, Brilliant, and Successful in Phoenix
- Spokane & Eastern WA Marijuana Business Networking

**Acronym-Based Names:**

- HOPE: Helping Other People Excel
- SMILE: See Miracles in Life Every Day
- TING: Temple Isaiah Networking Group

The name doesn't determine the group's value or philosophy, but it does offer clues about its focus and culture.

## THE BRING! PHILOSOPHY

Instead of merely describing these groups as "formal," we propose a new term: BRING! This term isn't just a name—it's a philosophy that defines the purpose and approach of these networking groups.

The BRING! philosophy revolves around two primary goals:

1) Facilitating business referrals among professionals who are bonded by strong relationships.
2) Encouraging interactive, reciprocal networking activities that benefit all members.

This philosophy is summarized in the acronym BRING!:

- **B** – Business
- **R** – Referrals (and)
- **I** – Interactive
- **N** – Networking
- **G** – Group

When we refer to BRING! groups, we're talking about formal networking groups that embody this philosophy. For example, a HOPE group could align with the BRING! principles, as could a Munch & Mingle group or a Chamber of Commerce group. The name doesn't matter—it's the alignment with the BRING! approach that makes the difference.

## THE BRING! PROTOTYPE

The group we belong to, BRING!, serves as a prototype for this philosophy. Located in Olympia, Washington, BRING! not only adopt the BRING! principles but also uses the name BRING! to emphasize its focus on business referrals and interactive networking.

Not all formal groups meet the BRING! standard, and that's okay. However, we urge you to look for—and expect—a group that embodies this philosophy. The BRING! approach is a cornerstone of this book and a proven framework for successful networking.

## UNDERSTANDING THE FOUR TYPES OF NETWORKING GROUPS

Before diving into the specifics of finding your perfect BRING! group, it's essential to understand how formal networking groups fit into the broader networking landscape. Networking opportunities generally fall into four categories:

- Family
- Casual
- Informal
- BRING! (Formal)

Your ability to navigate these categories and adapt to different networking environments is key to your success.

In the next chapter, we'll focus on identifying a BRING! group that fits your needs. We'll guide you through evaluating logistical factors, such as size, policies, and price. Then, in Chapter 10, we'll shift to the intangibles—how to assess potential groups' tone, personality, and professionalism to ensure they align with the BRING! philosophy.

# CHAPTER 9

# CONSIDER THE LOGISTICS OF A NETWORKING GROUP

Business people can and do benefit from attending formal, professional networking groups. That's just a fact. Networking groups provide invaluable professional contacts (**CC**) and provide always-welcomed relevant referrals (**RR**). They may also offer moral support, business ideas, mentorship, and a sense of identity and purpose. They also provide a place to practice the skills taught in this book. They are an absolute must for successful professional networking.

But not just any-ol' networking group will do. You want the right one for you and your trajectory. Whether you are new to networking, or just new to a location, you will need to find the right professional networking group that will advance your career and help you to reap the benefits that are just waiting for harvest.

Even if you are a seasoned professional networker, there may come a time when it would be advantageous to consider switching to a new group. Your choices obviously increase in larger communities and cities, and it may be worth a commute to attend the right group.

In networking, your primary aim is to expand the network in order to give and receive more referrals. And they need to be the right kind of referrals – relevant referrals (**RR**). A given group may claim to be able to provide a large number of referrals. But they may not be quality (relevant) referrals. The group may look like one that can meet your needs – but dig deeper. Don't accept a surface glance. Assess and observe more closely.

<u>Bottom-Line Rule Number One</u>:
Don't settle for less than what's the very best
for you, your business, and your goals.

Let's say you are fortunate enough to have a reasonable choice between several business groups. How do you go about evaluating which of the groups has the most value to you? What are some of the key indicators or characteristics that should be considered when selecting a networking group that is worth your time, effort, and money?

Don't rush your decision. An excellent rule-of-thumb is to attend a minimum of six different networking groups before deciding on a group to join. Few people will buy the first house they walk through or the first car they test drive. The same thing is true of professional networking groups. Attending this many groups will help you understand what is expected of its members. It will help you to assess the best fit for you.

## MEMBERSHIP POLICIES OF THE GROUP

Typically, you will attend each potential networking group as a guest. With only a few exceptions, going as a guest is free, and you will be enthusiastically and warmly received. That's great – who doesn't welcome a little TLC? Remember, though, you are visiting to make a hard business decision, not to join a social tea group. Carefully evaluate what you see and hear. Remember, too, the group will be – or should be – appraising you as much as you are evaluating the group.

There was a line from the old 1998 rom-com, *You've Got Mail* with Tom Hanks and Meg Ryan. The line said, "It isn't personal, it's business."[44] That you and many of the other members in the group will become good friends and allies is beside the point. This is business. You are there with a mission!

One thing you will discover very quickly is that different groups have different parameters on how much you can participate. Some groups have an exclusivity policy. This is often called a, locked group. That means that any given profession can only be represented by one person. For example, if a person is a residential real estate agent, there cannot be any other residential real estate agents in that group. Even if other real estate agents are invited to the same group as guests, he or she is hushed and not allowed to participate.

There may be some perceived benefits from such a policy, especially for those who are just beginning to network. They are able to hone their skills without worrying about any

---

[44] If you haven't seen this movie, check it out for a fun and romantic escape. The *Rotten Tomatoes* website summarizes it as: "Great chemistry between the leads made this a warm and charming delight." – see: www.rottentomatoes.com/m/youve_got_mail.

competition. As the only person in their profession, they will receive more referrals from the group because they are the only choice. The group is "locked in" to that person, as it were.

From our perspective, there are more downsides than upsides to exclusivity policies. It sounds good for those who are not yet seasoned networkers. Beginning networkers may benefit from this with a reduced anxiety about how they are doing. However, as a person's skills begin to accelerate, the downsides quickly overrun the perceived benefits and the limitations become glaringly obvious.

*First*, an exclusivity policy runs counter to the "Mindset of Abundance," discussed in Chapter 2. An exclusivity policy is an assumption of competition. It is not a philosophy of cooperation in a full field ready to harvest. You may prefer a group that welcomes people, not one that puts up walls and bars the door.

*Second*, it limits the ability for two professionals, say two financial planning agents or two marriage counselors, to help each other in a collegial manner. Sure, other group members in other endeavors can and will support you. But there is nothing like the ally-ship of a mentor or colleague in your same field of work. An exclusivity policy rules out the opportunity.

*Third*, if you apply the Rule of 12, as discussed in Chapter 3, you'll understand not every referral you receive as a potential customer will be a "good" client for you. Experienced networkers focus on clients who will work with them well, and with whom they work the best. This is especially true when the client is not just a one-time purchaser.

So, referrals in locked groups are not necessarily based on the best fit for a contact. They may come simply because there is no other choice than the person who happens to fit the slot for that business category. That would mean you could receive many referrals that are not relevant or profitable for you.

While there may be other good reasons to join a locked group, it may be more difficult to concentrate on the "cream of the crop" or the top 12% of your contacts. And remember, one goal in the formula is to create contacts (**CC**).

Even if you allow for the concept of "competitors," consider this. We all have competitors who do certain things better than our company does. That does not mean locking them out of our meetings is in our best interest. If we have a relationship with them, that allows us to, believe it or not, make referrals for clients who would be better served by one of our competitors rather than us. That demands a great amount of professionalism to understand and more to put into practice. It means accepting:

1) A "competitor" may actually have a better product or service than you
2) Your product or service would not be practical, cost-effective, or profitable to you at this time

3) The underlying philosophies of abundance over scarcity (Chapter 2) and service (Chapter 1) are valid philosophies that can be profitable to you down the road.

How are these three statements possible? Let's look at an example.

If you have a client with a specific need that is positive for you at this time, attempting to fill that need may not be wise, It may be financially risky – due to time and effort, if for no other reason. In other words, if that client would be a drain on resources, then send them to the competitor. Trust that your strengths may be your competitor's weakness and vice versa and a stream of referrals could result. If the competitor doesn't reciprocate, then find a different competitor to refer to next time. For this reason, rather than excluding different representatives from the same industry, it makes sense to encourage competitors, who may become colleagues. This way, you can build even more referral relationships.

*When we know our own and our company's strengths and weaknesses, we are better professional networkers.*

Sometimes it is a painful exercise to identify our weaknesses and let others fill the need. By going through the process, we can spend more time focusing on clients. The clients then end up with better results. When competitors are allied to give clients the best experience the entire industry represented is benefitted. When the industry is better, all the companies in that industry profit.

## ASSESS THE COSTS OF MEMBERSHIP

One immediate consideration is the costs of membership in the group. Those costs are not just monetary. There are also less obvious costs in such resources as time, commitment and energy.

### DO CHEAP FEES = CHEAP QUALITY?

One valid consideration is the financial cost of a membership. Groups need a budget for renting space, printing costs, website development, upkeep and the like. That usually means membership fees. But how much?

There are some groups that are free. Other groups may charge as much as $1,000 a year. That is no small difference. On the one hand, most of us like to save a buck whenever we can. Who doesn't appreciate a freebie? On the other hand, there's the old adage, you get what you pay for. Free or lower-cost groups may be overly-casual – too informal. They may even be chaotic. Sometimes, they lack structure and strong leadership.

But that's not necessarily the case. Low-cost groups can also be highly effective, especially for new members who are just starting out. These groups typically do not have a lockout system or an exclusivity in their group. They often have a more-or-less open-door policy. That's a plus. And they can be more personable and accepting. A group with no, or a low, membership fee may be the perfect one for you.

On the other hand, there may be much to be gained from a group that promotes itself as the Lamborghini of professional groups. They may provide prestige, credibility, and solid organization and leadership. But not necessarily. The group may or may not actually be worth the membership dues. If your company is footing the bill, that's fine, but if you're the one coughing up a large fee, the membership dues may be a deal breaker. You must decide whether or not the cost of the dues is just flushing money down the toilet.

And, even if the money isn't a stumbling block, remember that their charging a top premium is no guarantee that they are any better than an inexpensive group. A fee of $1,000 does not necessarily buy networking success.

The fact is there is often a valid correlation between quality and cost ...but only to an extent. You have your own experiences with buying cheap and being surprised with great quality; and paying top dollar and being disappointed with junk. We have all experienced both of those.

The cheapest or least costly group may, or may not, be the group that is the best fit for you. It's best to consider the membership fee as one, but only one, cost to consider. Annual dues can be a valuable investment in yourself and your career, but only when there is a good return-on-investment (ROI). The bottom line is that price, by itself, is not the best criterion for making your decision.

## NON-MONETARY COSTS – FIGURE PROFIT/LOSS

Remember there are other costs besides just money. A membership in a professional group entails a time commitment as well, especially if you volunteer or are elected as a group officer in any capacity of leadership.

There may also be a cost or benefit in terms of the prestige of your group. You want to impress, not depress, the prospects and guests who you will invite to visit the group you join. What will impress them? Will it be a large, corporately-owned and well-funded group with abundant resources and distinguished members? Perhaps a group connected with a Chamber of Commerce?

Maybe a coffee-shop collection of people who get together for an enjoyable sharing of stories and referrals? Which is best for you? Which is best for the guests you will invite to join you there? There are strengths and weaknesses to *all* of these.

The bottom line (and by that we mean the final analysis, not the financial situation), is you have to balance what you're putting in (money, time, identity, and loyalty) with what you're getting out. That is a simple cost/reward analysis.[45]

If all Rewards (minus) all Costs = positive,<br>
that is Profit – Steam ahead!<br>
If all Rewards (minus) all Costs = negative,<br>
that is Loss – Run away!

## FACTOR IN THE NUMERICAL SIZE OF THE GROUP

Another related question is the size of the professional networking group you are considering. Large groups provide more opportunities for expanding your network and, consequently, more relevant referrals. Smaller groups may be less daunting – especially for people who are just starting their careers. People may feel more comfortable in a smaller group. You may not want to be the proverbial small fish in a huge pond.

An ideal size for most professionals may be more than 20 (for contacts and referrals) but less than 50 (when cliques start splintering off). As the room gets larger and the population grows beyond that, conversation at one end of the room often becomes different from the conversations at the other end of the room. Also, as the size grows, it may become more difficult to develop trust relationships. You get lost or have to compete to be heard and recognized.

## CONSIDER GEOGRAPHY AND SCHEDULING

The location of the meetings will become very important to you. It may seem well worth it to travel to a larger town or another section of the city to attend the best meeting. Well and good …for the first few meetings. But will you want to do this – *will* you do this – week after week? Make no mistake, geography *will* affect your attendance.

So will scheduling. Meetings earlier in the morning are much better for most people. If you have a meeting that meets in the middle of the day, it probably should be very close to your office,

---

[45] For one example of a cost/benefit analysis, see the website, *Project Manager* at www.projectmanager.com/blog/cost-benefit-analysis-for-projects-a-step-by-step-guide

even in your office complex. That would make you more likely to attend regularly. However, the fact that it is scheduled in the middle of the day could still make it difficult to attend, no matter where the meeting is held, because of appointments and the flow of business.

If the meetings are in the late afternoon, it will still increase your participation if it is more-or-less on that geographic line between your office and your home. Detours across town in afternoon traffic, and especially commutes to another town or area of the city, will become heavy burdens you may decide to skip "just this once." Once will become twice, then thrice and, before you know it, a month or more will have somehow slipped by.

If the networking group you are considering meets in the evenings, it may be even more important to find a group that is close to your home. If you are fortunate enough to make it home for dinner, are you going to want to go back out? Meetings will simply not be as inviting when you are tired or discouraged from a long day. It is obvious that you will be much more likely to turn around and go back outside if the meeting is close, than if you have to make a long drive somewhere.

None of this is essential – but understanding geography and scheduling *will* impact your attendance and your commitment to the group. That, in turn, impacts how much you will profit from that group and what it has to offer you. The greater the detour or inconvenience, the less the group will benefit you – and you, the group. This is particularly true if you have a propensity to run late. Having a meeting close to your home or office will make it more likely to be on time and to participate fully.

## MEMBER'S PERCEIVED VALUE AS A BAROMETER

When you're investigating a group, it is absolutely fair game to ask members, in private conversations, exactly what they're getting out of their memberships. What is the return on their investment? Now, if you simply ask members, "How do you like the group?" you're going to get the standard, socially expected, response. They are going to be really positive because they want to validate their own membership, and they want to be loyal to the group who is trying to recruit you as a new member. Expect that, but don't settle for that. You've often heard and probably said, "There are no stupid questions." However, "How do you like the group" is approaching the stupid threshold.

Instead, start asking the harder questions. Try to avoid closed-ended formats where questions can be answered with simple yes/no or one-word responses. Substitute an open-ended format where questions require reflection and elaboration. And don't be afraid to push deep and hard. You want that barometer reading to be accurate!

- Ask about the number of referrals you are likely to receive if you become a member.
- Ask if the member you are interviewing (yes, "interviewing") learns at least something at every meeting attended and, if so, what specifically did he or she learn in the last 3 meetings attended.
- Ask your person to point out the most helpful member in the group, and how that person helps others and would help you.
- Ask who would be able and willing to offer you the best mentorship. Heck, you can even ask who to avoid.
- Ask what time and energy commitments you will be expected to make in addition to just the cost of dues.
- Ask about the history of this particular group.
- Ask about the quality, the reliability, and the integrity of the current group's leadership.

Pose any and every question you can think of to get the information that you need. Be polite – but be blunt and probing. This is for your professional future. The more you demonstrate that you are truly serious about getting information, the more you will be responded to with frankness and honesty.

Work over the person you are interviewing. Probe that person and don't let go. Like a dog with a bone, chew until you get to the marrow. This is a big deal.

Understand that the value of each referral is different for every person in every industry. A productive referral to a real estate agent may be worth $10,000, while a referral to a printing company may be only worth $10. You probably want to consider what the value of your average transaction is. Talk to people who have similar price-points for their products or services. Do the math. You don't have to necessarily tell them that you're doing that math, but you want to know if the networking group will be effective and profitable for you.

If you decide it is, join up. You may have stumbled on the perfect networking group that can truly advance your career and your agenda. You may have found a group that would be a great fit for you. If you judge the members you meet have reached an expert level you haven't yet achieved and that you will receive numerous relevant referrals (**RR**), count yourself richly blessed … join that group.

If, on the other hand, your assessment is that you already do better than the members of that group and you are already a better presenter than what you see in the meetings, that is an entirely different outcome. This may not be the group for you – expensive or free. If that is the case, politely and humbly thank the person who invited you to the meeting …and quietly move on.

All of these logistical characteristics and all the information you have collected so far are important. Just as important are intangible characteristics that make up the character, the feel, and the culture of a group. In the next chapter, we will discuss this tone: what it means and what to look for.

# CHAPTER 10

# ASSESS THE TONE OF A NETWORKING GROUP

In the previous chapter, we explored the logistics of formal networking groups—factors like membership policies, costs, group size, and meeting schedules. But choosing the right group isn't just about practicalities; it's also about how the group feels.

This chapter gets personal. It's about finding a group that resonates with you on a deeper level, a group where the tone, personality, and culture align with your professional values and networking goals. Think of it as finding your "business home-away-from-home."

What's the vibe of the group? How do the members interact? Does it feel welcoming, collaborative, and inspiring? Or does it feel cold, competitive, and disorganized? The answers to these questions matter because the group you choose will shape your networking experience and outcomes.

By understanding these less tangible factors, you'll be better equipped to choose a group where you can thrive. Let's dive in and explore how to assess the tone of a networking group to ensure it's the perfect fit for you.

## THE PERSONALITY STYLE OF THE LEADERS

One of the most important factors will be obvious immediately. It will occur almost automatically as a result of your mere attendance. The leader is your first real view of the group's culture and will create, or at least influence, your first impression of the group. Closely assess the personality style of the leadership. Place most importance on the president. Can you relate to that leader? Is he or she friendly and warm? Accessible? Do you feel intimidated or feel an instant rapport? Are you comfortable with the level of humor, of formality, or flexibility?

The group will largely be a reflection of the style and personality of its leaders – be they the president, the membership coordinator, the time-keeper and recorder, the treasurer, and so on. If the group is running like clockwork and the leader still has a long time to go in that position, expect that the style you see will continue for some time. This is a variable that you cannot control, but it is important. The BRING!-type meeting will be a significant part of your professional network for the foreseeable future. Do you feel comfortable in that milieu? Would you happily and eagerly return to that mood and tenor each week?

On the other hand, this is not junior high. You do not love or hate a class based on whether you love or hate the teacher. As an adult, you are certainly able to still learn a lot from a leader you don't particularly care for. You can still learn a lot, create contacts (**CC**), make and nurture friends (**NN**), and share relevant referrals (**RR**), even if you found the leadership dull, silly, or autocratic. But you may not feel quite as comfortable as you would like. The formula would still work, though not as efficiently or powerfully.

Then, too, you may be assuming the president was elected to a five-year term but, in fact, you may be looking at a substitute for that one day. Or, the leader may be brand new and feeling awkward and clumsy. If so, expect the style to morph and change. By contrast, the president may have been in that position for 6 months to a year, or more. Mistakes will be at minimum and any residual of nervousness will be long gone. If so, what you see will be what you get. So, try to find out where this individual falls in the typical tenure of the position.

Though the personality style of the leadership should not be a deal-breaker, it is at least a tie-breaker. It is at least another characteristic to throw in your decision pot. So, while considering the personality of the leadership, remember that personality is still only part of the picture. In other words, it is important that you avoid the rookie mistake of assessing the <u>leadership style</u>, and not the <u>leadership structure</u>, of the group. Leaders change; structure does not. A dynamic and energetic group leader who sprinkles humor into the conducting of the meeting, may be replaced by a dry and to-the-point manager. Both of them may be equally effective, but their styles may be in sharp contrast. When the leaders change, texture and tone usually do as well. You are not there to be entertained, but you must feel comfortable and confident in the leaders.

Leadership should not be the sole reason to join or not join a group.

## THE PROFESSIONALISM OF THE GROUP

The tone or culture of the meeting, itself, can also come into play. This is an important indicator of whether this is the right group for you.

When you walk into the first networking meeting, most of the people there will, of course, not know you. Pay particular attention to if, and how, they greet you. Regardless of the size of the group, there should be at least a handful of people who attempt to make you feel welcome. Make sure that happens. If it does not, strike one! Comfort level is essential and being warmly received is a large part of how comfortable you are made to feel.

A warm welcome may not seem that important to you. You may believe you can overlook a weak welcome if other factors are encouraging. Remember, though, you will be bringing guests to that group in the future. Even if *you* were able to overlook a tepid welcome, your guests may not feel the same way. You want them to feel welcome. You want them to know their attendance is appreciated.

**BRING!**
Business Referrals and Interactive Networking Group

- Pledge of Allegiance
- Welcome
- Networking Education
- Member Commercials
- Brought Introductions
- Member Presentations
- Stat Report
- Testimonials
- Reporting Results
- Member Announcements
- Member Gift Drawings*
- How to Join BRING!
- Open Networking

## PUT THE AGENDA ON YOUR AGENDA

In addition to the welcome, look closely at how the meetings are conducted. For example, make sure that any group that you are seriously considering joining has a set agenda. Ideally, that agenda will be published and followed. Look to see if the agenda is available to all its members. Why is this so important? When you can see what the agenda is, you can follow along. You'll see this when you're a guest at a group. If you don't know where you are on the agenda, you don't know how much longer you have left in this meeting. You don't know if you're going to make your next appointment on time. You don't know what to expect next. That can make you (and others) feel lost and overwhelmed.

In some cases, the meetings are going well, and you won't reference the agenda. That's fine. But not all groups have a set agenda and not all groups that do have an agenda follow the agenda. And not all groups that have and follow an agenda make that agenda available to all members. That's not fine.

Below is an agenda from a BRING!-type meeting that is also called, BRING! This group is the prototype of a BRING!-type meeting. It meets in Olympia, Washington, and is open to all invited guests.[46]

Find groups that use, publish, and distribute such an agenda. When you are first investigating a networking group, you will find that seeing an agenda will help you to understand what is

---

[46] The agenda page for this prototype BRING! group was designed and is maintained by Sheryl Miller at: http://site-impressions.com.

going on and help you to stay engaged. For those reasons, it is enormously relaxing. You know you will be taken care of by professionals who know how to conduct a professional meeting. In its absence, you may notice your discomfort at not knowing what the format of the meeting will be and when activities will occur. You have a right to expect to have that agenda followed, published, and accessible to you

You will also find that an agenda continues to be important to you when you are a full member of that group. Let's say you have invited one or more guests to the meeting. Armed with that agenda, you can turn to them and say, "This is what's coming next. This is what you can expect." Even better, you can review the agenda with your guests even before the meeting starts. That helps your possibly nervous guests to relax.

## DRESS AND SPEECH CAN REVEAL A LOT

Other factors to consider are the ways the other members present themselves in dress and speech. There is no dress code or preferred speech pattern other than that members should be at the top of their particular careers and occupations. A baker would not wear a business suit with a hanky in the pocket. That would be inappropriate for her field. But neither should she attend a BRING! meeting in shorts and a halter top with unkempt hair. There is nothing wrong with shorts around town or at the beach, but not at a formal networking function.

We are not talking about the quality of the meeting. A meeting of top CEOs will be very different than a meeting of people who get their hands dirty with ink, hair dye, bread dough, or engine oil. One is not better than the other. We are talking about fit for you. A CEO will be less comfortable in a room full of polo shirts and flowered blouses. A cake decorator and cosmologist will be less comfortable in a room full of business suits and briefcases.

If you work in construction or service, you will tend to dress more casually by virtue of the work you do. If you are a plumber, carpenter, or commercial artist, for example, but you attend a group that is made up primarily of "suits" (attorneys, financial planners, accountants), their dress and speech patterns may make you feel uncomfortable over time. It's not that attorneys don't need carpenters, and hair-stylists, and plumbers. An attorney's toilet gets clogged up as often as anyone else's. It's just, sooner-or-later, you're going to feel awkward if you dress and speak more casually and attend a meeting where you feel underdressed. Their silk ties and fancy grammar is going to get old over time.

On the other hand, if you're an attorney, financial planner, or accountant and you're going to a group that centers more around construction, maintenance, and repair, then you are probably, over time, going to feel awkward and over-dressed. It's not that carpenters and plumbers don't need the services of an attorney. It's that you may begin to feel out of place sitting in your three-piece pinstripe with your university grammar while most others are casual in their slacks and more relaxed communication style.

Take a look at all of this. You are not assessing value or quality. You are assessing fit for you based on the tone of the group. You may want to be in a group where most of the members are at least roughly similar to you.

We recommend looking for a comfortable mix of dress and language. Those are external trappings anyway. They are merely required tools of our various trades. We are basically all the same and status differences and class distinctions are best overcome by mixing together and finding out humans are humans. At our core, we all need each other and are all just looking for problems to be solved.

But no business professional wants to be a member of a group where the members dress in grunge, or work-soiled clothes, or lace their sentences with profanity. If you encounter that, this may not be the business group where you will be the most successful in sharing referrals and growing your business. You want to be in a group where members present themselves, through dress and speech, at the top of their appropriate career path, whatever it may be.

## ARE MEMBERS SELF- OR OTHER-ORIENTED?

There is one final tip for examining the tone and professionalism of the networking meeting. Are the members self-centered or are they other-centered? Do they recognize and support each other? Most meetings provide an opportunity for members to share. Look for that. There may be times when members stand out to give a public thanks or provide a shout-out to a colleague. If you hear one member offer a shout-out to another, listen to these very carefully. They will be one of two kinds:

<u>Self-Promoting</u>: Some public shout-outs look like an expression of gratitude – on the surface. Look deeper. In fact, they may be nothing more than an excuse to give another commercial about the person making the shout-out. For example, a member may stand and say something like: "I received a referral from Kathy, and I was able to help that referral do XYZ. My product helped that referral do much better. Thank you, Kathy, for the referral." That thank you was really just another commercial for the individual and a thinly-veiled attempt to promote a product or service.

<u>Other-Promoting</u>: Other public shout-outs truly focus on the other member and make the other shine. For example, the member stands and says something like: "I gave a referral to Audrey and she helped my friend with a makeover. My referral's hair looked super cute and she felt 10-years

younger. She felt a boost of confidence. It was wonderful to see. Thank you, Audrey, for what you did for her." That's not another commercial for the speaker, that's a praise for Audrey. It was truly thanking her for what she did. It was not an excuse to talk about the speaker's own business or product but to spotlight Audrey's business and product.

Listen to see if the group has a culture of self-promotion or mutual-support. That's a huge indicator of the atmosphere and culture of the networking group as a whole.

## OPPORTUNITIES FOR WEEKLY PRESENTATIONS

Another characteristic of tone to consider when you are selecting the ideal group is the degree to which you will be able to share with others, usually on a weekly basis. We will talk much more about this in the next few chapters. The point for now is that you want the group you join to provide opportunities for weekly sharing of what we will call, in later chapters, "networking commercials." You will also want times to receive information from others. Look for these opportunities.

Most groups routinely provide a great deal of time for longer presentations by their members on a rotational basis – say, every few months. This is good. You want this. But not all groups offer more regular and frequent mini-presentations (commercials). Look, specifically, for this. Hold out for this. Consider this a bottom line that you must have.

Why is this so? Why are mini-presentations (commercials) so important and why should you care if the group you are looking at allows for them?

First – Because Things Change. And they change all the time. Business is seldom stagnant. Let's say Audrey, a member of a group, is given an opportunity to make a long, once-every-six-month presentation. She does so very well, but then the next week, there is a product change. Now what? Or what if the big presentation comes off just fine, but a week later her supervisor leaves and a new manager is hired and changes the business practices? What now? Perhaps the day after the presentation, the company adopts new graphics or new slogans, maybe even a new name. Now what? Perhaps the member no sooner delivers the lecture than Audrey receives a big promotion, or a title change. What if she earns a new certificate or license? How does Audrey tell the group about these changes? She will have to wait several months to update her fellow members on these significant developments.

Second – Because the Member Just Wasn't "On" That Day. Let's say Audrey, who is only given a once-every-six-month opportunity to present, just wasn't in top form that day. There are any number of reasons for that.

- She was not fully prepared and was winging it just a little bit or doing it off the cuff.
- There had just been a major argument with her partner or an upsetting complaint from a customer
- Audrey experienced a reversal in her life, maybe the illness of a loved one or an unexpected large bill.
- It was as simple as her coming down with a cold, or she just couldn't sleep well the previous night.

We've all experienced those kinds of flat times. There could be a host of reasons why Audrey just wasn't sharp for the "big presentation." If any of those conditions were going on, she just blew a once-per-six-month opportunity. What a loss!

Third – Because Attendance is Not Regular. It only stands to reason that different group members attend on different days. What if a key networker for Audrey missed her one-shot presentation because of an illness or a scheduling problem. By definition, Audrey is limited to presenting to those who happen to attend on the day that she is presenting. In some cases, she may miss out on reaching the very ones who would have benefited her the most – or who Audrey could have helped the most. So, now Audrey has to wait another six months to try again.

That's no good! You do not want to be put in any of these positions. Shorter, more frequent, mini-presentations cut through all these problems. Weekly commercials fill all of these gaps. They account for unexpected changes, presentation variations, and attendance fluctuations. The amount of time that is provided to you, and the frequency with which you are allowed to feature yourself and/or your product or services, is an important characteristic to consider. You want the members of any group you join to be able to update often – ideally, weekly. This is important, so look for this.

## EDUCATION AND OTHER TRAININGS

As important as weekly presentations (commercials) are, longer presentations are also very important. Most networking groups also allow time for education trainings. Make sure those opportunities also exist in the group you are considering. The quality of a group's in-service offerings and trainings are important factors to consider.

The instruction is typically given by someone, usually a seasoned person, to provide points of information and share knowledge that can help you in your networking. It is highly advantageous to have quality educational times that focus on helping members advance their professional networks. If the group is not interested in your growth and learning, it is not the group for you. So, assess the opportunities for education and trainings, too.

Pay attention to these characteristics of a group's tone. Listen closely to what the educational opportunities are and how they are being presented. Are they structured or is everything loose and casual? How is humor used? That education time usually sets the tone for the entire meeting. If the moment is filled with humor, the next few presenters will usually communicate lightly. They will toss out jokes and informalities that are received by laughter and comments called-out from the audience. If the educational moment is filled with formal instruction and teaching aids, the rest of the meeting tends to be conducted by-the-book with the participants sitting attentively but quietly.

## PUTTING IT TOGETHER TO ASSESS FIT

Listen to people's commercials about themselves and the companies they represent. Hear what they are saying in those commercials. See if they are representing areas you are comfortable with and if they are areas where you'd be able to offer and receive referrals. Gather business cards and take a look at them.

In addition to emphasis, groups also differ in focus. Networking groups can vary greatly. For example, some groups are heavy with professionals whose careers focus on self-care, health, wellness, well-being, and beauty. The entire group will emphasize those career areas. Whether intentionally or not, these groups are geared toward, aimed at, or leaning in that direction. Other groups lean in other directions, such as consultations and advising. Some are heavy in product sales. Some in business administration. Some emphasize helping members increase their business. Other groups emphasize expanding members' networks. Some emphasize in-service training and mentoring. Some groups are primarily social clubs, coffee get-togethers, or lunch groups. Most groups have elements of all of these, and that is probably the best for most professionals ...but maybe not for you.

At the beginning of this section, we recommended that you visit at least six different networking groups before deciding which one to commit to. Having now done that, ask yourself again, "Exactly what am I looking for?" You are trying to produce a product – your business. Make your choice with at least as much proactive care as most bread makers would in choosing the type of flour to use. Do you want to bake with whole wheat flour, white whole wheat flour, white flour, enriched flour, bread flour, spelt flour, rye flour, pastry flour, cake flour, oat flour, self-rising flour, gluten-free flour, semolina flour, buckwheat flour, corn flour – phew! the list goes on....

## ASSESS THE TONE OF A NETWORKING GROUP

Choices, choices, choices!

All the factors and indicators are important individually. And, so far, we've looked at these individually as highly specific requirements of professional networking groups. We looked at where they are geographically located, how much the annual dues are, whether the leadership uses an agenda, whether the membership policy includes exclusivity, how members dress and speak, what kinds of educational opportunities exist, and so on. These are like the specialty flours of the pastry chef. At some point, you are going to want to put it all together. We recommend All-Purpose Flour. But there's nothing wrong with experimenting with one or more of the specialty flours.

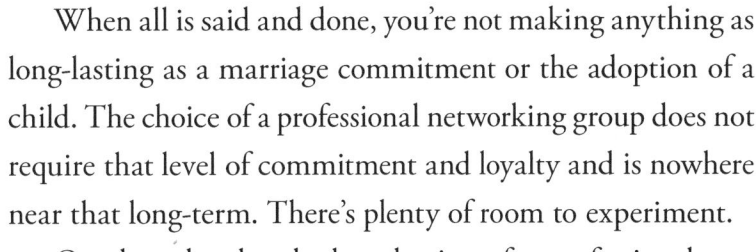

When all is said and done, you're not making anything as long-lasting as a marriage commitment or the adoption of a child. The choice of a professional networking group does not require that level of commitment and loyalty and is nowhere near that long-term. There's plenty of room to experiment.

On the other hand, the selection of a professional networking group is far more important than the toppings to put on a pizza.

So, approach your decision seriously, but flexibly.

We have identified several features and indicators to think about as you consider the very important decision of which professional networking group is the very best one for you. The bottom line is to find the one that best matches your strengths and best meets your needs. That will be the one to join.

Now that you have made a choice of what group you are going to attend and where you are going to expand your time and energy, let's turn to how to leverage group meetings for your business growth and as a target for your mindset of service to others.

# CHAPTER 11

## JOINING A GROUP AS A NEW "BROUGHT"

Up to now, we've talked about what networking is and we've given you a dynamic formula for achieving networking power. We've talked about assessing at least six professional groups to find one that seems just right for you. Hopefully, you've found one that uses the BRING! philosophy introduced earlier:

B — Business
R — Referrals (and)
I — Interactive
N — Networking
G — Group

Some of these groups may have allowed you to present material about your business goals and history, while some limit anything beyond a self-introduction to people who are not yet members.

And you are not yet a member. In fact, just what are you in the period between having decided which group you would like to join and actually becoming a full-fledged, dues-paying member? What can we call you and, more importantly, how do you act as you are transitioning into full membership.

### DEFINITION OF A "BROUGHT"

Unlike terms like "guest" or "visitor," which imply a casual or temporary presence, a Brought represents a more intentional step toward exploring the group's culture, connections, and opportunities. For many, being a Brought is part of the investigative process—evaluating whether the group aligns with their professional goals and networking philosophy.

The term "Brought" also acknowledges the shared responsibilities in this phase of networking:

The inviter's role to facilitate the introduction, offer guidance, and support the Brought in navigating the group.

The group's responsibility is to warmly welcome and engage the Brought, ensuring a positive and authentic experience.

For the Brought, this is a chance to observe, ask questions, and experience the group's dynamic while considering a potential deeper commitment. For the group, a Brought represents an opportunity to expand its reach and enrich its network by welcoming new perspectives and connections.

Whether you're an experienced professional seeking new opportunities, a curious first-time attendee, or someone exploring their fit within the group, being a Brought is a pivotal first step in building meaningful relationships. It's not just a title—it's a moment of exploration, engagement, and potential.

This chapter will guide both Broughts and group members through making the most of this crucial introduction, ensuring that the experience is positive, productive, and aligned with the principles of BRING!: Business, Referrals, Interactive Networking, and Group engagement.

## TIP #1: DON'T FORGET YOUR TOOLS

<u>Punctuality is a Tool</u>. Our modern western culture is faster paced than any other in history and excuses to be tardy abound. However, punctuality is usually under your control. Punctuality is a tool that can be used to make lasting impressions. Developing a habit of always being on time (or slightly early) shows reliability, dependability, and discipline. Broughts, as well as seasoned networkers, who are punctual, communicate to others they are dependable and disciplined, and they respect others. If you consider an agreed-upon meeting time as a promise, then keeping your promise is obviously important. In fact, it is important to arrive for meetings (big or small) early.

Opportunities to meet new people and re-acquaint with others are greatest before the meeting. Arriving early can turn any kind of meeting into a potential networking event. You just need to be there to seize the moment.

<u>Paper and Pen</u>. It is amazing how many people forget to carry something as simple yet essential as a pen or a piece of paper. Perhaps it is out of fashion now that we can enter contact information and even notes into smartphones. However, doing that leaves you with your head buried in a device, no longer listening, and not making eye contact. Staring down at hand-held devices leaves a bad impression on those around you. You don't want that – especially when you're new and creating first impressions in others. The pen is mightier than the device – at least in this situation. This holds true for paper, as well. Consider the lack of professionalism telegraphed by

having to say, "Just a sec. Let me write that down. Hmmm... Got a piece of paper? Here, I'll just use the back of this envelope...."

An old-fashioned small notebook and a pen will serve you much better than the smartest smartphone at a business meeting. But, if you must use your phone, at least have some way of recording your questions, thoughts, and observations. And, you *will* have those. You are going to hear things or see things during the meeting that will intrigue you. You may think you will remember them for later, but you won't. Why? Because there will be many other intriguing occurrences to remember, names to recall, and questions to ask someone later. There could be a dozen comments said to catch your attention. Write them all down.

Writing in a small notebook has none of the negatives of looking down to an electronic device and clicking buttons. Why? People know what you are doing with a notebook. With an electronic device, even if you are recording the exact same information, it appears to your peers as if you are totally bored and are surfing the Web, checking your email, or texting someone. You don't want to give that impression.

Be sure, too, to write down the name of the various people who made the comments as well as the context in which they occurred. Perhaps you didn't catch the various names because they didn't give their names. That would (should) be unusual. Speakers often garble their names, unconsciously assuming others know their names as well as they do themselves. In any case, you missed the names. In such cases, write down features of the presenters. For example, you could write down, "Blue shirt, third table, next to woman with hair in a bun" or whatever the case is. This will allow you to find those presenters later or ask another member about them. As a side-benefit, that will help you engage more people and give you something to talk about with them.

<u>Business Cards</u>. Another tool to remember is your business card. This is essential, especially for your first meeting. In a later chapter, we'll emphasize that the correct use of a business card is to convey, not spray, information. Never pass out your cards indiscriminately because it cheapens the card and leaves a negative impression on others. You don't want that. As a general rule, never give out your card unless you have shared your name and a handshake with the other person.

Keep in mind that avoiding spraying cards and avoiding cards are very different animals. Be judicial with how your hand them out, yes, but be absolutely sure you have business cards with you. They convey essential information. They put an exclamation mark on a one-on-one introduction and a face-to-face meeting.

<u>Name Badges</u>. Because of its small size, your networking group may not use name badges. Those are more typical of larger networking functions. But when name tags are used, resist the

temptation to treat them with disrespect. Professional networking is about relationships. The clear conveyance of your name is a benefit to others and helps build those relationships. When you use a name badge correctly, you help others feel comfortable meeting you. By "correctly," we mean mainly two things:

First, use both your first and your last name. This conveys a professionalism others will be drawn to. Using just your first name is too casual for a business environment.

Second, this is not the time for a clever gimmick. Don't try to initiate a professional relationship by wearing the label upside-down or sideways. That may create conversation; it may even be "sticky." However, it sets the first impression and needs to be an impression that is positive and professional.

<u>The Law of Primacy</u>. First impressions are critical for you as a Brought in a first networking meeting. Humor and goofiness may be better later. You only have one chance for this first impression, so it is a good idea to think this through carefully.

Although every reader knows what is meant by a first impression, it is worth looking at it a little closer. Edward Thorndike introduced several laws of learning including the Law of Primacy, or the Primacy Effect. Thorndike found that when he tested the memories of his subjects by giving them a list of objects to be recalled, they most clearly and accurately remembered the first few objects they saw.

This holds true in a networking meeting. People remember the first thing that triggers their senses. As we'll talk about in this chapter, this means the way you look and the way you speak. But it also includes their first contact with your name and the name of the company you represent. This is why you need to treat your name tag with respect.

In addition to the Law of Primacy, Thorndike also introduced the Law of Effect. This means that "learning is strengthened when accompanied by a pleasant or satisfying feeling." Introductions are more effective and memorable if some slight positive emotion is evoked. That can be surprise, humor, joy, and so on. Something as simple as saying, "Hello, I don't know you yet. My name is _____," evokes emotion. First, it puts the emphasis on the other person, not on you. Second, there is a twinge of warmth and humor to it – and that has been attached to your name. It can only help.

It follows from the Law of Effect that the first comments you make should be positive and uplifting, not critical or complaining. Your impression of something going on may be negative, but that doesn't mean their impression of you has to be negative. Similarly, since you are new, you may be tempted to hold back and answer with a nervous voice or in a mumbled, half-hearted tone. Avoid this. The impression you save may be your own! It will stick strongly with most people if you greet them with a smile and a clear strong statement of your name. They will always associate you with a positive tone and a relief of stress. This could only be a good thing.

Use Your Smile. You have a great smile. Everyone has. A smile costs nothing and gives much. And a smile is one thing you *can* spray! When greeting others, have the habit of smiling. Few things are more pleasant during a greeting than a genuine smile. A smile shows warmth. A smile shows praise. A smile shows gratitude. A smile shows enthusiasm. A smile shows passion. One blogger noted:

> *When the woman at the other end of the cash register smiles at me, I feel better about my purchase, about the store and about myself. In the same way, smiling at the woman or the man in your life will convey your sense of happiness, satisfaction and confidence in yourself and the other person.*[47]

You may not be at a cash register, but you are in a business context. As a new person at a BRING! meeting, you, too, want to feel these feelings and convey those traits. To do this, you need to show your smile. It is a free tool, and a powerful tool.

> *If you're not using your smile, you're like a man with a million dollars in the bank and no checkbook.*[48]

## TIP #2: EXPECT TO MEET PEOPLE

As we have repeatedly stressed throughout this book, formal meetings are a forum for meeting and networking, not selling.

### SELL THROUGH, NOT TO

Neither you nor the other networkers at the meeting intend to endure a sales pitch from other attendees. If you are attending networking meetings with the intent to sell your product, or service, you have set yourself up for disappointment. The pathway to success lies in seeking introductions, not sales. It doesn't matter if the function you were invited to is large or small. It doesn't matter if the event is formal or informal. It *does* matter if you try to sell to people while at networking functions, especially in your transition role as a "Brought."

An informal survey was taken at a large networking mixer of over 1,000 people in Las Vegas, Nevada, in 2012. People were asked if they had come to the event planning to sell their product

---

[47] See Sean Swaby, 2017, "How Your Smile Can Change Your Love Life and Improve Your Career" in https://goodmenproject.com/sex-relationships/smile-can-change-lovelife-improve-your-career-snsw.
[48] Les Giblin, 1968, *Skill with People* in: http://www.skillwithpeople.com/les-giblin.html.

or services. A second question asked how many were there with the intent of making a purchase. These two questions were asked again and again until over 500 professionals had been surveyed. The results proved to be consistent:

1. _Most_ responded said they were attending with the intent to sell to other attendees.
2. But _not a single person_ (zero, nada, rien) said they were there to purchase.

This means attending a networking meeting with the hope of selling to other attendees is fruitless. It is a flawed goal. The members are simply not there to buy your product or your services. The plan to sell at a meeting or other networking event does not serve you well. It portrays you as someone who is short-sighted and lacking an understanding of the true power of professional networking (**NP**).

An experienced 212-level networker would not fall into this trap. Advanced networkers sell _through_, not _to_ other professionals. You would be wise to follow their example. Attend the networking meeting with the goal of creating contacts (**CC**) so you can eventually share relevant referrals (**RR**). That is a much more realistic and effective goal. Plus, this will help you fit in much more quickly.

So, you're not going to the meeting expecting to sell. What are you going to do, then?

You're going to meet people. You're going to create contacts.

Either before the meeting or just afterwards, the person who invited you is going to make introductions for you. Be genuinely interested in these new acquaintances.

Here's a tip: don't sit down until the meeting begins. When you sit down, you make yourself less approachable and you make it harder on the person who invited you to support you. When you are standing up, people feel as if they can come up and introduce themselves to you. You will also find it more convenient to introduce yourself to the people around you and easier for your host to make introductions.

When those introductions are going on, be sure to ask questions. Remember their names. Make an attempt to recognize what you have in common and how you can help each other grow professionally.

Shake their hands professionally....

## WAIT, THERE'S A PROFESSIONAL HANDSHAKE?

There is, indeed. In Western culture, it is appropriate to shake hands. Our handshake has a tremendous impact on relationships. Avoiding the handshake is not really an option in business. Fortunately, we have a lot of opportunities to refine this skill.

The greeting process can be made awkward when a person doesn't know how to shake hands. The casual, localized handshakes of social interaction are not for the realm of professional networking. Thumb and palm grasps, high fives, and the like are too casual for a greeting in a professional setting. Here are some handshakes to avoid:

- The "sweaty drip" – This one demonstrates a nervous situation. If you need to, take a brief moment to wipe your hand before the shake.
- The "fist bump" – Another non-handshake. Popular recently, it conveys informality at best. It is not a business action.

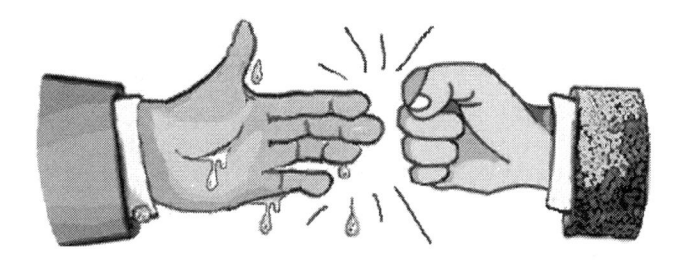

- The "limp fish" – This handshake conveys weakness and lack of confidence. It may also give the impression that you don't really want to be there.
- The "finger grab" – This handshake isn't really a handshake at all. At best, it's a finger shake. It may be popular in Europe, but save this one for admiring jewelry.
- The "hand crush" – Taking someone in a vice shake may suggest perceived dominance or exuberance. Be careful, your victim may have early arthritis. Don't hurt them!
- The "wet toad" – This one jumps into the hand, feels cold and lifeless, then leaps out of the hand.

If you are not already standing, do so. The person you're greeting deserves the respect standing up demonstrates. Only the Monarch shakes hands sitting down, and they have had many years of practice.

Your stance needs to communicate confidence and an interest in others. When you're shaking hands, stand confidently, and lean forward a bit. This will indicate assurance in yourself and an attentiveness to the other person.

Integrate eye contact as a standard part of your handshake. The importance of eye contact cannot be overstated. Eye contact starts even before the formal physical connection of the hands. Confidence in yourself and interest in the person you're greeting are best communicated when you look the other person directly in the eye. This is not an invitation to stare or hold the gaze an awkwardly long time.

Even though you are the new one at the meeting, try to be the one to initiate the handshake.

In our cultural history there have been various morés about who should initiate handshakes. Throw those away. *You* are responsible for your business. Even though you are new, do not be bashful about putting your hand out for a greeting.[49]

When you offer your hand for a handshake, put it about two feet away from your body, about waist height. Your palm should be facing sideways. Facing your palm down when offering your hand is rude; it indicates you are in a position of power and are determined to use this power. Put your hand out right now with the palm down. Do you see how dominating that can appear? Conversely, facing your palm up can indicate submission weakness. Again, try it right now. Do you see how it could have an implication of asking for a hand-out? You are new to the meeting, but you are not subservient to anyone.

Use a firm grip. In our culture, a firm handshake communicates an enthusiasm for the greeting. On the other hand (pun intended), don't hurt anyone. If you see gray hair, lighten up. Many people have arthritis in their fingers and enthusiasm, expressed as grip strength, is *not* appreciated. You won't know if your grip is too tight unless you ask friends. You might be surprised at what they say. On this same topic, be mindful of the ring or any sharp jewelry on your right hand. Folks don't want to be injured when greeting you. That pain can be so distracting that the greeting may be a negative experience for the other person.

## WAIT, WHERE DO I SIT?

When it is time to sit down, choose a place carefully. Where you sit, and who you sit near, is an important decision. Sitting near the front or near the back of the room is part of that decision. Being left or right of presenters is your decision. When you arrive early, you have a greater selection where to establish your place. If you arrive late, you are allowing others to put you in your place. Don't do that.

There are two benefits to sitting forward: 1) less distractions, and 2) better visibility. The fewer people between you and the presenter the more focused you will be. Attentive listeners are viewed as intelligent people. Visibility isn't all about you seeing the show. It's also about people seeing you; even if they only see the back of your head. The "I didn't see you there" comments are typically made by people who were in the front about people who were in the back. If you want people to know you're there, place yourself near the front.

---

[49] The only exception to shaking hands is if you are sick. Don't initiate or accept a handshake if you have a cold or flu. You don't want to spread illness and they don't want that either. Be apologetic when you deny the other person's offered hand and smile while you do that. It will be appreciated.

## TIP #3: DRESS WITH IMPACT

Talking about jewelry, consider the true story of a young and attractive woman who we'll call Lisa. She sold jewelry and was moderately successful in her career. Her target market was other young professionals so attending a networking meeting was a smart choice for Lisa. She could get relevant referrals (**RR**) there.

Here's the problem. Lisa attended her first meeting dressed as if the meeting was just something she was obligated to attend. One would think she had no ambition or incentive to be there. Either that, or she really didn't understand why she was at a networking function. The bottom line was that this created the first impression. The Law of Primacy worked against her.

Worse, the impression continued. It was not uncommon for Lisa to show up in sweats, with no makeup, and her hair grabbed and loosely tied up into a disorganized bun with stray ends poking out. If Lisa wore any of her own jewelry, it never accentuated or matched the outfits that she wore. Someone commented that, "It looked as if she had rolled out of bed 10-minutes earlier."

Now, none of this is to suggest people who are dressed in sweats cannot be successful or are not appropriately dressed for certain events. However, for a business meeting, which is what a networking meeting is. She was underdressed to a fault.

Lisa would have been much more effective had she dressed as if she were the most successful jewelry salesperson in her career field. Jewelry is a tough sell at the best of times. Why make it harder? Lisa could have catapulted her effectiveness had she dressed in style, with class, and in a way portraying excitement about what she represented. She could have conveyed the impression she was excited about meeting the members who attended the meeting. Her dress did not instill confidence and thereby encourage others to refer their best contacts to her. She forgot (or did not know):

*Good Attire = Good Referrals*

Lisa did not do that. For Lisa, dressing like the most successful jewelry salesperson in the county would have been a monumental change. But it would have been worth it. Granted, the networking function may have been scheduled at a time that was inconvenient for her to attend. But this doesn't mean she can just blow it off.

Add to all this the fact, even if she now made the change, it was too late in many ways. The Law of Primacy was already in place. It would have taken a long time to undo the damage she had caused to her career. The other professionals cannot unsee the sweats and the tossed-up hair-bun. She has made her first impression. Would it not have been more effective, even if it was inconvenient, to have made a better first impression by dressing a little bit better in the first few meetings?

Now, you are not Lisa. And presumably this is your first or second meeting to attend. It is not too late for you. Attend in such a way that you modestly impress everyone in the room. Then you will not have to un-do any bad impression. We live in a society that seems to be encouraging more relaxed clothing – the so-called, "grunge look" that started in the 90s. Professionally ripped jeans, sometimes all up and down the leg, may be the rage, but is it the style for you? This passing style also includes "thrift-store clothing often worn in a loose, androgynous manner."[50] Rather than imitating what others are doing, think about what statement you are making. In the never-ending search to be "new and different," the style imitates poverty. This is not what you want to convey. A better idea is to convey success.

Instead, dress to impress. Dress as the most successful person in your own career field. An example of this is Randy who sells and installs window blinds. He arrives dressed as if he is already highly successful. There are solid reasons for Randy to present himself with a success-minded appearance. It isn't that Randy wants to present an image he is not. Rather, Randy wants to be successful in the field he has chosen and in which he has set career goals. If this is the case, then why not dress as if he has already achieved those goals? By doing so, Randy will attract a higher clientele and generate greater success. This will attract a higher level of relevant referrals (**RR**). What you want is to create a self-fulfilling prophecy.

> *You can think of a self-fulfilling prophecy as a circular pattern. Our actions toward others impact their beliefs about us, which dictates their actions towards us, which then reinforces our beliefs about ourselves. This, in turn, influences our actions towards others, which brings us back to the beginning of the cycle.*[51]

Randy created this kind of circular self-fulfilling prophecy when he attended his first few meetings. If we had seen Randy in an overly casual and sloppy way, we would have simply imagined him as a handy-man who puts up $20 blinds from a Big Box store. We would refer contacts, if we referred them at all, who were looking to save a buck and do the work on the cheap. "Want the cheapest blinds? Randy's your man!"

On the other hand, because Randy dressed as if he were at the top of his career field, we perceived him as an energized and motivated home designer who was involved in quality home decoration. We imagined him as well able to provide a complete and quality window treatment including the best quality blinds, expensive curtains, decorative curtain rods, sheers, a valence, and everything else that goes with it. We're going to naturally refer to Randy those people who are at that higher level of expectation and are willing to pay for it.

---

[50] Quote from: https://en.wikipedia.org/wiki/Grunge_fashion.

[51] Quote from: https://study.com/academy/lesson/self-fulfilling- prophecies-in-psychology-definition-examples.html

"Want beauty and quality for your window? Randy can meet your needs." That's obviously a better ticket for Randy.

This doesn't mean that Randy can't still install $20 blinds. It just means his best clients are the higher-end ones who are eager to have their windows done completely. The way he presents himself – and a large part of this is how he dresses – will communicate he routinely provides full quality window dressing, not just putting up cheapie blinds. Because of his quality presentation, we will subconsciously want to give him our best top-end referrals.

These effects of careful business attire apply to all fields. If you present as a high-end professional, you will be perceived as a high-end professional. The mere sight of you as a professional creates the expectation of your professionalism. It suggests that you provide top-quality work for high-end clients who will easily pay you whatever you say it is worth – and without batting an eye. Wouldn't we all prefer to work with clients who have the budget for the top end of our line?

Now, nobody is suggesting that Randy show up to his first few meetings in a tux and cummerbund. This would be over-the-top and inappropriate. The idea is that he dresses as if he were the most successful window designer around – wearing clothes appropriate for that image.

Let's change it up. Instead of a blinds salesman, let's imagine Randy is a highly successful real estate agent showing luxury homes. It would be quite appropriate for him to wear well-pressed slacks and a polo shirt with the logo of his realty embroidered on the breast. He could add a smart blazer. But no more than that. People wouldn't feel comfortable being shown homes by an agent in a three-piece business suit. They would feel sloppy in Randy's presence and we don't want to create any kind of discomfort in our customers.

So, what about a person in the trades? Let's say Randy is now a successful plumber, meaning one who has a crew doing the manual labor. He would still wear the polo shirt and dress slacks, as if he were going to bid on an expensive remodel of a bathroom suite in an upscale home. If Randy, as plumber, were to wear a white shirt and tie similar to an attorney, that would be foolish and send the wrong message to his colleagues and clients. Even the most successful plumbers don't dress like that.

What if Randy were going to do the plumbing labor himself? He would still not attend the meeting in bib overalls and boots. Even if he had brand new coveralls and was on the way to a job, it would not be appropriate for him to attend a networking group dressed in that. And dirty overalls? Forget it! It may mean he needs to have a change of clothing in the truck.

So be it. It is worth the effort.

It all comes down to the kind of impression you want to make. There are even people who have attended professional networking meetings in tattered jeans and t-shirts week after week after week. They have tried to have other professionals at the meetings give them referrals. Ain't happenin'! The other professionals would be uncomfortable referring a high-end purchaser to someone who presents in tattered clothes.

There is scientific evidence for what we are saying. Several studies support the idea that people who were dressed in more formal clothing felt better, performed better, and were perceived in a more positive light than those wearing informal clothing. One study, reported in the *Journal of Experimental Psychology,* found:

> *Male participants donned clothing that signaled either upper-class (business-suit) or lower-class (sweatpants) rank prior to engaging in a modified negotiation task with another participant unaware of the clothing manipulation. Wearing upper-class, compared to lower-class, clothing induced dominance…in participants.*[52]

As a Brought at a networking meeting, you're going to be meeting people who you have never met before. Like it or not, this is when the Law of First Impressions is going to kick in. Before you have opened your mouth, before you have flashed your award-winning smile, before you have extended your hand for that professional handshake, you will have already made a first impression by how you are dressed. This is how you will be remembered. There will be some members who were at the meeting and will, perhaps unfairly, describe you to others who were absent based on what you were wearing.

"Sorry we missed you at the meeting, Frank. There was a new young woman at the meeting yesterday. I think her name was Lisa. She sold jewelry. Let's see…. What can I tell you about her…"

Keep the significance of that in your mind!

## TIP #4: SPEAK WITH IMPACT

How you present yourself orally is as important as how you present yourself in dress. It is a major component of the first impression you create. For that reason, speech is another critical factor to look at in a professional networking meeting.

Let's set aside speech characteristics that cannot be changed. Those would include speech impediments. Networkers will look past those problems. If the group you visit can't see beyond

---

[52] M. Kraus and W. Mendes, ""Sartorial symbols of social class elicit class-consistent behavioral and physiological responses: A dyadic approach." *Journal of Experimental Psychology: General, 143*(6), pp. 2330-2340; abstract available at: https://psycnet. apa.org/record/ 2014-38364-001.

a speech impediment, find another group. Similarly, networkers will also look past, or even enjoy, the accents of non-native speakers who learned English at a young age. Such accents can be modified, but only with great effort and practice. Those who learned English after the age of 10 are more-or-less locked in.[53] Many listeners find accents to be endearing.

The point here is some speech characteristics will be limiting and are 100% under your control. They can be modified. For example, it is a myth that some people have "soft voices." If you are one who is frequently asked to "Speak up!" – correct the problem. It is easily done. There are excellent YouTube videos that can help.[54] A "soft voice" is simply not knowing how to project the voice. The resonance of your voice will affect your credibility. Why not learn this skill?

In the same vein, those who speak too loudly falsely equate volume with enthusiasm and have great difficulty lowering their voices when excited. Loud enthusiasm may be appreciated, but only in small doses. The payoff for networking with both problems is worth the relatively small struggle.

## FIVE SPEECH HABITS YOU CAN ABANDON

The speech characteristics we are talking about are primarily just bad habits. Once pointed out and with some commitment, these habits can be changed and dropped. The effort required varies from speech pattern to speech pattern, but all can be corrected. The small effort required to break these avoidable habits will result in significantly improved networking success. Those bad habits to avoid include:

<u>1. Avoid Speaking Too Rapidly</u> S-l-o-w d-o-w-n your rate of speech. Talking too rapidly may be the result of nerves. However, rapid speech is often a learned habit. If people you're meeting keep saying, "Sorry, I missed that" or "Say that again," it could be a clue that you are speaking too quickly. This is particularly common among younger Americans. The speed with which they talk can sometimes require subtitles. Rather than rudely repeating, "I didn't get that, I didn't get that" some of the BRING! members will just thank a new Brought and then walk away. That is absolutely <u>*not*</u> what you want if you are serious about transitioning into the new networking group, creating business contacts (**CC**), and building a network. There is no time-card to be

---

[53] Accents are learned in the crib, even before speech starts. This is discussed on several websites. For example, see Edwin Kiester, 2001, "Accents are Forever," *Smithsonian Magazine* available at: www.smithsonianmag.com/science-nature/accents-are-forever-35886605.

[54] For two among many example, see 1) www.youtube.com/watch?v=de65Xk25lWI and 2) www.google.com/search?q=Youtube+how+to+project+your+voice&rlz=1C1CHBF_ en&oq=Youtube+how+to+project+your+voice&aqs=-chrome..69i57.8145j0j7&sourceid=chrome&ie=UTF-8#kpvalbx=1 xx https://www.youtube.com/watch?v=YvaRSyfO3PY

punched at any BRING! meeting. Slow down for impact and understanding – especially when you are giving your name. Pause between your first name and your surname. Be quick to listen, not so quick to speak.

2. <u>Avoid Failing to Complete the Ends of Your Sentences.</u> If you're thinking about your second sentence before you have finished the first, you will invariably clip off or garble the last few words of the first sentence.

This is very common. Humans think much faster than they can speak. This situation is similar to a baseball player who tries to throw a ball to 1st base before it's safely in his glove. It's like a football player who starts to run for the end zone before he has secured the pass.

Cutting off the ends of sentences may also be caused by a lifetime of having others interrupt you as soon as you pause for a breath. In networking, people are not going to cut you off. As you are introduced to new people at a meeting, take the time to completely finish your idea before moving on to the next thought. This problem is a fully correctable speech issue.

Look at it from the perspective of those you are meeting. They may need half a second to process your sentence and another 2 or 3 seconds to store your name in their memory banks. You know what you want to say; they do not. Give them their three seconds. It will dramatically help you as you meet people.

3. <u>Avoid External Fillers While Thinking Internally.</u> Back in the 60s to 80s, an entire generation of Americans sprinkled a loud and audible "umm" and "errr" every time they had to search for a thought. "So, I, er… think that, umm… you are, umm…. nice…."

That disruptive habit was replaced in the 90s with the phrase, "you know," which was often abbreviated to the shortcut, "y-oh." It came out as, "So, I, you know… think that, y'oh… you are, y'oh… nice." We once counted 13 "y'oh" fillers in one single run-on sentence. That creates the wrong kind of impression. Notice, too, we were counting rather than listening. Do you want people to whom you are being introduced to count your y'oh's instead of listening to your name and background? You will make a more positive first impression if you drop this bad – and avoidable – habit.

As the new century dawned, what used to be called, "Valley Girl Teen Speech" (also called, "Valspeak"[55]) was popularized by a few movies. Almost overnight, young people replaced the "y'oh" filler with a new filler: the word, "like." "So, I, like… think that, like… you are, like… nice." Hearing multiple "likes" in a single sentence can be off-putting for anyone wanting to hear what you say. "Like" is often used 4 or more times in the same sentence. Don't spray business cards, and don't spray "likes." This usage also gives the impression of being distracted. Watch

---

[55] See: https://en.wikipedia.org/wiki/Valleyspeak.

people while they speak. Those who saturate their speech with "like" are often not making eye-contact. As a result, it comes across as them being distracted.

Some organizations, such as *Toastmasters International,* provide professionals with opportunities to give short, off-the-cuff speeches and to avoid fillers. Their mission statement reads:

> *Toastmasters International helps men and women learn the arts of speaking, listening and thinking – vital skills that promote self-actualization, enhance leadership potential, foster human understanding, and contribute to the betterment of mankind.*[56]

In many Toastmaster clubs, members vote on who they thought gave the best impromptu speech. Their annual World Championship of Public Speaking involves over 33,000 participants in 141 countries making it the world's largest speech contest.[57] Some people even refer to Toastmasters as the "Umm Busters"! That's great! They may be the "Like Busters" too.

As we have said, most networking groups also offer their members opportunities to stand up and present short networking presentations. Your professionalism and credibility in meetings will increase 100-fold if you resist using fillers as you pause to think while being introduced to people. Here's a tip: there's absolutely nothing wrong with a few seconds of silence while you are thinking!

4. Avoid Trendy Slang and Informality. Granted, you don't want to put on airs when you meet people, but neither do you want to come across as too informal. The popular trend in the US is to try to level the field and make everyone "equal" in every way. That's okay in many situations, but there really are status differences that need to be respected. As a few quick examples:

- "Madam Speaker of the House" is a more appropriate way to refer to Ms. Pelosi, at least in a government role, than to refer to her as Nancy
- "President Balderdash set a policy for all new freshmen" is preferable to "Bob set a policy for all new freshmen"
- "Mom" and "Grandma Smith" are more respectful than "Jane" and "Michelle"
- "The Reverend Rebecca White" communicates greater respect for her office than "Becky" or even "Reverend Becky"

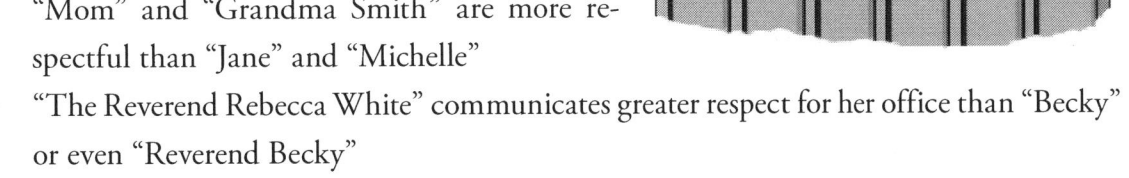

---

[56] Mission statement from: https://sunrise.toastmastersclubs.org/values.html
[57] Statistic from: https://en.wikipedia.org/wiki/Toastmasters_International

Similarly, you sound more credible and professional if you refer to the people around you in the networking group as "people" or "networkers" rather than as "guys." Similarly, avoid trendy and invented words even if they seem popular. You want your listeners to pay attention to your meaning, not your vocabulary. This means:

- Avoid trendy and made-up words. Say "gigantic" and "enormous" rather than "ginormous"
- Similarly, use "sick" to mean sick and "wicked" to mean wicked; neither one means good or wonderful
- Refer to cannabis and marijuana – and not "grass" or "weed"
- BFF is teen talk, not networking talk. Avoid it.
- Remember when "far-out!" meant, "great"? Fortunately, that has now gone back to its original meaning of, far away
- Remember when "bread" meant money? That worked in the 60s and 70s, not today. Now, they are just silly phrases from a time long gone. Modern, trendy vocabulary will suffer the same fate.

You will be more successful and make a better impression at your first or second formal networking meeting if you avoid slang expressions and colloquial speech. As one writer put it so well:

> *To your grandparents, "busted" probably meant that something was broken. To your parents, it means getting caught doing some-thing wrong. The latest use? As an adjective to mean "ugly." "No, I won't go out with your little sister. She's busted."* [58]

5. Avoid Sprinkling Your Speech with Profanity. Profanity is simply not welcome in all professional settings. There are definitely people who use profanity as punctuation marks in their sentences. The F-bomb has become a noun, a verb, an adverb, and an adjective. However, if you sprinkle profanity in your speech as you are milling around in a meeting you will alienate more people than you will attract.

There is no question, profanity is on the rise. The 1939 movie, *Gone with the Wind*, shocked the world when it had Rhett Butler use profanity in front of a lady. He said to Scarlett O'Hara, "Frankly, my dear, I simply don't give a damn…." Hollywood's products have evolved (devolved?) from there. Some movies use 30 to 40 F-bombs in a single film.

Recently, a student at a local university dropped the F-bomb several times in a class discussion. The professor told him during class break that such language was inappropriate in a class

---

[58] See: https://examples.yourdictionary.com/20-examples-of-slang-language.html

that was teaching professional practice. "Oh, you're just out-of-touch," he replied. "That's how young people talk today."

No, it isn't. At least not among young professionals. Despite what this student and many Hollywood directors seem to believe, strong profanity is not welcome in settings such as networking groups.

The word, profanity, does not just mean to swear or cuss, it means "to treat with irreverence or contempt."[59] You do not want to treat your first networking meeting with "irreverence or contempt." Profane words will not serve you well as you meet members. The point is to make and nurture friends (**NN**), not draw attention to unfortunate speech patterns that limit the effectiveness of networking and block contacts you are trying to create (**CC**).

You are going to be introduced to several people as a new Brought at a networking meeting. Be sure you have your tools (pen, paper, business cards, and smile). Meet members confidently and avoid anything that sounds, smells, or looks like sales. Shake hands professionally with good eye-contact. Dress at the top of your business field. Speak clearly and slowly, particularly when you give your name. You may also be called on to recite your elevator speech a few times. Know your answer to the question, "What do you do?" Make sure your answer is concise and generates interest. That attention to detail will help to present yourself in the best possible light

Be sure to ask to be introduced to the leadership of the group. Also ask to be introduced to other members who are well networked. You may even ask for introductions to people who are not in attendance, but who you heard brought up repeatedly. That provides opportunities for follow-up away from the event.

There comes a time when conversations conclude and functions end. Express gratitude for the introductions and invitations. Don't loiter – transition. Too much of a good thing is still too much.

Now that the meeting is over and everyone has gone home, remember to follow-up, follow-up, follow-up. New contacts don't mean much until they are cultivated (**CC**). Schedule time in the days following a networking function to follow-ups with your new contacts. If there are introductions to make, arrange for them quickly.

If you have incorporated the tips and guidelines presented in this chapter, you should do just fine. You will see the incredible value of a group, and you will understand what networking is and what it can do for you professionally and personally.

---

[59] Definition from: https://www.merriam-webster.com/dictionary/profane

## BRING! MEMBERS: INVITE BROUGHTS FOR SOCIABILITY & CREDIBILITY

There are at least 6 excellent reasons and clear benefits of extending invitations to, specifically, your business clients or prospects. Your invitation to business Broughts bring at least the following benefits:

1. There Will Be No Pressure for a Sale. Your prospects already know they are on your radar. It can be a great relief to them to learn your invitation does not include you closing a sale. They do not have to make any kind of commitment. They can enjoy this largely social occasion. It is also your desire to impress them to enhance your credibility in their eyes. That's fine. But nowhere is there an expectation that a sale will be requested. There will be plenty of time later to request referrals or sell products. When you invite the Broughts into your professional meeting, make it about them.

Think of it this way: You are doing them a favor. If you are genuinely helping them or their people to solve a problem or fill a need, then the product or services you represent is a benefit and solution for them. But it won't happen at the meeting

2. Invitations Establish Your Credibility. If your networking group is professional and impressive, then, by extension, you look professional and impressive. That can't hurt. Make it a point to introduce your Broughts to group leadership and to key members. Most people like to be introduced to power people because it elevates and validates them. And, it builds your credibility to be in a position to extend that level of introduction. They are important enough to be introduced, and you're important enough to introduce them. Your credibility will sky-rocket.

- "Audrey, let me introduce you to our BRING! president. I just couldn't wait to get you two together because you have so much in common."
- "I'd like you to meet the owner of 'Bud's Barbeque,' the most exclusive restaurant in town. I know you appreciate quality. Well, this is true quality in dining."

3. Invitations Strengthen Relationships. After one or two of your Broughts have attended an event with you, there is a natural enthusiasm in your conversation. You will have common ground for a stronger relationship. If you want to look at it in these terms, you now have far more than a "foot in the door" with your business prospect or future referral partner. They are now friends.

4. Invitations Mean Access to New Networks. You are not the only one with a network. The Broughts also have their own family, personal, casual, and professional networks. Because of the

service you have rendered, they will give you access to at least parts of those networks. According to the Rule of 12, some of those new contacts will instantly want to associate with you. Think of what those additional referrals, sales opportunities, and friends would mean in your life and in your business. You want this! As they give you this access to their networks, seize it. If you are invited to attend your prospects' networks, ATTEND. These Broughts have just offered you the "pot of gold" you've been looking for. Think about what this means:

- It's an unmistakable sign they trust you.
- They want what you're offering, even though the timing may not be quite right.
- It shows they want *you* to be a part of their professional networks.
- They want you to meet their friends. Don't git no better 'n that!

5. Invitations Showcase You and Your Products. Now, how is that possible? We've emphasized that meetings aren't about selling…. That's still true. You are not selling anything to the Broughts. But even though networking time is not a time to sell, it is an opportunity to describe the services you offer, the growth and change in your industry, the type of referrals you seek, or a myriad of information that invokes curiosity. And the Broughts are watching you do that. They see your commercial.

6. Invitations Help Your Broughts. They will benefit from meeting the other members at the meeting. Encourage them to note, during the meeting, people who caught their attention. Ask who they would like to meet. You can then make those introductions after the meeting. That way, you are providing your Broughts with valued opportunities to grow their business. Professional networking is a powerful tool in business development. If your Broughts are new to networking, they will appreciate the help.

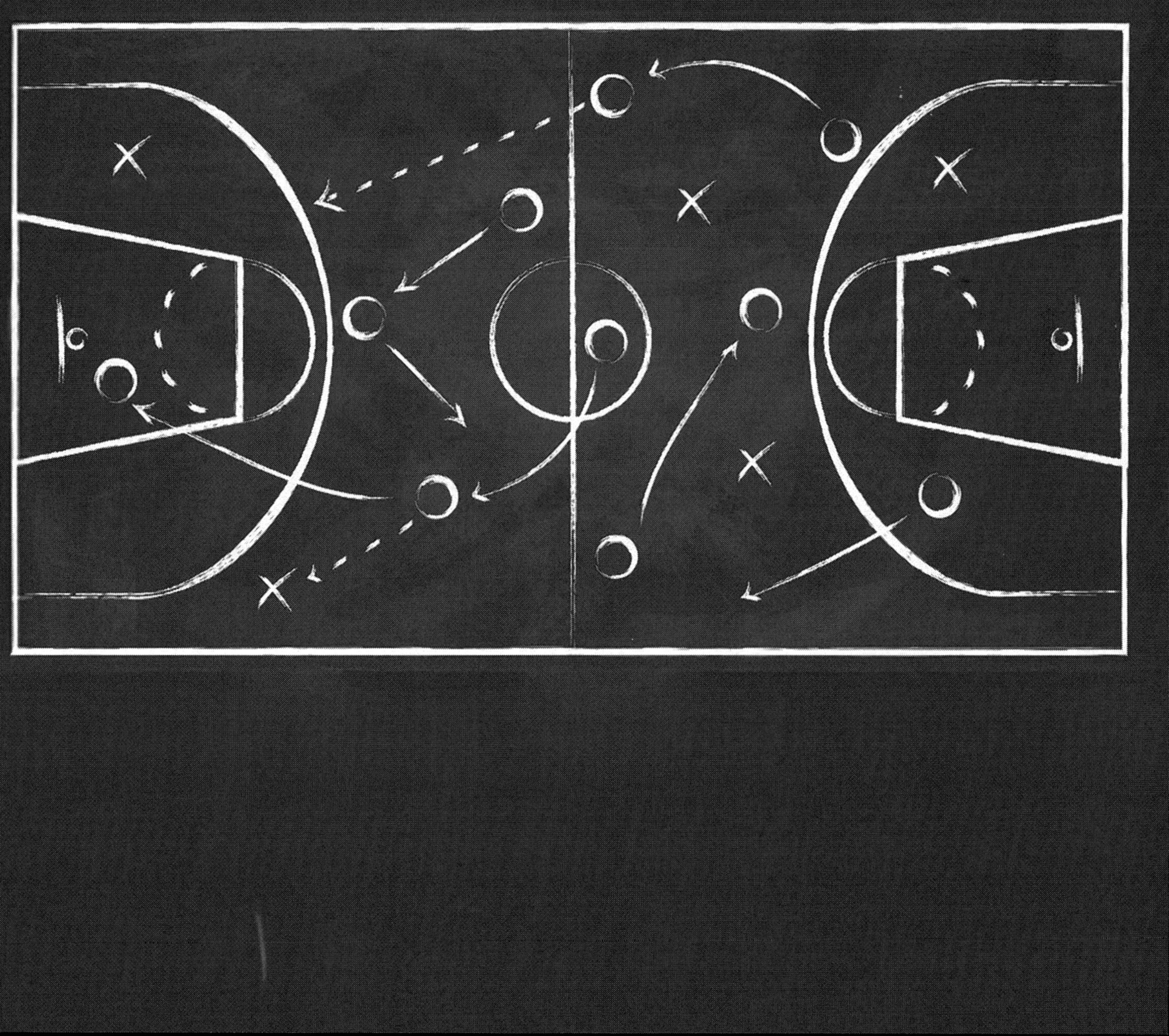

# CHAPTER 12

# STICKY COMMERCIALS: THE CONCEPT

Imagine having a short, memorable, label that elevated your business to a household phrase that became known all over the United States. What would this do for your business? Just think of it!

Have you ever heard of the California Milk Advisory Board (CMAB), an instrumentality of the California Department of Food and Agriculture?[60] Didn't think so.... But what you *have* heard of is their slogan:

*"Got milk?"*

That simple two-word tag has been called "one of the most famous commodity brands and influential campaigns in advertising history."[61] It was developed by an agency named Goodby, Silverstein & Partners over 25 years ago. It only ran two years. Yet it is still widely known. Part of that is because it has been spoofed on numerous TV shows such as *Friends, The Weird Al Show,* and *Roseanne*. It has been printed on t-shirts, *Hot Wheel* cars, and other places. It's even been used as a gag line in the major motion picture, *Nutty Professor II*. This two-word question explosively branded the product. As such, it was worth millions of dollars. The tag, *Got Milk*, sold many thousands of gallons of extra milk, especially in California. The same thing happened with Wendy's three-word question:

*"Where's the beef?"*

Many commercials are fun like these but, unfortunately, most are quite forgettable. You want one that is truly memorable – like "got milk?" and "where's the beef?" We call the memorable

---
[60] See: https://www.realcaliforniamilk.com/about-us/
[61] This statement comes from: https://en.wikipedia.org/wiki/Got_Milk%3F

ones, the commercials that remain in our heads for a very long time, "sticky commercials." This means they will stick into a listener's memory, much like a song you can't get out of your head.

Being "sticky" is the "why" of commercials. In this chapter, and the two that follow, we will discuss the concept of a sticky commercial including:

- What a sticky commercial is
- Why it is of incalculable benefit to you
- and above all, how to make it sticky.

The opportunity to present networking commercials is one of the main reasons why networking groups exist in the first place. A professional networking group is not a social club, although you will invariably make and nurture many friends. A networking group exists primarily to give you the opportunity to present and hear sticky commercials and to give and receive networking referrals.

## JUST WHAT IS A "STICKY" COMMERCIAL?

Let's begin by talking about the commercials you are most familiar with. Those are, of course, TV spots – the 30 second or 60 second ad pitches that you love to hate.

The practice of preparing statements to market merchandise is thousands of years old and was placed on papyrus, pottery, or animal hide. However, the first legal TV commercial, one for Bulova watches, ran just before a baseball game on July 1, 1941.[62] Since then, television commercials have become a standard feature of popular culture. Like it or not, they are now deeply ingrained into our way of life. According to researchers at the University of Southern California, viewers in the 1970s watched an average of 200,000 TV commercials per year. That number has since increased to a staggering 2,000,000 per year today.

Commercials seize and hold viewers' attention through tricks like increasing the volume, using flashy colors, and especially appealing to emotions. In fact, researchers have found that viewers' "emotional responses to an ad has far greater influence on a consumer's purchasing than the ad's content does."[63] Commercials can abruptly break the illusion of a fantasy movie or interrupt the tension of an adventure or a mystery. They can instantly switch viewers' moods from one of anxiety or romance to one of boredom and indifference. Some experts believe that commercials

---

[62] See Lily Slate, 2016, "Watch the First Commercial in TV History, Which Aired 75 Years Ago This Weekend, July 3rd - see *Business Insider*, at www.businessinsider.com/watch-the-first-commercial-in-tv-history-bulova-watch-2016-7.

[63] Statistics and quotes from Dana and David Dornsife, University of Southern California: https://appliedpsychologydegree.usc.edu/blog/thinking-vs-feeling-the-psychology-of-advertising/

make us jaded and increasingly unable to feel true emotion. Whether that is true or not, you are manipulated by commercials.

You may protest that you are immune. You aren't. There's a reason why a 30-second spot during a Superbowl Game costs advertisers a staggering amounts[64] Commercials work.

You may also claim you are indifferent to them. You're not that, either. Commercials invariably elicit unconscious emotion, either love or hate, in essentially everyone who views them.

When you *love* them, they work because you feel a subconscious bond that translates to a higher likelihood of a sale. You may feel the most affinity for the ones that are funny. For example, a camel walking through a business office or a talking block of cheese with an attitude. You may be attracted to the ones that feature an endearing cartoon or a cute, fuzzy animal – even a tiny lizard. You may be a sucker for the ones that have a catchy tune or a memorable image.

When you *hate* them, they still work – through name recognition. You feel such an aversion that the name sticks, subconsciously. The next time you are at the store and you see the product on a shelf, you think to yourself, "Ahh, yes, I've heard of that. 'Can't quite remember where... Somewhere...." Advertisers know that; they manipulate with that. It's the same with offensive negative political ads. People hate them, but they work.

Those are TV commercials. What about what we will call business or networking commercials? Are they the same thing, just in a different setting? The answer is, no. The most obvious difference is this:

- TV commercials are trying to sell a product to the listener.
- Networking commercials are not designed to sell anything.

There isn't, or shouldn't be, any attempt to make a sale at a networking meeting. Remember, you are networking. Your goal needs to be to sell through... not to.

So, why do almost all formal networking groups provide their members with opportunities to present 30- to 40-second networking commercials in group meetings, usually on a weekly basis? Answer: because they are of incredible value in areas other than sales. The value of a network commercial shows itself in many ways. Commercials may provide any or all of the following:

- Introduce new members and/or provide their mini biographies
- Request specific referrals to key people
- Highlight a new product in someone's sales line
- Inform about sales going on in a company

---

[64] Cost from: https://en.wikipedia.org/wiki/Super_Bowl_commercials

- Tell stories of how products help in aspects of people's lives
- Announce a new sales direction that the presenter is planning
- Tell about a new credential/qualification the presenter earned

The only thing that a business networking commercial is _not_, is what a TV commercial _is_: namely, a sales pitch to listeners. Given all of that, let's define the term. For the purposes of this book, we define a networking commercial as:

> *A 30- to 60-second opportunity, provided as a part of a formal networking meeting, for group members to communicate information to be recalled when a referral opportunity presents itself in their day-to-day lives.*

In a networking group of 30 members, commercials can take up a quarter to a half of the total meeting time. So, they are obviously considered an extremely important activity. True, members may occasionally have an opportunity to present a longer and more in-depth discussion of their product or service, but we aren't talking about that. We are talking about the 30- to 60-second commercials that are presented on a weekly basis.

Did you catch the "weekly" part? Unlike an elevator speech that doesn't change and you will use again and again to create contacts (**CC**), you are going to create a new commercial each and every week. For this reason, we need to discuss the components that make up the most effective networking commercials possible. We will do this in the next chapter.

It is important here, while we are introducing the concept of a networking commercial, to keep in mind the most important goal, by far, of any business commercial. That goal is to deliver a commercial that listeners will remember – ones that will be sticky. They may include catchy phrases such as "got milk?" or "where's the beef?" They may involve the audience seeing the products for themselves or carrying away color photographs of the product. They usually involve humor and/or enthusiasm. Those are the kinds of elements that make commercials sticky.

## THE CURSE OF KNOWLEDGE

In attempting to understand the concept of a networking commercial, you need to be aware of what has been called the "Curse of Knowledge."

> *The Curse of Knowledge is when people forget that they didn't always know what they now know.*

# STICKY COMMERCIALS: THE CONCEPT

The Curse of Knowledge is most often revealed when presenters use references (usually terminology or jargon) that is specific to their company or industry and/or are known only to a select few within their cadré or circle. It usually occurs in one of two related ways:

1) When they use abbreviations, acronyms, and jargon that are old hat to them, but are foreign to their audience.
2) When they assume that an audience has the same knowledge they do, and the audience does not.

## TYPE 1: INDUSTRY JARGON

When you start using industry jargon that is unique to your area, you run a significant risk of dismissing people who are not part of that industry. A sure sign of the Curse of Knowledge is if you experience pride or feel special and important because of the vocabulary you're using. But even if you aren't using terms to show off, the price of using jargon may be alienating the very audience you are trying to reach.

Examples of industry jargon include casually talking about a 401K, a CAPEX, or a PIP as if every reasonable person knows what those are. Most people don't. They also don't know how a toilet, a tracking cookie, or an internal combustion engine works, they just know they do. "Check the 4Cs of a stud to make sure it is not a CZ that is flush set," is not referring to racehorses, carpentry, or toilets. "The prima facie discovery suggests dissimulation" is not referring to moon exploration or dissecting a cadaver.

If you feel like the Big Man or Big Woman on campus because you can talk like this, that's fine. But keep in mind these kinds of sentences confuse and distance people. Worse, they turn off your listeners. Think about it. You've had the experience of hearing people refer to something that's funny when you have no idea what they're talking about. Then they laugh between themselves at their own inside joke. You know intellectually they're not making fun of you at all, but at some level, you still feel mocked.

Industry jargon in your commercials can have the same effect. You are using terminology only a few people use. By doing so, you're marginalizing your audience, and they will feel that way – marginalized and unimportant. They will feel put off. They won't remember your commercial, and they will **_not_** refer their friends to you.

Some very good networkers, who are otherwise skilled at creating contacts (**CC**) and nurturing them into friends (**NN**), have failed miserably at giving effective commercials. They just can't figure out why their commercials aren't effective. "Why can't I get the attention I need to help my business grow?" they wonder. It could be because their commercials are using terminology that just doesn't resonate with the majority of the listeners.

Think of this the next time you present your commercial. Your terminology needs to be appropriate for your audience. There's a delicate balance between being too simple and condescending and being too complicated and technical. You want the sweet spot between those two.

## TYPE 2: YOU FORGET WHAT YOU DIDN'T KNOW

The second type of the Curse of Knowledge is you didn't always know what you now know. Think about times in your life when people have spoken down to you as if you should have known some specific fact. They may have even talked in a mocking tone. When people do this to you, they are forgetting they didn't always know the fact either.

An example of this form of the Curse of Knowledge happened when one father began teaching his 15-year-old son to drive. He took him to an empty parking lot. It was the very first time the boy had ever sat behind the wheel, but there was absolutely no danger of any problems – or so Dad thought.

They circled here and there and cruised around cement dividers. With a big grin, the boy accelerated and slowed down – he turned left, he turned right. He was having a great time becoming used to steering the vehicle and handling small differences in speed. It seemed like a good next step to have him try parking. The boy slowly maneuvered this 4,000-pound vehicle into the parking stall. He did just fine, including leaving an appropriate space on each side of the car. "Good…, good." And then …right through and out the other end.

"Whoa, stop! Stop! What happened? The idea is to park! You know, as in, park."

It was clear from the son's face that the young man had forgotten one small item. This was not one of his video games. A video game would have automatically stopped, parked, and shut everything down for him when he got into the spot. But, not, _he_ was the one who had to complete the action of fully stopping the vehicle, shifting the car into neutral, and turning the car off. It had never dawned on Dad that there would be an issue here. Never, for one second, had this father anticipated that his son would not know how to stop the car.

The take-away from this story is this father had a vital piece of knowledge that he hadn't thought to share. He assumed everyone knew about stopping a vehicle. The reality was that the teen simply didn't know about something this basic, important, and as Dad thought, obvious. It was a result of the father's Curse of Knowledge.

This is something to keep clearly in mind if you want to make your commercials sticky. You have an abundance of knowledge in a specific area. The way you present that information can either leave people feeling left out or sound condescending. Be mindful of your audience. Don't leave them feeling like children. The Curse of Knowledge can be brutal.

## BE SPECIFICALLY SPECIFIC

Another issue to help you understand the concept of a sticky commercial is exactly how specific you can be in your networking commercials. The answer is: very! If you want to do business with a specific company, you can ask in your group meeting for *specific* referrals and *specific* introductions to *specific* people in that *specific* company. That's how specific you can be.

Let's say you sell ink and you're looking for local print shops that need ink. You specifically need contact with the buyer at the largest of them, which is *ABC Printing*. You just can't seem to figure out how to get past the gatekeeper. So, ask your network group. "I need an introduction to some key people at *ABC Printing*. I would like an introduction to whoever makes decisions about their supply needs." A networking group is exactly the forum to do this. Being this specific helps people understand what is valuable to you, and it sets a model for others to follow.

You may think being this specific will be limiting. You're afraid listeners will assume you only want to do business with *ABC Printing* and no other company. This just isn't the case. The reality is one of the listeners in the room may come to you after the meeting and say, "Well, I don't know the folks at *ABC Printing*, but I do know a guy at *XYZ Printing*. My neighbor is the supply manager at *XYZ Printing*. Would you like an introduction to her?"

"Yes, yes, I would."

By being specific about the company where you were seeking introductions, you draw an image in your listeners' minds. They will make the connection, mentally, about how the first company is similar to a second company and confirm with you that you'd like a connection to that second company, also.

If you know a person's name and especially if you know the person's title, ask your network. "Do you guys know Janet Capella-Smith at *ABC Printing*? I'd really like to be introduced to Janet."

Maybe Nova Caine, a friend of yours from the networking group, will come up after the meeting and say, "I know Janet. She's in my book club that meets Wednesday nights. I never even thought about her working there and how that would be good for you. I'll talk to her." Nova is going to eagerly work to make that introduction the very next Wednesday when she sees Janet.

Or maybe none of the members know Ms. Capella-Smith, but someone will come up to you after the meeting and say, "I don't know Janet Capella-Smith at *ABC Printing*, but I do know Patty Owen who also works there. In fact, she's the vice-president. She could help me get that introduction for you." Either way, you've really expanded your chances to get to Janet Capella-Smith.

This also works for specific categories of people or specific areas of interest. Let's assume you are a photographer and your specialty is capturing the elegance and magic of antique cars. You want to assemble collections of photos of antique cars into coffee-table books to sell. You love putting them into rural settings with the light falling on them just right to bring out the nostalgia of yesteryear. Your commercial can reflect all of that.

"I'm looking for people who restore very old automobiles. The condition doesn't matter. They can be broken hulks rusting at the edge of some rural field. That would be great! Or, they can be fully restored and shiny vehicles that are road-ready and show-ready. I want to take striking photos of all those cars for a book I'm preparing. Can you help me connect with owners of these kinds of antiques?"

If any members at that meeting know people who fit your description, they won't hesitate one second in sharing this information with you. People like to feel helpful; they will respond.

As another example, let's say you sell insurance. You want an introduction to skydivers because that is a high-risk hobby. Perhaps you share the hobby and know something about it. You at least know that skydivers don't always think about protecting their families. Some are underinsured. So, in your networking group, you give a commercial where you ask for introductions to skydivers.

"Do any of you know someone who is really into skydiving? I'd love an introduction to a person like that because, a lot of times, their insurance isn't where it needs to be. I'd love an opportunity to review their insurance and help them out."

Even if the listeners can't think of anyone off the top of their heads, they will recall your request. Skydiving is one of those categories where people will either think, "That would be so cool!" or they'll think, "That's nuts! Jumping out a plane with nothing to stop your fall but a hunk of cloth? I would never do that!" Either way, that's an emotional response. The emotion makes it sticky. The next time anyone, ever, brings up skydiving, they'll think, "Oh, yeah! That member last month wanted an introduction to someone who was interested in skydiving." It will pull that string back to the image of you talking about skydiving. That's what you want.

Perhaps you're thinking that you're limiting your referral base by being this specific. You are not. You are actually expanding it. You are drawing mental images for people to remember. Long after you have finished your commercial and they have gone on about their lives, your commercial is still sticky in their heads. Sometimes they can't even get it out of their heads, and that's exactly what you want. The whole purpose of giving your commercial is to make them so sticky that people will remember them.

## SELL THROUGH... NOT TO

Throughout this book, we have talked about the importance of selling _through_ your network and not _to_ your network. You want them to leave the meeting and get on with their busy lives, including talking with the hundreds of people who they know and meet each week. The goal is to have group members remember your commercials and then to remember you when the time is right. But you are not selling _to_ them, you are selling _through_ them.

### THE POWER OF SELLING THROUGH... NOT TO

Selling through your audience does not mean you are sending them out as your own private salesforce. You are not. You are hoping, in the course of their daily lives, they will happen to talk to someone (a friend or a network contact) who has a problem you can solve. If that happens:

1) You want them to remember your commercial (it was "sticky") and then...
2) You want them to refer back to you, i.e., to make a connection between you and the person they were talking to so that you can then solve that person's problem with your products or services.

If your product or service is not a one-time purchase, that means a repeat customer. That's wonderful! But that's not all. Another benefit comes because you probably didn't yet know that person. So, it isn't just another sale, it is a new contact to add to your network. That new contact may then create further contacts (**CC**), which could mean more sales. That is network power (**NP**).

Consider the difference between selling through... and selling to... in more concrete images. Let's say you still insist on selling _to_... your networking group. That's a huge mistake, but let's say you can't be talked out of it. Let's be generous and pretend the impossible: You sell your product to all 30 networkers at the meeting that day.

That makes 30 sales. That's great! Or, is it...?

Let's change the scenario and say that you sell _through_... your networking group. This means that you present a sticky commercial and, after the meeting, all 30 group members go out into the world and talk to 10+ people each. Further, they refer all of them to you and all of those referrals purchase your product. That's 300 sales! And that's just one week. Your commercial is actually like the gift that keeps on giving. If your commercial was sticky enough, the listeners will also remember it the following week and make more referrals. That will continue the week after that, and so on. Referrals could even continue into the following month, or even the following year. That could be thousands of sales!

Which would you prefer: 30 sales or 30,000 sales?

Of course, that's not remotely realistic, but you get the idea. Let's try this again, but let's be realistic this time. Not a single person is attending that networking function to buy anything but let's say you try selling *to* them anyway, and you make one sale. That's nothing compared to the potential 3 or 4 *dozen* sales that could come from their later referrals if you sell *through* them. This is why it is essential your networking commercials be sticky. Stop trying to sell; start trying to network. Quit swimming upstream or trying to put a round peg into a square hole.[65] Fix in your mind that group members are there for either one or both of two reasons:

1) To request your help by introducing them to people who they could then help through their products or services.
2) To help the other members succeed by making introductions and referrals that can help them.

What they are *not* there for is to purchase a product.

This rather startling perspective may require a paradigm shift. Make the shift! You are not there to sell products; you are there to fill needs. You are the problem-solver, not the salesperson. You have the network people need to quietly solve their problems. In short, a networking function is not the time or place to get people to buy your product. There are other times when it will be appropriate to sell, but not now. It is your time to network.

## HOW TO DISTINGUISH SELLING THROUGH... FROM SELLING TO

You may not be totally clear on how to tell the difference between selling and networking. Here is the primary way to determine whether you are selling through… or selling to…. Listen carefully to the words being used. It's a dead giveaway. You can use it to evaluate the wording of your own commercials or other people's commercials. Just listen to the words. If you hear the following types of phrases, the commercial is trying to sell *to*… the networking group:

---

[65] As a piece of meaningless trivia, it has been proven, mathematically, that a round peg fits better into a square hole than a square peg fits into a round hole; see: http://mathworld.wolfram.com/Peg.html

## STICKY COMMERCIALS: THE CONCEPT

- *"You need this because this will make your life richer, happier, and better in many ways"*
- *"I've significantly helped other people. May I help you, too?"*
- *"Today, I would like to demonstrate a product (or service) that will solve your problems."*
- *"Did I mention the price of my product (or services)?"*
- *"I can provide a wonderful service that would be of great interest to you."*

Those are all indicators that you are selling to the group.

By contrast, if you hear the following types of phrases, the commercial is selling *through*… the networking group:

- *"What my company is offering can help many of your friends and contacts."*
- *"Do you know a person who has this issue?"*
- *"I'm sure some of you know this specific person, Mr. Caddie Lack, at this car company on Main Street. We were able to help him. We can help others you know in the same way.*
- *"I'm needing an introduction to people who love languages (or who collect stamps, or who go salmon fishing, or who are wanting to upgrade their furniture, etc.)"*

Those are all examples of wording that is focused on selling through the group, not selling to them. These differences can be difficult to spot, and you may tend to morph back and forth between selling *through*… and selling *to*…. A lot of presenters do this. A sticky commercial is definitely not something most people can create on the fly. You can't just "wing it."

Don't hesitate to enlist the help of other members to evaluate your networking commercials. Better yet, partner up with a teammate in this process and evaluate each other. "Did I sell *through*… or did I sell *to*…?" You can get very good at hearing the difference by tag-teaming like this. The distinction between selling *through*… and selling *to*… is very important to make. When you are selling through your networking professionals, they will be eager to help their friends through you and/or eager to help you directly. If they pick up on you wanting to sell something to them, they will tune you out. If this happens, your commercials will definitely not be sticky.

Below are five brief scenarios that may help clarify the concept of "sell _through_... not _to_...."

| *Sell Thru...*  *Opportunities to Network with a Contact* | *Sell To...*  *Opportunities to Sell to a Customer* |
|---|---|
| Both people are looking for Introductions to _other_ people who can benefit from the product available. | One person is _looking for_ a product that the other one represents and that can be used to solve a problem. |
| The conversation is a _two-way_ sharing of stories covering a variety of thoughts and opinions. | The conversation is _one-sided_ and focuses on a specific product or services that are available. |
| A discussion of one person's problem results in the second making an introduction to a third who holds a key to fill the need. | A person is caught off-guard in a casual conversation by a sudden attempt to close a deal and to generate a sale from what is now a trapped situation. |
| The intent of the interaction is primarily social to create or strengthen a relationship. | All parties in a conversation know a potential business transaction is imminent. |
| Both people in a conversation enjoy a pleasant exchange of ideas or experiences that help identify other new introductions. | One person feels cornered and has the desire to be out of the situation, while the other continues to extol the virtues of a product. |

Okay, so we have addressed the concepts of what networking commercials are and the value of making them sticky. Part of this is stressing that networking is networking, while selling is selling. There is a time and place for each activity. Fine.... But how do you create these commercials? Are there any power plays in your playbook that are available to help you? The happy answer is, yes!

The content of effective commercials – the "what" – will be the topic of the next chapter.

# CHAPTER 13

# STICKY COMMERCIALS: THE CONTENT

The idea of giving weekly commercials to a room full of your peers may sound overwhelming. It may be totally outside your wheelhouse. For many people, having others silently look at them and listen to them is terrifying.

Remember you are not alone. You have friends who will guide you to help make your networking commercials sticky. Plus, there are tried and tested plays that you can add to your playbook. In this chapter, we will discuss three power plays that will help you in achieving networking success and the importance of a Plan B.

## THE POWER PLAY OF A GOOD STORY

Let's start with the importance of creating imagery. Don't be afraid to try telling a story. We can't over-emphasize the stickiness of storytelling. For millennia, humans have sat around glowing fires at night telling each other stories. The mental pictures created by memorable stories are truly worth a thousand words. That's why we use stories, anecdotes, and dialogue in this book. It is to make this book sticky. An academic treatise doesn't have the power of discussions illustrated by fun and memorable stories.

The same is true for your network commercials. One of the great things you can do is learn how to tell a short story in the amount of time that you've been allotted. It's a powerful skill to tell about an event or situation that just happened to you. Or, you could tell about a client who was bettered by what you had to offer. How much more effective is it if that story wraps up in a way that's truly meaningful and takes the audience from a lower place of understanding to a deeper place of better understanding. That contributes to your network power (**NP**).

When you tell your stories, you create imagery. The emotions you draw out of your listeners remain with them much longer than words can or will. One writer put the idea this way:

> *Think about your favorite movie. What was the name of the main character? What did you like about him or her? What happened to the character throughout the movie? You can probably recall the plot in great detail. Now think back to the last quarterly update your organization's leadership sent around internally. Maybe you can recall a statistic or two, but I'll bet you'd be hard pressed to recount any significant portion of the report to your colleague who hasn't read it yet.*[66]

Tell stories about people who you've helped to solve a problem. Don't forget those times when you've helped indirectly by making a connection to a third person in your network who has helped out. Put those experiences into a quick story format. Talk about those people, who they are, what their products or services were. Talk about the issues they had, and how they couldn't overcome them alone. Talk about how, with your help or your product, they overcame problems and had successful experiences. If you can do that, you'll be surprised how many people will also want to experience that same success by coming to you. That's what you want to have them do. You want to draw the mental stories for your listeners.

Later, they will be going about their lives and meeting different people. They won't even be thinking about you. Suddenly, a person they're speaking with reveals having an issue or problem in that exact same area. You will immediately flash into their minds. "Oh, yes!" they will say, "I know a great person for that!" They will remember you were speaking about solving that problem, and you know how to solve it. It becomes an easy introduction for them to eagerly connect their friend with you because your story was sticky, and they care about you.

Think back to the things you've wanted to pursue or learn in your past. That interest probably came because there was a story behind it; it wasn't just a piece of data handed to you. So often in networking, and in sales in general, we just announce to people that we have product XYZ. When we start telling stories about that product it begins to resonate with people. Later, when they are in a conversation with a person you don't know, they recall the story you told. This is what word-of-mouth advertising is all about. They'll remember the story as it relates to them.

---

[66] Quote from Noah Zandan, n/d, "Does Telling Stories Really Make You 22 Times More Memorable?" Quantified Communications; see: www.quantified communications.com/ blog/storytelling-22-times-more-memorable

They will draw the connection. The story will come first in their memory. Then, the relationship between you and your product follows.

For example, it really doesn't make much sense to say, "Hey, I know Audrey." Okay, that's fine – you know Audrey. How is that relevant? Why is that memorable? Now, add the back story. It makes all the difference. If you tell the group about how Audrey made an impact on your life, and how she could make an impact on their lives, they will suddenly have the desire to meet her.

When you are telling a story to make a commercial sticky, there is a rule-of-thumb you can use. Spend roughly 60% of your story time fully developing the problem to be solved. Describe it as monumental in the life of someone. Frame it as a dilemma. Avoid the idea that the dilemma is unique or unusual. The idea is you want your audience to identify with the story. You want them to say, "Wow! That's me! That's exactly what happens to me!" When that happens, the audience members feel the problem is, or could be, their individual problem. You want the story to be common to people without saying it's common. Then spend 10% of your time explaining how your product offers a simple solution – it is the magic pill. If the problem takes a long time to form, and you can solve it with a few simple steps, that creates power for the listeners. Spend the last 30% of your time talking about the rewards of having the problem solved, how different the listeners' lives will be with this problem solved. Your goal is to conclude on a happy note and with the message the solution to the monumental problem is simple and satisfying. Remember, the story is not to sell; the story is to make the commercial sticky. So, the 60-10-30 formula of story-telling is:

> Spend **60%** of the story time describing the problem as monumental but common, **10%** how your product will solve it, and **30%** how satisfying the outcome will be.

Be eager to tell stories. Be eager to relate case studies about things that have happened. Practice telling multiple stories. Bounce them off other people. Share the stories in casual encounters and tell them in informal conversations. You'll be surprised how sticky that is for people. They don't let it go. It pops into their heads when they least expect it. Of course, that is exactly what you want. You don't want people going around saying your name all the time and trying to remember to give you a referral. You want people to think about you at exactly the right moment and in exactly the right place. That will happen if your commercial is sticky.

In this discussion of running the play of storytelling, there are five cautions to consider. Each one is important, but none are deal killers.

<u>Caution 1: Secure Permissions</u>. If you choose to present case studies of living people, make sure you have their explicit and, ideally, written permission to do so.

Caution 2: Be Careful with First Person Stories. Similarly, you may have heard about people in your career path who have been helped by a product and you want to tell their stories, too. That's fine, but don't tell it in the first person because that would be disingenuous and misleading.

Caution 3: Don't Tell a Story That Asks for Help. If the story reveals failure or other negative outcomes, reflect carefully before putting it in the first person, even if it really is about you. You run the risk of presenting yourself as a victim and in need of help. It may seem like an expression of polite modesty, but tread lightly. If the listeners perceive they need to rescue you, the emphasis on networking benefits or the product as a solution to an issue or problem will be smothered. Instead, the listeners will have pity elicited. Examples include a marriage breakup, disgruntled customers, a death in your family, a wayward child, a product failure, loss of a job, and so on.

You could also damage your credibility in the eyes of your listeners. That will be difficult to win back. You don't want either of those two reactions to your story.

Caution #4: Don't Tell a Self-aggrandizing Story. By contrast, be very careful about telling grandiose stories that make you sound as if you are the greatest of all time. You do not want to give the impression that you believe no one else on the planet could do something better than you. In fact, you don't want to make the stories about *you* in any case.

What you want to do is craft stories where you were able to help someone else succeed. The other person needs to be the hero, not you. The other person did it. All you did was to help. Another way of saying this is you want the people who come to you to feel as if they, themselves, have conquered their problems. They are not coming to you to fix their issues. They are coming to you for a tool to help them to solve their own problems.

Caution #5: Vary Your Story Lengths. If you're going to use a story format often, alternate between a large view and a small one. One time present a large story of a major problem being solved. Another time share a smaller story of a little problem being solved. What will happen is people will remember both types. They'll remember you solve problems, big and small, especially in those particular areas.

## THE POWER PLAY OF CATCHY TAGLINES

One of the best power plays in your playbook is what is usually called a "tagline." These are catchy slogans, ditties, or 3- or 4-word labels that lock you or your products into the memories of your listeners. And memory = sticky.

We started Chapter 11 by talking about "got milk?" and "where's the beef?" Those two-word questions went around the world. They were taglines. If your listeners come to associate effective taglines with you, even if they are not as effective as those two, you are two-thirds of the way toward many, many, new contacts (**CC**), relevant referrals (**RR**), and sales.

## CATCH A CATCHY TAGLINE

Whether you are aware of it or not, you've heard taglines all your life. If you're old enough, you'll remember:

> *Brylcreem: A little dab'll do ya!"* [67]

Brylcreem was a paste of mineral oil stabilized with beeswax. The idea was that men would grease the sides of their hair and comb it back and then make a curl in the center, all held in place with wax. This was billed as irresistible to young women. Despite the unlikelihood that anyone would truly want to run their fingernails through greased up hair, it lasted until the British band, the Beatles, arrived in New York City in 1964 sporting long – and dry – hair.

If you are old enough to remember them, other highly successful taglines from yesteryear were:

- Alka Seltzer: Plop, plop, fizz, fizz; Oh, what a relief it is!
- Roto-Rooter: Away go troubles, down the drain
- Band-Aid: I am stuck on Band-Aid 'cause band-aid's stuck on me
- Oscar Mayer: Oh, I wish I were an Oscar Mayer wiener [68]

More modern taglines surround us like an avalanche. There seems to be no escaping them. Some taglines that are particularly known include:

- Nike: Just Do It
- L'Oréal Paris: Because *you're* worth it
- Bounty: The quicker Picker Upper
- State Farm: Like a good neighbor
- KFC: Finger lickin' good
- US Marines: The few, The proud, the marines [69]

---

[67] The lyrics and history were taken from: https://en.wikipedia.org/wiki/Brylcreem.
[68] See http://www.americanmusicconcepts.com/blog/18-time-greatest-radio-tv-commercial-jingles/ for other vintage taglines.
[69] These well-known taglines were taken from: https://blog.hubspot.com/marketing/brand-slogans-and-taglines.

Dentists often use taglines, many of them with the questionable idea that people with whiter teeth will feel more confident, so will smile more often:

- Where beautiful smiles begin
- Caring for you and your smile
- Your smile is our passion
- Gentle hands, healing touch.
- New smile; New life
- We love to see you smile
- Putting a smile on every face
- Where smiles come alive
- Dentistry with heart [70]

A few taglines for barbers are:

- Rock the cut
- Barbering at its best
- Hairstyles that fit your lifestyle
- Because salons are for girls
- It's not just a haircut, it's an experience.[71]

There is no reason you can't come up with similar kinds of taglines that are sure to powerfully identify you and your career track. Those would be dropped into your commercial, often at the end.

That's catchy; that's sticky. That's network power (**NP**).

You can develop some really cool taglines. Here are a few guidelines for developing a good tagline that you can use.

1) Remember it has to be attached to you. You must own this because it will partly define you.
2) It should be short – ideally 8 words or less – and able to be almost instantly memorized by the listener.
3) It should illustrate the results you want to highlight.

---

[70] Dental taglines are from: www.everydayknow.com/dental-slogans.
[71] Selected from barber taglines at: https://brandongaille.com/ 34-catchy-barber-shop-slogans-and-taglines.

## STICKY COMMERCIALS: THE CONTENT

**GET CREATIVE – THE SKY'S THE LIMIT**

Taglines don't have to be at the end of your commercial. The end is usually where we think about putting them since a lot of research shows that people remember that last item the best. But don't get stuck on the idea that it has to be anchored at the end. It doesn't. It can be in the middle, or even the lead-in to the rest of the commercial.

If you have a good tagline, after a while people will start to recite it with you. At first, you may feel uncomfortable with that, but think about it: If they're remembering it with you, they are remembering it without you, too.

There was one networker who would start every one of his commercials by saying, "So, there's this movie…." Then he would relate a past or present movie back to his business in some interesting, funny, and creative way. That always got a laugh. People would anticipate it as he stood up to give his commercials. The only question was what movie he was going to reference. But if it were only creating a laugh, that wouldn't be very effective, just funny. It only became an effective tagline because he tied it to his business in some creative way.

One of this man's movie references was to a baseball movie that happened to be playing at the time. A listener who had heard the commercial happened to be at a ballgame the following week with a friend who mentioned that same baseball movie. The man who had heard the commercial instantly remembered it – and, more importantly – the networking member who had given it at the last meeting. That memorable tagline, "So, there's this movie…," which had led-off the commercial is what made his commercial sticky.

Although we wouldn't necessarily suggest it, do you see how you could use that exact same tagline at the beginning of each of _your_ networking commercials? And, it wouldn't matter what profession you had, or what movie came out that week.

You can pretty much tie any movie to any business if you have enough irreverence. Be willing to bring your personality into it. If it's something that's way out there, and out of bounds, but you own it and that's part of what you do, that could really work for you. It could make your commercial sticky.

Give your tagline with _confidence_. Then, after you use it, whether at the beginning, in the middle, or at the end… STOP TALKING – for at least 3 seconds!! Don't say anything else. Let the tagline attach itself in your listeners' minds. Let it percolate and do its work.

If you immediately say something else, you surrender its power. You give away its effectiveness.

So many people simply do not understand what silence can do. Or they are afraid of silence, so they fill the silence themselves. Don't do that. That's like driving a golf ball down the green and then immediately hitting another one before the first ball has landed. It's like putting a huge forkful of iced birthday cake into your mouth and then putting in another one before you have tasted, chewed, and swallowed the first mouth full. You don't want to do any of those things. STOP TALKING!! Three seconds of silence should not be too difficult. Yet, many people seem unable to do it. As a result, they end up sabotaging their own commercials.

Similarly, if your tagline comes at the beginning of the commercial, don't spoil it by first introducing yourself. Start with your tagline. Then, give it 3 seconds of silence – 6 if the audience laughs. If you deliver your tagline in the middle, bookend it with 3 seconds of silence on each side. If your tagline comes at the end, say NOTHING MORE. Just smile and go sit down.

This is not rocket science. A few seconds of silence will give your tagline more punch and more power. It will create the focus that you want it to have. It will allow your tagline to create more stickiness in your commercial. A baker would never mix bread dough and immediately pop it into a bread pan and put it in the oven. It has to prove until it has doubled in size. If you bake it without proving it, you won't end up with a fluffy loaf of bread; you will end up with a hard brick fit only to be a door stop. Likewise, give your taglines a few seconds to prove. Think of silence as the exclamation mark of speaking.

## THE POWER PLAY OF MEMORY HOOKS

As powerful as taglines are, they are only a part of a larger memory hook. Think, again, of the discussion of the taglines, "got milk?" and "where's the beef?" from the beginning of Chapter 11. Those taglines only took off because they were a part of a larger and catchy scenario. It was the full commercial that was the "hook." For example, "got milk?"...

> *...the advertisements would typically feature people in various situations involving dry or sticky foods and treats such as cakes and cookies. The person then would find himself in an uncomfortable situation due to a full mouth and no milk to wash it down. [One] ...commercial was a cruel businessman getting hit by a truck seconds after insulting someone over the phone and seemingly going to Heaven, only find out it is actually Hell when he finds a huge plate of cookies and an endless supply of completely empty milk cartons.*

Without the memory hook of the funny commercial (the man in Hell with dry cookies but no milk to wash them down), the two-word question, "got milk?" has little real power. The full joke of the commercial was the memory hook that drove the engine of the tagline to stick into people's memories.

You can use similar memory hooks (with or without taglines) to make your commercials pop. The memory hooks work by giving the audience something unique and memorable. That's why they are called hooks – because they hook your audience in the same way an angler would hook a fish. You give them something yummy to chew on and then reel them in. If the hooks create lasting memories, that makes networking commercials sticky.

## VERBAL MEMORY HOOKS

Memory hooks are usually (but not always) verbal. Verbal memory hooks might include memorable stories that catch people's imagination and stay with them. Sayings, quotes, or poetic turns of phrase that create a sudden image or emotion are great. They could be a joke or be verbally jarring. They could be something unexpected, like suddenly singing a phrase.

Some people create a memory hook out of a specific story. Others create the verbal memory hook with a single phrase that they deliver early on in the commercial. Then they refer back to that story or phrase again and again – like a running gag in a comedy. The single-phrase gag becomes the memory hook to remind people of the commercial long after they have left and gone. The hook has made the commercial sticky.

One insurance broker uses the saying, "It takes 8,460 bolts to assemble an automobile, and one nut to scatter it all over the freeway." That saying, though not coined by her, is her adopted memory hook.[72] It always gets a chuckle because it's true; we've all seen that nut on the freeway. The insurance broker's phrase, which is really a mini story, becomes a memory hook.

Creating or adopting these kinds of memory hooks can take some time and practice. You likely will need to experiment and get feedback until you have it dialed in exactly the way you want it.

One thing to remember when creating a good memory hook is that you have to own it. It has to be _yours_ (even if you have adopted it). You have to feel like it is truly you. It's okay if it feels awkward at first, but you have to reach a point where it no longer feels awkward. If you remain timid about laying down your memory hook, that will be instantly revealed by the way you deliver it.

So, use it! Own it! Enjoy it! Love it! Live it!

## VISUAL MEMORY HOOKS

Memory hooks aren't limited to just the words you say. They can be nonverbal, too. A great example is the comedy of Robin Williams. He had one that his audience didn't usually recognize. He

---

[72] The origin of the quote is unknown, but it has been used in several places, for example: https://warehousestories.wordpress.com/2007/06/20/it-takes-8460-bolts-to-assemble-an-automobile-and-one-nut-to-scatter-it-all-over-the-road-C2%A9-unknown-author.

would place an "anchor" on the stage. It was often a tall wooden stool. During one of his standup routines, he would first touch that anchor and then deliver the punchline of the joke. If the joke bombed, he would go back, touch that memory hook (the stool) again, and then repeat the line. That would trigger a laugh. People didn't even recognize that they were being tricked into a laugh.

You can also use such nonverbal memory hooks. It could be a fist pump that you sprinkle into your commercial. It could be spinning in a circle. It could be a certain way you stand. One good-sized man would put a hand on his hip and kick his hip out a little bit. It would always get a laugh from his audience who were waiting in rapt attention for that hip jiggle. Years later, several people said that anytime they saw anyone else do anything similar, they would think of this large man doing his jaunty hip jiggle in a professional setting.

One young woman chewed bubblegum and periodically blew bubbles as a sight-gag memory hook. It brought the house down and made her whole commercial become sticky – in more ways than one. It was her trademark. People remembered not just what she said but how she said it. Maybe that wouldn't fit your personality, but it fit her personality to a tee.

One caution: Make your commercials _sticky_, but don't make them _stupid_. If the audience remembers your costume or your shrieking in some weird accent, but not your name or your business ...well, then, the whole point of the commercial has been lost. "Ha, ha, that young woman blowing bubblegum bubbles was sure funny! I'll remember that for a long time!!" Okay, but what was her business? What was her name? "Hmmm, not sure I got those parts...." Oops! Don't get so caught up in antics that you forget you are running a business. The idea is to make your commercials memorable, not annoying.

## GIVE-AWAYS AS MEMORY HOOKS

Another thing you can use as a memory hook is a gift or give-away, usually of a product you are selling. You can use that hook once in a while, and it can be effective. However, it is difficult to use, especially to use consistently.

One of the problems with a give-away is the time allotment. It takes time to pass anything tangible out to everyone in an audience. That's true even in a small room or coffee house, and even with helpers to pass them out. If you are allotted only 30 to 60 seconds, you have to distribute your give-away while still presenting your commercial. How are you going to do that?

As an example, let's imagine you are a baker and you decide your giveaway will be a decorated cupcake for everyone. Fine and good. But do the math. Let's say you have as little as 30 total seconds. You allow yourself 10 seconds to introduce the giveaway and 10 second to wrap-up the commercial. That leaves you only 10 seconds to distribute 30 cupcakes, 30 napkins, and 30 plastic forks to 30 people in a large room. OK! That's about one-third of a second per cupcake. Did you remember to wear in-line roller-skates with a jetpack on your back? 'Ain't happ'ning!

The other consideration with a give-away is that the medium needs to be part of the message. Ignoring the impossibility of the time, it at least makes logical sense to give away sample cupcakes if you're a baker. It makes no sense to give away cupcakes if you're an insurance broker or a roofer. Then it just becomes an extremely cheap bribe, not a memory hook. Or worse, your commercial becomes the group members' memory of what *not* to do!

There's one way around this. You could always distribute just a couple of giveaways. You could make them a door prize for a lucky few. You could tape cards to the underside of a few chairs for a few people to find. One easy way to do this is to randomly throw 3 or 4 give-aways into the crowd for people to catch. That could work.

One downside is this solution only fits certain types of give-aways. Don't throw iced cupcakes! That would be a mess. And don't throw anything pointed – or a heavy object that could land on someone's head!

Another downside is, if the give-away is desirable and you can't give one to every person there (think, cupcakes or a tech-toy), some may feel left out or passed over. You don't want anyone feeling like that.

A third downside is the ones who got the give-aways may be trying out the sample, maybe eating them or, worse, showing them around to others at their table. All that time they're doing that, they are not listening to your words.

Still, it could work. Important point though: You would want to relate the give-aways to your presentation with some clever logical connection.

- A nutritional advisor throws a couple of Dollar Store yo-yo's out into the audience. "Here, catch!" Then she tells the audience, "Remember folks, yo-yo diets don't work." That would be an effective and sticky memory hook. Few people would feel left out if they didn't get a cheap yo-yo, and even those who didn't catch a yo-yo would still think back to that nutrition commercial the next time they saw a yo-yo or heard a friend discuss dieting.
- A dentist who was asking for referrals from the group places a sample toothbrush and a roll of dental floss at everyone's place on their tables. When it is time for the commercial, the dentist jokes: "Give these to your friends and tell them they have bad breath. They need me!" *That* would be sticky!

- A financial advisor tosses 5 or 6 individual packets of baker's yeast, wrapped in play dollar bills, out into the audience. She says, "That's what I do as a financial advisor. I 'double' people's money so they can see their assets 'rise'!" That would be sticky, too.

None of the tools talked about in this chapter are gimmicks. They are serious elements that will help your commercials to be sticky and help you in your career. However, in considering such tools, remember to use them together with your personality, your enthusiasm, and your style.

Above all, don't be afraid to experiment and play. Those 30-, 45- or 60-second commercials give you invaluable opportunities to look people in the eye – even stare at the audience. Look at the people in the room, look to the right and left, look at those close to you and those far away. Address the audience as a whole or try calling out one or two by name.

Experiment each and every week. Try a joke or two (keep it clean). The people will absolutely not criticize you or your iffy humor. The worst that could happen is they will snicker but not laugh out loud. So what? The leadership will not ask you to leave. There is not a pot of hot tar and a bag of feathers waiting in the broom closet. You will be fine.

## PRACTICE PLAN A AND PREPARE PLAN B

We have repeatedly encouraged you to develop confidence, and we stand by it. But confidence does not mean over-confidence. One sign of over-confidence or pride is the belief that you are good enough to "wing it" when it comes time to deliver your business commercial.

Never, never fail to make the time to be thoroughly prepared with your commercial. Being fully prepared is absolutely essential. It has been said:

*If You fail to prepare,*
*you prepare to fail.*[73]

Do not accept any excuse for not being prepared. It is sadly but surprisingly common to see at least some group members simply compose their commercials as they deliver them. Some have even walked into a BRING! meeting, stood up to give a commercial, and started by apologizing. "I'm really not prepared…" or "I don't know what I'm going to say." Some seasoned professionals have even announced, "I'm scheduled for a big 10-minute presentation later in the meeting, so I'm not going to use my time now," and then sit down.

Don't do that.

---

[73] This truism, another chiasm, has been credited to Benjamin Franklin, but that is unlikely. See: https://quoteinvestigator.com/2018/07/08/plan for other attributions.

## STICKY COMMERCIALS: THE CONTENT

You're a professional. Use *every* opportunity you're given. You're enthusiastic about your business and you're enthusiastic about giving service and helping others in their lives and careers. Show it! Don't model negative behaviors like indifference and lack of preparation. Being prepared is the key to all networking success.[74] When Broughts see you giving a fully prepared and quality commercial, it helps them do the same. In the long run, you are helping them succeed in their lives and their careers.

But what if the unthinkable happens? What if you cannot deliver the Plan A commercial that you have composed and practiced? What if an earlier presenter stole your thunder by talking about the same subject you're talking about? Ouch! Now what?

Have a Plan B in your back pocket.

Without a back-up plan B commercial, all you could do is piggy-back on what the other person said. That's not good! There are at least three negatives to piggy-backing o n someone else:

1. If you repeat elements of another person's commercial, you sound impotent and weak. The audience has already heard it, and only a few moments ago. You sound boring.
2. You essentially just gave away the precious time that you were allotted and, by doing so, lost the attention of the entire group.
3. You are actually making a second commercial for the *other person!*

Imagine how the following comments would sound, and who they would highlight:

- "As *Mary* said in her excellent commercial a little earlier…."
- "I can only echo what *Sue* explained to you…."
- "So, thanks to *Jeff* for telling us all about…."

Naah, don't put yourself in a position where you have to do that. We are all about serving others and giving to others …usually. Not now and not here! You need to be a little selfish on the small amount of commercial time you have been allotted. This is not a time to serve; this is a time to present. You have been given 30 to 60 precious seconds. Keep them. Don't throw them away. Anchor them to you.

Suppose you are an insurance broker and have prepared a commercial that talks about some new auto insurance rates that have just become available. If another broker talks about those same

---

[74] Alexander Graham Bell is credited with saying, "Before anything else, preparation is the key to success." See: https://www.brainyquote.com/ quotes/alexander_graham_ bell_387728

— 165 —

rate advantages, you need to have a backup. A piggyback commercial will not be effective and have network power (**NP**). It will just fall flat on its face.

This is a completely avoidable problem. Just have that backup. If you have that plan B at least partially ready, you won't have to hit the panic button. So, always have two commercials prepared every week. Of course, one will be better rehearsed. You were ready to go with that one. You've got it nailed down, and it was the perfect commercial.

Too bad. You've lost the opportunity to give plan A.

Give plan B.

It is perfectly acceptable if your plan B backup is only a rough draft or even one you used a couple of months ago. Far better to go with the one that is less prepared than to represent someone else's commercial that has already been given that day.

No, have a Plan B in your back pocket.

We've now discussed several helpful tools and plays you can put in your playbook. They will work.

In the next chapter, we'll consider style elements. Style refers to how you deliver your commercials. The "comm" in commercials is the way you communicate. It is the YOU that you bring to your audience. It is your personality and your style that will make your listeners "comm" to you and remember you.

# CHAPTER 14

# STICKY COMMERCIALS: PRESENTATION STYLE

In the last chapter, we talked about content that makes commercials sticky. The content of your commercials is very important. But just as important is style. It is hard to over-emphasize the importance of the way in which you deliver your commercial. Weak content and mediocre substance can be overcome by memorably delivery. Unfortunately, it is also true that amazing and significant content can be buried by a clumsy and ineffective presentation style.

To help you deal with the pressure of effectively presenting a commercial in a public setting, this chapter will focus on several tried and true tips. We'll give you some style elements for the "how" of presenting. Those will help make your commercials sticky and memorable.

## STYLE TIPS FOR A STICKY COMMERCIAL

One of the most important elements you can add to your commercials is enthusiasm and confidence about what you do and what you offer. If you are enthusiastic, you will automatically speak positively and be excited to help other people. This will show,

### CULTIVATE ENTHUSIASM AND CONFIDENCE

Confidence covers a multitude of sins and flaws that you otherwise have. It always goes a long way to your commercials being sticky and remembered by other people. You become known for your enthusiasm and confidence.

"Look, here comes Joleen," members will whisper. "Her commercials are always excellent!"

Do you hear what just happened? Joleen's networking commercials are sticky …by anticipation. They are sticky before she even opens her mouth. It's a little like being a singer, an actor, or an author. If they are already known and loved, their albums, movies, or novels are guaranteed to be grabbed by producers and publishers and snapped up by the public. If it's a new album by Adele or a song by Taylor Swift, it's number one on the charts before it's played for the first time. If it's a movie starring Tom Hanks or Meryl Streep, it's a box-office smash before the credits roll. If it is a novel by Steven King or J.K. Rowling, it's automatically a best seller. In reality, the song can be a yawn job, the movie a downer, and the novel a dog, but it will be well petted and well fed all the same. Other singers, actors, and writers can be even more talented, but they will not appear on the radio or the big screen and their book proposals will be dumped in the trash sight-unseen. That's just how it works.

To a much lesser degree, this is also how it works for you as a networker. If you are known for quality networking commercials, service to others, and contagious enthusiasm, your commercials will be sticky before you even present them. Relevant referrals will roll in faster than you can process them.

However, if you are known for lacking commitment and enthusiasm, your commercials will bomb no matter how many memory hooks, catchy taglines, or jokes they contain. And your referrals will be few and far between.

This is really the essence of what you want to communicate in your commercials. It is enthusiasm and confidence that will be the most sticky. A good dose of enthusiasm is worth a dozen memory hooks and the catchiest of taglines.

Fortunately, enthusiasm and confidence are style characteristics that can be learned and cultivated. It is amazing what a little confidence can mean to you in your networking success.

## STAND, SMILE, SPEAK WITH BOLDNESS AND CLARITY

Delivering your business commercial with enthusiasm and conviction is "numero uno." The person who stares down at a pad of paper and reads a text will never captivate an audience like the presenter who can verbally play with an audience. But knowing this fact is very different from knowing exactly how to pull it off. Fortunately, there are some simple tips you can easily do to help.

1. Stand Like the Rock of Gibraltar. Posture is a frequent error, but one that is simple to correct. Never deliver a commercial while sitting down, even if others in the group do. Stand up! Give your commercials the respect they deserve by getting up on your feet.

And, once there, stand firm. Nervous people rock and pace. Confident people stand firm. That doesn't mean you become a statue. It just means your posture tends to convey your convictions. When you move, move with a purpose. Don't stroll back and forth and switch your weight from leg to leg. Adopt power positions. Your commercial is not wishy-washy; don't let your posture be wishy-washy. Waves are for sailors, not presenters.

Posture is usually unconscious. It is vital that you make it conscious. Once you know to look for this, you will see the two posture habits everywhere you go.

- You'll see people who command a crowd by how they stand.
- You will also see aimless rocking.

Swaying is a sure sign of nerves and lack of confidence. Research has demonstrated you can be in control of this and it will make a significant difference.[75]

You may have heard the same advice given to young singers on television talent programs. "Work the stage!" the judges say. "Interact with the audience. Everyone here can sing. Not everyone can relate to the crowd." They are right. And this doesn't only hold for a TV show, it is a truism of life. People look solid when they stand solid. When they sway and rock back and forth, they simply look weak. So, before you open your mouth to speak, consider how you stand.

2. Smile with Sincerity and Confidence. Add to power posture a sincere smile. Even if the audience members are looking down and not looking at you, which would be very rare, people can actually "hear" a smile in your voice inflection.[76] Your enthusiasm will be portrayed if you have a smile.

When you stand up, stand up with a smile on your face. This is an exciting moment for you. Own your audience with your posture and your smile. They are not doing you a favor by listening to you; you are doing them a favor by speaking to them. (Say this last sentence to yourself three times before getting up and delivering your commercial with a smile.)

3. Look Straight at Your Audience. Make eye contact. If you have difficulty doing this, at least avoid looking down. People who are uncomfortable in front of a group often fail to make eye contact. They spend a lot of their time looking down at their hands or feet. This body language conveys timidity and embarrassment.

---

[75] See Albert E. Scheflen, 2016, "The Significance of Posture in Communication Systems," *Psychiatry: Interpersonal and Biological Process*, Vol. 27, No. 4, pp 316-331.

[76] For one example of this, see the article: "Hearing a Smile in Tone of Voice," NPR, Jan. 19, 2008 at https://www.npr.org/templates/story/story.php?storyId=18255131.

If you're having trouble looking directly at members of the audience, it would be better to at least look above the heads of the people. This will accomplish two things. 1) Keeping your head up will demonstrate, visually, some enthusiasm. 2) Raising your head will also change the tone in which you speak by opening your windpipe. It will raise your tones a little bit so it sounds like there's some enthusiasm and excitement about what you're doing. Even here, there's a trade-off. Looking up triggers people to speak clearly, while looking down encourages them to mumble.

The best plan, though, is to look at your audience and make eye-contact. Try to ignore anyone who is talking, reading, or otherwise showing no interest, no matter how much that behavior will hook you (and it will). Instead, try to find those people who look interested and supportive. Talk directly to them. Feed off them. Project to them your enthusiasm about what you represent. See them seeing you. They are friends. They want you to succeed. They want to connect with you as much as you want to connect with them. Look at them. Use them as your lifeline.

4. Speak with Power and Authority. Talk loudly enough for the entire room to hear. You don't have to shout, but you will need to project your voice. Despite what you have heard, there is no such thing as having a "soft-spoken voice." That is a cop-out. Soft-spoken just means the person has never learned to project the voice. This is a learned skill. You can learn how to do this. People are no more soft-spoken or loud by nature than they are angry or morose by nature. All of this can be changed. So, change it. If you don't know how to project your voice, there are people who can teach you, usually for free. It's all about lowering your voice by a note or two and breathing from the diaphragm. If you can't find someone to teach you, there are many excellent websites and YouTube videos to show you how.[77]

Think about how big your room is and how many people are in there. If there are a hundred people in the room, you need to project really well. Hopefully, there will be a microphone. But if not, you will need to speak up. If it's a smaller group of 10, 15, or 20 people, there may not be a microphone but, certainly, you need to speak in such a way that people can hear you clearly. An audience will only listen to a muffled voice for so long. But a loud, clear voice will engage the room.

5. Observe the Speed Limit. If you are like many Americans, you probably need to *slow down* in your speaking. Because humans think faster than they speak, this is a problem for almost everyone. Again, it can be overcome. It *must* be overcome if we are to have maximum effectiveness with our networking commercials. People want to be informed, not to have to scramble to follow a torrent of words.

---

[77] One excellent website is from WikiHow; see www.wikihow.com/ Project-Your-Normal-Speaking-Voice

Nerves can be a factor in this. It's normal to be nervous when you give a commercial in public. Nerves = speed. This is true especially if you're new to networking, but even those who are seasoned can often get nervous. Slow down! Take your time in saying what you're saying. Generally, slow speech = powerful speech.

6. Speak, Don't Read. It is important to know what you're going to say ahead of time. At least know the first line you're going to say and where you're going to end. You can fill in the gaps in between without memorizing the content. Both 1) memorizing and 2) reading from a card result in far more negatives than positives. Sure, either one is a comfortable crutch …if you like crutches. But you don't need a crutch, so avoid these two bad habits. If you have memorized your text, you will have a greater tendency to rush and speak even faster. And if you read, your voice will take on a different rhythm than the rhythm of speaking. Reading and speaking sound very different. TV news anchors and show hosts train very hard to make their reading from a teleprompter sound natural.[78]

If those negatives about reading a script are not enough, consider also that it is extremely difficult to develop a rapport with an audience when reading. The eye contact is painfully missing; the presentation becomes one-way, not two-way.

7. Articulate and Enunciate. Be careful that you're not mumbling. It is important to enunciate your comments and articulate your words, especially words that have more than two syllables. Slowing down will help you to enunciate better. Have you heard the phrase:

*"Sup? Jeet jet?"*

That is meaningless garble to most listeners. Slow it down and enunciate and you listeners will hear what you are really asking:

*"What's up? Did you eat yet?"*

Talking about eating, "eating your letters and syllables" is not a good thing unless you're eating alphabet soup. Swallowing consonants and syllables is a wide-spread shortcut in casual speech. Avoid that in public speaking. That bad habit is guaranteed to confuse your audience. The longer they spend translating your words, the more of the next sentence they will miss.

Actors practice articulating by putting marbles in their mouths and then trying to speak. It forces them to make the mouth motions needed to clearly pronounce words.

---

[78] See, for example: http://www.mrmediatraining.com/2017/01/16/four-tips-when-speaking-from-a-teleprompter

Here are some quick examples of phrases that will stop the flow of understanding by making your listeners have to do a half-second translation. People often drop letters, especially the middle "t" in many words. We've emphasized the sounds, syllables, or letters that have been swallowed.

| <u>Many People Say:</u> | <u>When What They Mean Is:</u> |
|---|---|
| Profes'ial den'is | pro-fes-si**on**-al den-**t**is-**t** |
| Bi'ness cus'mer | bu**s**-**in**-ess cus-**to**-mer |
| Ne'workin 'spdeez | ne**t**working **ex**per**t**ise |
| Winner med'e'olist | win-**t**er met-e-**or**-ol-**og**ist |

It's okay for you to need a microphone; it's not okay to make your audience need subtitles. When you mumble and "eat your words," it may also send the message that you're not confident or that you don't have enthusiasm about your product or service. You don't want to give the impression you are ashamed of your own career.

Be aware, at a distance of over 20 to 30 feet, your audience stops hearing consonants being spoken. They mainly hear vowels. Fortunately, most listener's brains are quick enough to be able to unconsciously replace the consonants and insert them where they are essentially now missing. But this only works to a point. The more consonants you mumble and the greater the distance between your mouth and your ear the less the audience will understand. The audience will finally just tune you out.

<u>8. Own Your Own Name.</u> This last one sounds obvious and simple. Yet, it is probably the most important of all, and it is often the most neglected. Be sure to articulate clearly *the most essential* items in your commercials. What are those essential items? How about your name and the name of your company?

Obvious? Apparently not.

At a recent networking meeting, the participants were asked to give their names and the names of the businesses they represented.

The first very first person to stand up said, "Hello everyone. I'm J'nfrwmmson, N'spird-'ands-ms'age, and I'm thrilled to be here with you." She then delivered her commercial. But now she was using clear articulate speech and a professional voice. Then, in conclusion, and to make sure we had heard her name and business the first time, she again rushed over her name, effectively slurring, "I'm J'nfrwmmson, N'spird-'ands-ms'age."

What? What? We totally missed her name and her company's name both times.

We were later told that it was Jennifer Williamson, owner and lead massage therapist of *Inspired Hands Massage*. Some people in the audience, those who were part of her network, already knew Jen and her company. Several did not. We did not.

Just why would Jennifer do that? Why would she garble the most important words of any commercial she could give? Why was it more important for us to know that she was "thrilled to be here" than for us to know her name and the name of her massage therapy business?

Nor was J'nfr-Wmmson alone. Over half of all those who presented that day did the exact same thing. There was El'nkolr 'f Pujit-Snd-Relty, (Ellen Koler of Puget Sound Realty), Shremdsn 'f Limpic-B'rnGrl (Sherry Madson of Olympic Bar and Grill), and on and on. We clearly learned of specials being offered and successful contacts made that week (both less essential information). However, we did not learn the <u>most essential</u> information, the names of the presenters and the businesses they represented. Why is that? If we asked any of those presenters the question: "Of all the many things that you could say in a business commercial, what are the most important words?" Every one of them would give the correct answer. They would each reply: "The most essential words are my name and the name of my business."

So why were they garbling these essential words?

Familiarity = garble. This is another example of the Curse of Knowledge. You may be the victim of your own unconscious assumptions that everyone knows your name as well as you do. They don't. You probably give out your name, perhaps the most precious thing you own, a dozen times a day. You may give out the name of your businesses a hundred times a day. If you're answering your own phone, you give your own name and your business name a thousand times a day. The question is, do you say,

"Hello, this is J'nfrwmmson, N'spird-'ands-ms'age. How may I help you?"

Or do you say,

"Hello, I'm (PAUSE) <u>Jennifer</u> (tiny pause) <u>Williamson</u> (tiny pause) of (tiny pause) <u>Inspired</u> (tiny pause) <u>Hands</u> (tiny pause) <u>Massage</u> (PAUSE). How may I help you?"

If you don't say your names clearly – set off by pauses – why not?

Think about it. You spent weeks coming up with the perfect name for your company. Perhaps you considered and rejected ideas for names like *"Needed Kneads"* or *"Soothing Solutions."* You threw around *"Body by Jennifer"* and *"Healing Touching"* before settling on *"Inspired Hands Massage."* It was perfect! Then you had to go online to register that business name. You paid good money, and a lot of it, to have a neon sign made with that name. You put it on your letterhead and on your business cards. That name became the identity of your company. It became the essence of what you do. Does it make sense to sluff off your core identities by garbling the names? Just because those precious names have become second-nature to you, does not mean they are second-nature to your networking contacts. To you, those names are obvious.

Remember, to others, they are not. Enunciate the most essential feature of your trade – own your own name.

## TIC TOC, TIME YOUR COMMERCIAL

Since we're talking about the mechanics of delivering a power commercial, let's consider the timing issue. That involves the length of your commercial and its location on the agenda.

### TIME YOUR COMMERCIAL TO THE SECOND

As with so many things in life, timing is critical. We are creatures of the clock. This applies to networking commercials as well.

Professional networking groups vary as to how dogmatically they monitor the length of member commercials. You will need to gauge how structured your networking group really is. This will affect how you deliver your commercials. Group policies and practices range all the way across the spectrum. At one end are groups that are sloppy and extremely casual. The group doesn't have an assigned timekeeper and commercials are only approximately – timed if at all. If they run long but are interesting, the members don't care. If the meeting ends early because the presenter doesn't have much to say that week, that's fine, too. So, the entire set of commercials may take up a quarter of the meeting, half the meeting, or the bulk of the meeting. Nobody really knows. This is extremely casual.

At the other end of the spectrum are meetings that are structured to the point of being rigid. Almost all groups have a timekeeper. That's fine, and it's usually appreciated. But some groups carry it much further. If the presentation goes long, some group leaders will cut the speaker off in mid-sentence. If it ends early, the clock continues to run, and the presenter is expected to not sit down but to stand there in silence until the time runs down. This is not silence as a tool, this is silence as a punishment and a humiliation. That is extremely rigid.

Of course, there are many points in between. You need to clearly know the policies and culture of your group and where they fall between those two extremes. This will obviously affect how members give their networking commercials.

For most groups, running short or long by a few seconds is no big deal. However, don't make a habit of running long, even by a few seconds. Just don't do it. People will notice. It is like being late to places. Both become more of a habit than you think they will, and others come to think about you, or joke about you, as the one that always runs long or arrives late. "Oh, yeah! Here comes Karl to the podium. This one's going overtime. Did anyone send out for dinner? Chuckle,

chuckle. Do you have your sleeping bags? Ha, ha!" You don't want that reputation. If you fill all the time you are given but never go over, that's really powerful. This is the way you want people to think of you. You want them to see your network power (**NP**), not be the butt of their jokes or, even worse, scorn.

If you don't know your group's policies on timing commercials, assume they are flexible but not rigid. Still, always respect the time. Like Goldilocks and the three bears. You don't want your porridge or your presentations either too long or too short; you want them *j-u-s-t* right. Your commercial should always be timed to fit exactly within the time frame that was allotted to you. If you're allotted 30 seconds, don't exceed that parameter. On the other hand, be prepared to fill up that entire time frame. Failing to use up all of the time allotted implies a lack of attention or a lack of interest.

If you attend more than one networking meeting where one group gives you 30 seconds while the other gives you 60 seconds, know that ahead of time. Decide what can be either: 1) cut out of a longer commercial or 2) add to a shorter commercial. The time for this decision is *before* you present. Feeling flustered and having to fumble through your notes in front of the microphone with the audience watching is *not* what you want to be doing. That is a confidence destroyer and a credibility destroyer.

This applies to both too much content and too little content. To have to say, "One last thing I want to squeeze in, and then I'm finished" or "I'll just close with this one last comment" is rude, arrogant, and selfish. It is putting yourself above others. It is also embarrassing. On the flip side, having to say, "Well, that's all I have…. Guess the next person can have a little extra time" is disrespectful to the group and communicates a lack of organization. Worst of all, either too short or too long is off-putting to your fellow group members. You want to reach them, not offend them.

## LOCATE YOUR COMMERCIAL IN THE AGENDA

Know exactly where in the rotation you will be giving your presentation. Are you going to be the first, the last, or somewhere in between?

Being the first to present is not a bad thing. First impressions make lasting impressions. If you can strategically place yourself first, you will set the bar for all the other commercials. You will be amazed by how many later presenters will refer back to your commercial. This is especially true for those who are new, those who are less prepared, or those who are not implementing the kinds of content or style tips we are discussing. They will

*Seize Control of the Time and the Timing*

refer back to you and, when they do, they are placing the spotlight directly on you. In effect, these other people are giving commercials *for* you. Instead of one commercial, you get one + a third of someone else's + honorable mention in another + a quarter of yet another. How good is that? It is a victory for you. It is free airtime.

As enriching as that is, being the last person to present a networking commercial is also powerful. Why is that? Because of the law of recency. The last thing we hear sinks into our minds deeply. The last commercial sticks in our memories the longest – i.e., it is sticky just by virtue of being the last. If it is also sticky for other reasons, then it is double-sticky. In TV reality competitions like *The Voice, American Idol,* or *America's Got Talent,* the first act never gets the golden buzzer. The role of the first act is to set the bar for the show, but it is less likely to be remembered by the audience. No, it is the show-ender that is remembered because of the law of recency.

Of course, we can't always be the first or the last presenter. We can't control that. So, what can you do when you are in the middle of the pack? That's where you will usually be. There can only be one person to start and one to finish and you can't engineer either of those positions every week. So, what can you do?

One tip is to use the tool of _silence_. When you stand up, give 2 or even 3 solid seconds of pure silence. It will cause your audience to look up and wonder, "What? What's happening? What am I missing here?" They will turn their attention toward you. It creates a separation between you and the previous presenter. In a way, it is a start-over. You have made yourself the first presenter after all.

Suppose you find you are following a great commercial by someone else and it has gotten everyone's attention. Maybe the presenter knocked it out of the park. People are laughing or giggling, or they're emotionally involved or even upset. Here is another time when you need to create a gap between that presentation and your presentation. Otherwise they will be thinking about the previous commercial and not yet listening to yours.

Again, you do not want to piggy-back that commercial. Don't say, "Well, Sue just nailed that presentation, didn't she! Good ole' Sue. Thanks, Sue!" That would be giving her another commercial. You would be ceding your time to her.

Better to cede the time to the wind. This time don't just have 2 or 3 seconds of silence; make it 4 or 5 seconds. That sounds like a long time wasted, but it isn't. It is time well spent. Besides, those seconds are _lost anyway_! The audience is still reeling from the previous commercial. They aren't ready for you.

Be warned, when you are pausing for that long and all eyes are upon you, it will feel like forever. But it isn't. And, in fact, it isn't silent at all – not in your mind. You are doing your self-talk, "If you speak, you lose. Do Not speak! Let silence work." Count it out in silence in your mind: "One thousand one, one thousand two…." Imagine the audience calming down and transitioning to you. Build that wall of silence between the previous presentation and yours. Make silence work for you. Lower the theatrical curtain on that last act and raise it back up on your own act. You have become the next "first presenter" again.

A second tip if you find your presentation in the middle of a dozen or more is to use <u>movement</u>. Don't just rise from your chair; move away from the people around you. Eyes will track your movement. Heads will turn. They will track you to where you give your commercial and they will track you back to your seat. In effect, you are creating bookends for your commercial. That will make it stand out. That will help make it sticky.

## THE POWER PLAY OF PRACTICE

We've given you several very helpful tools and plays. They will be no good at all unless you are willing to...

# Practice, practice, practice!

Networking commercials are both self-correcting and self-improving – *if* you are willing to practice. The more you give the commercials, the better they become. In this way, sharing weekly commercials is like the "School of Soft Knocks." They teach you skill after skill in a real-time setting with an audience who will support and encourage you through every stumble and every fall. In this way, your network group is like a mini-graduate school in networking and public speaking.

Look at it this way. Each and every time you give a network commercial with your best effort, it is like a dress rehearsal for the following week. There are 52 weeks in a year. Allowing for sickness and holidays, you will stand up in front of a group of your peers around 45 times per year. How can that amount of practice fail to help you?

- If you didn't know how to swim, but you got into a pool 45 times, wouldn't you end up being a strong swimmer by the end of the year?
- If your bowling average started out at 90, but you went bowling 45 times, wouldn't your average rise?
- If you couldn't walk around the block without wheezing and leg pain, but you went out for a brisk walk 45 times a year, wouldn't you be able to walk to the store and back without breaking a sweat in a year's time?

- If you are a terrible cook and barely know how to boil an egg, but you baked cupcakes or cookies for the local homeless shelter 45, wouldn't you be considered a "dessert chef" by the time the year ended?

Why would public speaking be any different? It only stands to reason. Practice in anything brings improvement. If standing in front of a small group and chatting about your career now causes goosebumps, ringing in your ears, and a cold chill, after a year or so it will become a fun highlight of your week. You will look forward to sharing your new ideas and telling a joke or two with your friends.

That's simple cause-and-effect.

It's not that doing a task repeatedly, on an ongoing basis, makes the task any simpler. It doesn't. What repeated practice will do is dramatically increase your ability to do the task well.

We assume you'll have quite a bit of apprehension and raw nerves the first time you deliver a commercial.

That's normal anytime that you stand up and face a group of listeners. Just being able to stand up, smile and even *begin* to speak can be a challenge for many people.

Some people even say they *hate* to speak in public and they *hate* to meet new people. People with this degree of fear will sometimes avoid even going to networking meetings simply because of their trepidation.

Yet, in most formal networking groups, they are asked to stand up and speak. The fact they've even shown up and are willing to be put on the spot, says a lot about them. They're willing to overcome their fears. So, with great reluctance they do it. And so will you.

With this kind of practice, you will grow from being able to make a simple introduction, to sharing something about yourself, and finally talking about your business or industry in short 30- to 60-second commercials. How will you fare?

Actually, you will fare very well.

Remember, you know this topic. You are not being asked to lecture about the jet fuel, the gluten content of foods, or the fjords of Norway. You are being asked to talk about something you know and love: your career, your field, your business. You can do this. You are the expert in the room on your career.

Here's an idea: it will help to memorize the first sentence of your commercial before you begin.

If you are one of those people who freeze up and blank out as soon as they stand up in front of the podium, this will help you. Practice it. It's only one sentence. Knowing the first sentence that you're going to say will help you break through that curtain of fear that so many people feel at the beginning of a presentation. It's like diving into the deep end. Once you're in there, you can swim okay. It's just diving off the edge of the pool that is the scary part. It's like dropping the spark into the tinder. Once the flame catches, the fire will take care of itself.

Remind yourself, too, your fellow networkers are not your judge and jury; they are your friends, or soon will be. Many of your listeners are in your top 12%. They are there to help you succeed. Many times, one or two of them will come up afterwards to compliment you on various elements of your commercials. That kind of positive feedback will make you feel wonderful. It is a tremendous boost to hear. We aren't talking flattery; we are talking validation.

Seasoned networkers in your group know you can benefit from their assistance. You are far from the first new member of the group to struggle, and you won't be the last. People come into networking all the time. They want to help you and other new networkers understand the power of networking and how to harness that power (**NP**). Helping you is an opportunity for them to grow through service. Senior networkers fully understand the truism that we quoted in the *Introduction* to this book: "celebrate the success of others" for the rising tide of their successes will "float all ships."[79] With those kinds of positives, many people have gone from being extremely timid to extremely comfortable in just 6 months to a year. This will happen to you, too. Then, if you ever have to face an audience of people who are not your friends, you'll have the skills, the facility, and the confidence to pull it off successfully.

Commercials are not long, and yet they present a priceless opportunity to hone your public speaking skills, build your confidence, and overcome your fears. But you must be willing to practice by giving commercials often, preferably weekly. So, the first power play for you is to practice your commercials often in group meetings that are full of supportive senior networkers.

In this chapter, we have looked at how to effectively present networking commercials in a group meeting. In the next chapter, we turn to the very important topic of how to make the most out of networking BRING!-type meeting meetings.

---

[79] Quote taken from Phillips, Susan Elizabeth, 2001, in *Romance Writer's Report*; see: http://quotationsbywomen.com/authorq/52222/

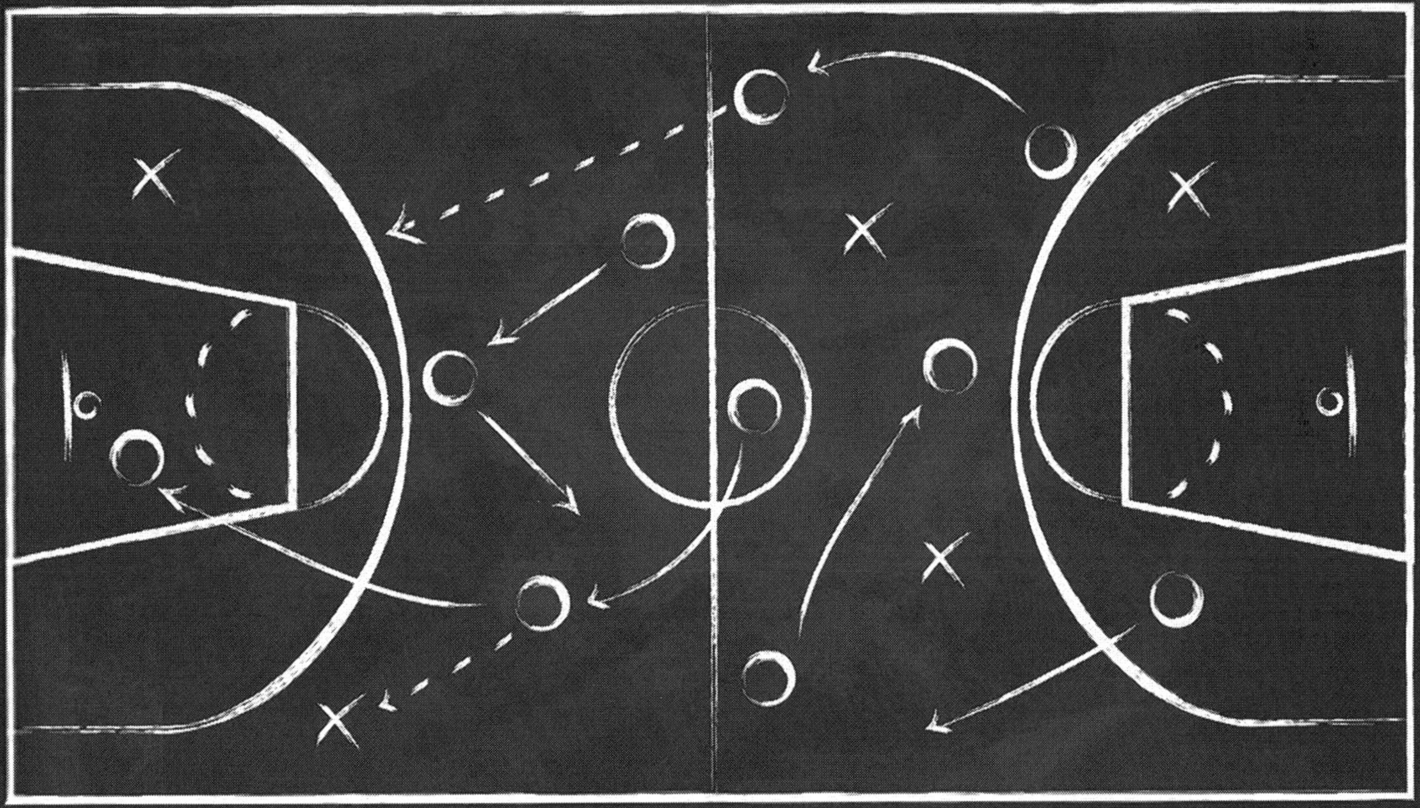

# CHAPTER 15

# BECOMING A MEMBER OF A BRING!-TYPE MEETING

Congratulations! You've mastered a lot. In Part One, you learned about networking, networking mindsets, the Rule of 12, and the formula for network power (**NP**). In Part Two, you learned about types of networking groups and how to assess them for logistics and tone. Hopefully, you've now selected not just a group, but a BRING!-type meeting that is just right for you. Then, in Part Three, you learned about networking commercials including what they are and power plays and style elements to make them sticky.

This chapter will put all that together and address your benefits and your role as a group member. It will provide tips for making your regular attendance at the group meetings and other networking functions pay off in many important ways – most importantly in the giving and receiving of relevant referrals (**RR**).

## MEMBERS SELL THROUGH... NOT TO

There's a time to Network, and a time to Sell.

Remember the networking formula. You maximize the power of a network (**NP**) by creating contacts (**CC**), nurturing your network (**NN**), and sharing relevant referrals (**RR**). Therefore, the goal in a meeting is to network, not attempt to sell products or services. In fact, the attempt to increase **NP** by selling at a meeting actually results in a decrease of **NP**. Why?

First, it won't work. Selling to other salespeople when they are networking is almost always an immediate turn-off. It's not nurturing them (**NN**). You won't make a sale, you won't make a friend, and you won't nurture your existing friendships. In fact, you may lose a friend.

Second, it is usually a wasted opportunity. Creating contacts (**CC**) is about meeting and making new friends – not intruding on them. Use the precious time at a meeting to create and strengthen relationships and friendships (**NN**). The point is to not let a chance to meet people or share relevant referrals (**RR**) go to waste. Your agenda at a networking meeting is truly just to make contacts, share referrals, and serve others. As a member of a BRING!-type meeting, do the things that you know how to do in order to make other people feel important and to build relationships.

## PUT AWAY HAND-HELD DISTRACTIONS

You can only accomplish these objectives if you interact with the people around you, not with an electronic device. We get it – you're at a networking event and the presenter is boring. So, you have three choices:

1) Pay attention and learn what you can,
2) *Act* like you're paying attention, or
3) Get out the electronic device that is beckoning to you.

Current technology is amazing. We can do so much in the palm of our hand. However, smartphones are highly addictive and distracting.[80] According to one researcher, these devices "… act like a stimulant, not unlike caffeine, amphetamines, or cocaine."[81] Don't just mute them, put them away during a business meeting. As your mother taught you, there is a time and place for all things.

Are you one of those folks that *think* you are concealing the use of your device while using it?

Think again. If you are looking down at your hands and your fingers are moving, we know what you're doing. If your face is slightly lit up by a blue-ish glow, we know where you're looking. The very fact you are attempting to conceal the use of a device reveals you know it is rude. It is not what group members need to be doing. Even if the presenter is oblivious to your actions, those around you are not. The impression you're leaving your fellow attendees is unmistakable. It communicates that either:

---
[80] To learn about smartphone addiction, see: https://www.helpguide.org/articles/addictions/smartphone-addiction.htm.
[81] Victoria Dunckley, 2016, "Autism and Screen Time: Special Brains, Special Risks," *Psychology Today* – see: https://www.psychologytoday.com/us/blog/mental-wealth/ 201612/autism-and-screen-time-special-brains-special-risks.

- You don't have either the time or patience to spend building professional relationships.
- You appear to be self-important.
- The only reason you're attending the event is out of obligation.
- You don't want to be bothered by other group members.

Do you really want to be sending any of these messages? Remember, there will come a time when you will be the presenter at an event. You will hope that others are listening to what you have to say. You'll want to hear about the impact of your comments. You will *not* want an audience distracted by a plastic and glass competitor.

When you are part of the audience, be a good listener. The world is not in your hand, it is all around you. You must disconnect in order to connect. As we have been emphasizing, the primary reason to attend BRING!-type meetings as a member is to network. That usually means building others up and putting your device down.

## MEMBERS BUILD OTHERS WITH TESTIMONIALS

One way to build others up is to support them by oral testimonials. Testimonials are extremely valuable. A testimonial can be defined as a personal endorsement or professional recommendation affirming the character, expertise, and value of an individual or business, highlighting their efficacy and contributing in a professional setting.

When was the last time you invested five minutes and gave a testimonial for a person in your network? Your opinion matters and can make a tremendous impact. When you provide a brief testimonial, keep five basic rules in mind.

1. <u>Keep it positive</u> – You are giving a testimonial, not a review. Listeners want to know the good qualities. They want to know the reasons it's good to do business with this person. They want to know why this person is an asset in your life.
2. <u>Be specific</u> – Point out precise traits. Tell what experiences you've had that demonstrate specific attributes such as determination, charisma, communication, and quality. Be abundant in your praise, but also be specific in how you know this.
3. <u>Remember a mother may hear this</u> – Don't ever embarrass the person. Say things a mother would love to hear. Use the person's name a few times throughout the testimonial.
4. <u>Encourage the reader to use the product or services</u> – Testimonials can help move a sale along are extremely valuable. The testimonial is a format for you to do referral marketing. Use this forum to say you will be a repeat customer. Recommend the person to your friends so they can feel confident in using this person to solve their issues.

5. <u>Express gratitude for your experience</u> – Convey appreciation by saying how happy you are with the results. If you have known this person for a long time, point it out. Let them know you are happy to have this person as part of your network.

Consider putting your oral endorsement into written form where it can be posted on social media sites, passed to potential clients, and even used in advertising. Give permission for the person to utilize your testimonial in ways that will help. Send a copy as an attachment to an email. Post it on a social media page. When you take the time to write a testimonial, the impact can be significant. It can strengthen relationships, assist in business development, and give someone a much-needed emotional boost.

## MEMBERS LISTEN MORE – TALK LESS

An easy way to build people up is as simple as listening to them. A rookie mistake in networking is to talk too much. To be an effective member of any BRING!-type meeting, try listening more and speaking less. That's how you hit a home run or score a touchdown in your networking group.

### THE HUNGER TO BE HEARD

One of the undiagnosed diseases of our society is a great emptiness deep within each one of us. Truly can it be said that there is a "famine in the land." It is "not a famine of food, nor a thirst for water."[82] It is a hunger to be heard, a thirst to be listened to, a ravishing need to be validated and acknowledged. The pervasive famine is occurring from sea to shining sea. You can be a refuge from the famine.

Listening is a lost art. We have become a nation of talkers; an ocean of one-uppers. Test this for yourself. At your next social gathering, listen to what is happening around you. People will politely appear to be listening to others. In reality, most are only waiting for the speaker to pause. Then they swoop in with their own favorite story, or opinion, or theory. What they think or have experienced is always a little better, bigger, and of course more interesting than what the speaker had been saying. Their truth is always more true than the other guy's truth.

Some people don't even wait for the pause. They just talk over the other person. Interrupting seems to be a national pastime. Husbands do this to wives; wives do this to husbands. We have all experienced it; you probably do it, too. As Stephen R. Covey summarized, "Most people do not listen with the intent to understand; they listen with the intent to reply."[83]

---

[82] Amos 8: 11 KJV.
[83] Covey, Stephen R. *The 7 Habits of Highly Effective People: Powerful Lessons in Personal Change*. Free Press.

For a very few people, it's not like this. For them, listening is a part of their lives. They have always listened well. No surprise that they draw others to them. Such listeners may end up in sales or in one of the helping professions. When asked, "What made you seek a career working with people?" they typically respond:

- "People always came to me wanting to talk. I figured I might as well make a career of it."
- "I was always a listener; people gravitated toward me."
- "Even in high school, people came to me because I had what they called a listening ear."
- "I've often had people come to me to share their sad stories."

Such listeners are the rare and lucky few who developed this skill in childhood. Others learned it and became intentional listeners. Either way, they are very attractive to those starving to be heard. You may be one of those natural or intentional listeners who nourish others through listening. But many, if not most, people are too hungry themselves to feed those around them. And, yes, you are feeding – by listening

That's why, as a listener, your value to others increases. Because you are not just a great listener; you become a great validator. You pay others the ultimate respect of sincerely valuing opinions and stories, which is to say, you validate other people's core selves.

Oprah Winfrey knew this truth. Her popular *Oprah Winfrey Show* ran for 25 years and 4,561 episodes. On the final episode of that final show, she made the following significant summary:

> *I've talked to nearly 30,000 people on this show, and all 30,000 had one thing in common: They all wanted validation. If I could reach through this television and sit on your sofa or sit on a stool in your kitchen right now, I would tell you that every single person you will ever meet shares that common desire. They want to know: "Do you see me? Do you hear me? Does what I say mean anything to you?"* [84]

This begs the questions: Exactly why are people so hungry to be heard? Why is the need so deep and so pervasive? A partial answer is offered by Blake Ostler who wrote in *Fire on the Horizon*:

> *We have all received the message at some point: I am no darn good. I am stupid. I will never be enough. I am not worthy. No one likes me. While we have all been on the receiving end of these messages, the shift occurs when we truly believe these lies about ourselves. When we accept the belief that we are truly worthless and are merely pieces of meat destined to rot in the earth, then we sell out on ourselves. We forget our*

---

[84] Quote from: www.oprah.com/oprahshow/the-oprah-winfrey-show-finale_1/7

*magnificence.... Moreover, it hurts at the very core to accept such beliefs about ourselves. My heart hurts when I feel rejected, stupid, unworthy, and inadequate.*

If you will listen to others – to their jokes or their theories or their stories, then maybe, just maybe, that core hurt will hurt a little less. If you don't believe the lie that they are fundamentally worthless and unworthy, then maybe, in some small way, they won't have to believe it either. So, keep trying. Validate others, again and again, with the goal of feeding the hole they feel inside.

Social media proves this point about feeding and satisfying this hunger. How much time is spent adding friend, after friend, after friend in a search for attention – in a search for a "life"? But there is always someone else who receives more comments or has more followers. The principle of "loneliest when in a crowd" holds true in the often-frustrating world of social media. We can never have enough "online friends" to fill the holes in our hearts. If you have 10, someone else has 100. If you have 100, someone else has 1,000.

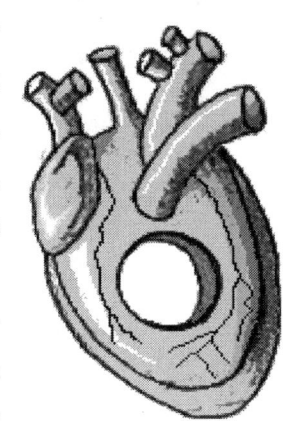

## CULTIVATING THE ART OF LISTENING

Fortunately, the art of listening can be cultivated, at least to some degree. Listening, not talking, is a skill and a mindset that you can, and should, develop. Warning! We are asking for a tremendous sacrifice to acquire this skill. You will have to put off your own hunger in order to feed the hunger of others. The reward will be well worth any sacrifice. Below are two introductions by two different people at a networking event. With which one would you rather create a contact?

> *Introduction 1: Hello. Audrey told me that <u>you</u> are the one to meet. They say <u>you</u> own that wonderful French restaurant downtown. People rave about <u>your</u> place! <u>Your</u> story of how <u>you</u> got into French cuisine has got to be a great one. How did <u>you</u> turn <u>your</u> interest in France into <u>your</u> success in <u>your</u> restaurant? (Big pause – silence – wait – listen.)*

Did you notice the sincere build-ups and validations included in the first introduction? Did you listen to the listening? This is feeding the hungry. We should add that listening actively and showing sincere interest in others is not a parlor trick designed to serve only you. It must be born of a love of others. Anything insincere will be immediately sniffed out for the falsehood that it is.

When sincere, though, it will shock the listener. It will bring flushed cheeks. "You want to know about *me*? I want to hang around nearby and feed more on your validation of my existence."

Compare that first introduction to the next one:

> *Introduction 2:* Hello. Let *me* introduce *myself*. *I'm* an artist with *my* own studio. *I'm* pretty good, too, even if *I* do say so *myself*, especially since *I have* arthritis in *my* thumb. *I've* got arthritis in *my* knees and *my* neck. Just *my* burden in *my* life. *I* guess *I'm* getting old, ha, ha! Anyway, more about *me*: *My* art skill was obvious to *me* and *my* parents. *I* guess *I'd* been given an eye for art. *My* business is called, "Bob's *I* for Art." Catchy, huh! *I* made that up *myself*, ha, ha! Anyway, *I've* done *my* art all *my* life. *My* career started with *me* sharing *my* art free. *I'd* never do that now. *I'm* too busy, and *I'm* too in demand. In *my* first job, *I* saw *my* future in front of *me*, staring at *me* right in *my* face. *I* was destined to… wait, why are you walking away?

Okay, okay.… This is admittedly extreme but notice the self-aggrandizements in the awkward and failed introduction. Did you also hear the hunger for validation? For some readers, even reading through the text is an ordeal. They want to skip reading and move on as their minds wander. That gut-reaction is just as real in spoken words. Talking about yourself does little to fill the hunger for validation that gnaws in the hungry stomachs of your listeners and potential contacts.

## MEMBERS BUILD OTHERS WITH HUMOR

There's another way to use your group membership. Build up others in addition to listening to them. Use sincere compliments and awe factors. However, be cautious with your choice of humor.

At a recent networking event, the group leader stood up to begin the meeting. As she looked out over the 38 professionals seated in front of her and saw the anticipation on their faces and their bright smiles, she was overcome with emotion. With great sincerity and feeling she said, "What a lovely sight you all are! You are all so attractive – both outside and inside. What handsome men and women! How beautiful you all are!" That was a confidence builder that built up.

Three or four friends were sitting around one table near the back. One of them, Helen, had spent a long time on makeup and had put on her favorite business suit. One of her friends whispered. "All but you, Helen! She didn't mean you. Not wearing a man's suit. Ha, ha!" That was a confidence crusher that tore down.

Why do people do that? Why do they think that negative humor and sarcasm is funny? Can you imagine a member of a BRING!-type meeting saying such a thing? Like most people, Helen was already insecure, and she was broadsided by the thoughtless jest. She didn't have her normal defenses up to protect herself; she hadn't expected to need them – not among friends. As a result, the joke ripped off the scab that she had carefully grown over long-forgotten wounds. Her confidence was shattered in an instant.

How much more positive would it have been to emphasize Helen's success at her business persona, not joke about pretend deficiencies? There is not a single person who would have joked about her "being fat" if she really were overweight. And there is not a single person who would have joked about her "ugly mouth" if she really had a slight cleft lip. Yet, people feel free in joking about her not being one of the "lovely ones." Why? Ironically, it's because she looks just fine. But what if *she* doesn't believe she looks fine? Most people don't. Helen's "friend" had inadvertently reopened a secret sore.

And, here's the irony: positive humor would have been just as easy. The group member could have leaned over and joked, "She must have been looking right at you, Helen! We're just lucky to be basking in your glow. Ha, ha!" It would have been just as funny, and it would have built her up. That's the kind of humor we would expect a group member to use. A light compliment brightens anyone's day and helps build confidence in both the teller and the hearer.

## QUIT NEGATIVE HUMOR; EMBRACE POSITIVE HUMOR

According to an article in *Psychology Today*, psychologists have identified four types of humor.[85] The first two tear down, while the last two build up. It is important to know the difference so that you can eliminate the first two from your networking efforts and embrace the last two.

> *1. Aggressive Humor – Involves put-downs or insults targeting individuals. This is the humor used by aggressive comedians – the put-down artists, such as Don Rickles or Joan Rivers.*

Aggressive humor is often funny, at least on the surface. It is not difficult to recognize this kind of humor. There is always:

1. Someone who is the victim – the butt of the joke
2. It is usually followed by some kind of cringing gesture.

---

[85] From Ronald E. Riggio, 2015, "The Four Styles of Humor: What do You Find Funny? How do You Use Humor?" *Psychology Today* in https://www.psychologytoday.com/ us/blog/cutting-edge-leadership/201504/the-4-styles-humor; This brief article summarizes research by Martin, Puhlik-Doris, Larsen, Gray, & Weir, 2003, "Individual Differences in Uses of Humor and Their Relation to Psychological Well-being," *Journal of Research in Personality*, 37 (1), pp. 48-75.

Funny it may be – but look deeper. Psychologists point out that <u>subconsciously</u> this humor may be intended to harm. This is the type of humor used by psychological bullies. It is "disparagement humor."[86] If confronted, the joke-teller simply denies the aggression claiming, "It was just a joke!"

In front of an audience, this is called, "roasting," and it can include extremely personal, even vicious, insults made "in jest." Another author pointed out that the "motto of these events is, 'We only roast the ones we love,' which is intended to capture the idea that these insults are …born of affection."[87] The humor usually goes too far, not that the target would ever admit to the hurt felt.

Without an audience, this is called "repartee," which is "a succession or interchange of clever retorts: amusing and usually light sparring with words."[88] But when does "light sparring" become "heavy hurt"? The target will try to dismiss the sting and laugh it off, but that is a cover-up. So, they return it in kind and the hurt is inflicted on both sides.

Sometimes, the aggressive humor is only what was taught. It is a bad habit learned in childhood. Aggressive humor was the kind used by Helen's insensitive "friend." This kind of humor has no place in professional networking. You want to share many things in your professional network – pain is not one of those. Your goal as a member of a BRING!-type meeting is to build confidence in others, not destroy it.

> *2. Self-Defeating Humor* – *Putting yourself down in a "poor me" fashion…. The late comedian Rodney Dangerfield would be an example. ("I don't get no respect" or "I was an ugly baby.")*

Instead of putting down others, self-deprecating humor puts down self. It can be based on false modesty or self-hatred. Either way, it's destructive to your confidence. Jokes like the following may be funny at first, but they may also be revelatory:

- *I specialize in screw-ups. It is a job that's commensurate with my abilities.*
- *It's trash day? Whatta ya know, a day named after me!*
- *LOL – I'll mess that up too. It's my modus operandi….*
- *What problems do I have – other than just being ugly, fat, and stupid? Ha, ha!*

There may be a hidden desire that the listener will disagree with the self-attack and contradict it. That seems like a rather sad and desperate way to get a compliment. Positive feedback that

---

[86] Thomas Ford, 2016, "Psychology Behind the Unfunny Consequences of Jokes That Denigrate." See: http://theconversation.com/psychology-behind-the-unfunny-consequences-of-jokes-that-denigrate-63855
[87] Jesse Marczyk, 2017, "Why Do We Roast the Ones We Love?" in *Psychology Today*. See www.psychologytoday.com/us/blog/pop-psych/201705/why-do-we-roast-the-ones-we-love
[88] Definition from: www.merriam-webster.com/dictionary/repartee

is derived through manipulation isn't going to build much confidence. It's kind of like buying yourself a Christmas present and then putting it under the tree. Somehow, it doesn't quite have the same magic.

Seasoned professional networkers can avoid the first kind of (aggressive) humor fairly easily. The second kind (self-defeating) is harder to overcome. Sometimes that's because they, like many people, don't yet understand the inherent and destructive nature of this kind of humor. Maybe it is also another bad habit picked up from the playground or an older sibling. As a group member, this is another habit to break immediately and completely. It is not only self-defeating; it is also networking group-defeating.

> *3. Self-Enhancing Humor – Laughing at yourself, such as making a joke when something bad has happened to you. [It is] trying to find the humor in everyday situations and making yourself the target of the humor in a good-natured way.*

If the first two kinds of humor are, sadly enough, easy to use, self-enhancing humor can be much more difficult to pull off. There is a fine line between being funny and being arrogant and self-absorbed. Here are two examples that succeeded moderately well:

- "Well, what do you know. I seem to be a genius after all!"
- "Explain that to me, would you? Don't worry; I'm a quick learner."

You can be the judge of how well the next three work:

- "Here, come sit next to me. You've managed to make it to the front of a very long line of my admirers!"
- "If my network grew any larger, they'd have to call it a phone book. Ha, ha!"
- "I know the answer to that, of course, but if I told you, I'd have to kill you."

There is nothing wrong with using this type of humor in your networking – if you can successfully navigate the tightrope between entertaining and arrogance.

> *4. Affiliative Humor – Using humor to bring people together to find the humor in everyday life – the types of jokes told by comedians like Jerry Seinfeld....*

"Affiliative" is defined as "the formation of social/emotional bonds with others or the desire to create such bonds."[89] Now, that sounds a lot like networking! The word comes from Latin,

---

[89] Definition from: https://www.merriam-webster.com/dictionary/affiliative.

*affiliare,* meaning "to adopt" and *filius,* or "son." So, the researchers clearly had in mind humor that bonds the listeners together. That certainly belongs in your network. The trick is to know what bonds and what divides. What is funny to one person may not be to another. Be careful! Humor about one political party may bond followers but alienate the other side. With true affiliative humor, we all come together because we all laugh together, much like coming together by eating together, rejoicing together, or experiencing tragedy together. We laugh together at the following:[90]

- "Doctor, when my hand gets better, will I be able to play the piano?" "Of course," replies the doctor. "That's great, because I could never play the piano before!"
- Mother to son: "Did you take a bath today?" Son: "No. Is one missing?"
- I didn't believe that my dad was stealing from his job as a road worker until I got home and all the signs were there.

Truly, humor is the best medicine.[91] This kind of humor neither builds anyone up or tears anyone down; it builds a shared bond making it a must for your networking – it *is* networking. This will build confidence in self and others.

As good as Affiliative Humor is, however, these researchers missed a fifth type of humor. The fifth type of humor that we suggest is called:

## THE BEST: CONFIDENCE-ENHANCING HUMOR

*Building others up in a constructive manner that compliments and enhances them, all delivered as humor.*

Earlier we proposed that the other ladies in the group could have built up Helen's confidence by saying, "The President must have been looking at you, Helen! We're just lucky to be basking in your glow." This is confidence-enhancing humor. This is how group members should use humor. Other examples of Confidence-Enhancing humor include any of the following and anything you dream up (but *make sure you are sincere*):

- "I'm not the professional you are, Helen. I'd like to be you when I grow up!"

---

[90] Examples taken from: https://examples.yourdictionary.com/examples- of-humor.html
[91] The origin of this phrase is very old. It was used by Readers' Digest magazine but predates that. It may date from the Bible. Proverbs 17: 22 in ASV reads, "A cheerful heart is a good medicine," while KJV reads, "A merry heart maketh a cheerful countenance," and the GNT renders it as "Being cheerful keeps you healthy."

- *"If you keep up your business successes, Helen, your child care business will soon become one of those blue-chip Fortune 500 companies!"*
- *"It's okay, everyone, Helen is here! We have a networking expert who can straighten us all out."*

With a little practice, you'll soon become a master. This is the kind of humor that James (Chapter 6) and Tanya (Chapter 7) use. In fact, if you look around, you'll begin to see this type of humor already being used by senior networkers. It will be a little bit like buying a Volvo. Suddenly, you notice Volvos being driven all over town. The point is, you can do this, too. It takes a little effort, but the end product is well worth it and you have another way to build others in your meetings and elsewhere.

A seasoned '212-level' professional networker is well aware of the first two types of negative humor (Aggressive and Self-defeating). They can quickly identify insulting roasts and repartee. They will find ways to take the sting out of any negative attack of self or others by deflecting the jab. For example, someone says, "Hey, late again, eh Bob!" the seasoned networker will interject, "Oh, but he's so worth waiting for!" If they overhear someone saying, "Say, Sally, isn't that the same commercial you gave last month? Are you trying to get it right? Ha, ha!" they will interject something like, "I liked it! That's what makes a classic commercial; it deserves to be heard again and again!" When a new networker puts himself down with a "joke" like, "Well, here I go to make a fool out of myself again!" they counter with, "Frank, I love seeing the progress you're making. I find it inspiring."

These 212-level networkers typically become masters at all three types of positive humor (Self-Enhancing, Affiliative, and most of all Confidence-Building). You can train yourself to do the same. And, if you are guilty of using either a negative aggressive humor or self-defeating humor, resolve now to make a change and give it up. When you think of a snappy _put-down_, pause a moment. See if you can shift it to a _put-up_. Your joke will be just as funny – maybe funnier – and it will build confidence rather than crush confidence.

## MEMBERS CONVEY, THEY DON'T SPRAY

Is there a place for a physical business card in our world? Is that a place for them at a BRING! meeting? The answer is a resounding yes. Business cards have not gone out of style. They still fill several essential functions. But business cards never _replace_ networking, they _supplement_ networking. Their best role is to convey simple, though essential, bits of information. Other uses can actually damage your networking efforts.

## BUSINESS CARDS CAN HELP OR HURT

Some business professionals believe business cards are a waste of money. That could not be further from the truth – *if* they are used properly. There are two ways that business cards can help you.

1. Cards Create a Positive Impression and Enhance Credibility. A well-designed business card makes a statement about you. It can be tempting to save a few dollars by printing your own cards at home. That is like insincere flattery – most recipients can see right through it. Rather than conveying professionalism, homemade cards convey cheapness and shortcuts.

When preceded by a solid handshake and eye-to-eye contact, a well-designed card makes a positive statement about your professionalism that will stick with the contact. By contrast, a casually dropped name is instantly forgotten. As has been pointed out:

> *A well thought out card…is the one tangible thing a person will take away from a chance meeting.*[92]

Avoid the mistake of overcrowding a card with information clutter. Clutter reduces credibility. Instead, use a large print and keep it simple and clean. Avoid a font size that requires a magnifying glass. You want to convey information, yes, but a business card is a classic case of less being more.

2. Cards Are a Cost-effective Way to Convey Simple Information. How often have you wanted to exchange phone numbers before or after a meeting, but neither of you had a pen? Either that or you couldn't find a scrap of paper. You fumble around and come up with the back of a shopping receipt. The information is written down, but in an awkward, forgettable place. Worse, information can easily be mis-transcribed. Incorrect phone numbers can cancel otherwise hard-won networking contacts (the precious **CC** in the formula). Website addresses can be bungled. The classic example is the difference between writing down, "whitehouse.*com*" and "whitehouse.*gov*."[93] Even if the paper and pen are found, and the information is written down without a mistake, it has been written down in an odd place. It will likely be tossed or lost. Enter the business card. For minimal cost, names, phone numbers, company logos, and web addresses are exchanged without error.

---

[92] Quote from: http://thestartupmag.com/business-card-value

[93] Whitehouse.com is an adult website that started in 1997. At one point, it contained explicit content including uncensored discussion of politics and soft porn. At one point, the site claimed an annual income of a million dollars and 80,000 hits a day. Some were intentional; some were mis-typings of people trying to find whitehouse.gov. In 2006, PC World ranked whitehouse.com as #13 on its list of "The 25 worst web sites." See: https://en.wikipedia.org/wiki/Whitehouse.com

THE PROFESSIONAL NETWORKER'S PLAYBOOK

There are also two ways in which business cards can hurt you:

1. Business Cards can be Intrusive and Unwelcome. In a sense, business cards are like mothers-in-law: sometimes they are welcome, sometimes not. We have all been attacked during a group meeting by a person going through the room handing out business cards as fast as possible with little, if any, introduction. These people are "sprayers" because they spray the room with their business cards. It seems to be vital to the sprayer that every person has *his* or *her* business card. Someone should tell these sprayers this action can turn around and bite them. Rather than convey a positive impression, it can betray them.

When you see an individual going through a crowd and asking for, or distributing, business cards, look out. You can be sure some form of contact you don't necessarily want is not far behind. Because business cards can be intrusive and unwelcome, many seasoned professionals become guarded about giving out their cards – especially to a sprayer.[94]

2. Distributing Cards Too Lightly Cheapens the Cards. You have probably endured the misery of watching really bad travel slides. It typically goes something like this:

> *Yes, well, this one's blurry, but you can kind of make out Mary feeding the chipmunks. This next one's not as good, though. I took it into the sun by mistake. You can sort-of make out Junior getting his face licked by a buffalo – the big lump behind the light-burst is the buffalo.*

Why in the world can't people throw away the ones that are blurry, cut off, or have the light-burst and just show the photos that turned out well? The slide show would be so much better. It would hold the viewer's interest. It's a little like that with business cards. Treat them as the valuable tools that they are. Don't pass them out lightly and dilute their value. Never just spray them around the room. Don't cheapen business cards into disposable nothings by using them where they won't be received with the respect you want and need them to have.

Business cards are a little bit like salt at a fancy dinner. A bit can greatly enhance the flavor. But too much can spoil the steak or destroy the intent. So, sprinkle, don't spray.

---

[94] Some professionals have been known to carry an alternate business card to give out to sprayers or drop in collections being circulated in meetings. Rather than containing correct information that will bring unwanted follow-up, it contains non-working contact information that will guarantee the card will end up in recycling.

Business cards are an excellent tool to convey basic information in a few basic and appropriate situations:

1. A chance or unexpected introduction
2. Relaxed moments at a casual networking function
3. Before or just after a formal networking meeting
4. Exchange information after setting an appointment

At the beginning or ending of a meeting, you are likely to meet others with whom you want to connect. Exchanging business cards with these few (emphasis on, few) allows you to follow up the introductions with vital contact information without being clumsy or discourteous.

Business cards do not belong in the formal, business part of a meeting. It is neither the time nor the place for spraying. Unbelievably, there are some networking meetings that encourage the sprayer. When a meeting passes around baskets for business cards, spraying is being encouraged. This is really "card abuse." It really doesn't matter if the cards are being passed loosely, in a box, binder, or as a stack. In addition to cheapening the cares, passing them around during the actual meeting interrupts the flow of the activities. When the stack of cards arrives at a table, the meeting is suspended for everyone there. There is no good way to sift and take cards while listening and participating in the meeting. The meeting has been interrupted. You are no longer listening to the presenter while you fumble for the card and read it. If you knew the perfect referral for the presenter delivering the business commercial, due to the disruption you may miss the opportunity. The moment will pass because the cards were passed around. Oops! The sprayer has struck again. Only this time the whole room has turned into a group of sprayers.

Formal networking meetings should not create a target-rich environment for the sprayer. But what can you do if the practice is group-wide? There are actually several things you can do:

<u>1. Speak up</u>! If this practice is sanctioned by the group's policies, consider politely but frankly talking to the leadership. Explain the situation. Discuss how cards are much more effective if they are accompanied with face-to-face introductions. Express how extremely disruptive the spraying of business cards is to the meeting content that the leaders want to facilitate.

<u>2. Limit the Disruption</u>. Recommend as an alternative that a small stack of business cards be placed at the doorway. After the meeting, people could pick one up for a later phone call if the person they want to meet is involved in a conversation. Although not ideal, this practice is far better than disrupting the meeting.

In almost every case, a business card needs to be accompanied with a firm handshake and a verbal exchange. Then the card means something; then the card has power. A business card functions best when it records and/or summarizes information that has already been conveyed orally between two professionals.

Think of it this way. Professional business cards cost around five cents each. If sprayers spray their cards all over a meeting group of 40 people, that's only two dollars. So, if they spray them in one group meeting, what's to stop them from spraying them in other groups or in other locations? Certainly not cost.

It still would be under $15 or $20. That's only the cost of taking one prospect out for coffee or hot chocolate one time. So, from an economic point of view, there's not much incentive for sprayers to control themselves.

Try this. Let's increase the perceived value of a card. Let's pretend, for a moment, that the cards don't cost five *cents*, they cost five *dollars*. They don't – in money. But they certainly do in credibility. You would never spray $5.00 bills everywhere in a meeting, nor would you pass around a box full of $5.00 bills. Handing out business cards like that would cost you $200. And spraying them elsewhere would quickly increase to $1,000 and even more. Who would do this?

Keep in mind the reasons to avoid spraying cards go far beyond economics. However, thinking of it in dollars and cents may just give you the pause and incentive you need to give up the destructive temptation to spray your business cards.

If you think about it, spraying cards doesn't just mean they no longer have the credibility value they deserve, it actually equates to a **negative** value – at least in credibility and effectiveness. Not only do people not want your card, they now think less of you because you forced your business card upon them unwanted and uninvited. This was obviously not your intention.

The professional way to use a business card is to summarize a one-to-one interaction; not to violate a large group meeting. While it is essential to convey, please don't spray.

## ABC POCKETS FOR BUSINESS CARDS

When you attend any informal networking group and some larger formal networking groups, be prepared to receive a *lot* of business cards – some sprayed, some not. You will sometimes get a ridiculous amount of them. What can you do about that? Here is a helpful strategy for filtering those cards as they come in. They can be sorted into three categories: A, B, and C.

"A" Cards from A+ Contacts. Some of the business cards will come from new contacts you have just created (**CC**) and the summary information on those cards will be very important to you.

These are people with whom you've just had a productive conversation. It was probably a short conversation since a networking function where you are trying to meet people is not the right place to have long and involved conversations. The point is that you are genuinely interested in remembering that new person.

Designate one of your pockets as an "A pocket" for "A+ people." These are people at the top of your list. By the time you leave the meeting or event, you only have two to five cards in this pocket. These are people who you want to have immediate contact with. They are people you want to remember.

<u>"B" Cards Mean They'll "B for Another Time."</u> Most of the contacts we make, or renew, will be B-type contacts. They do not have the immediacy of an A-type contact. There will be others who you are going to contact within the next week or so. You know you had a conversation with them, but a follow-up is pushed out by several weeks before you renew that connection.

When you do re-contact those people, it is a good idea to reference the function where you met. Hopefully, you scribbled a note or two on the back of their cards so you will know how to refer to the person. If it was a mixer at a convention, then reference the convention, the mixer, and something positive about the convention you really enjoyed. See where that contact goes from there.

That is your "B" pocket.

<u>"C" Cards Mean "C You Later!"</u> Then there's the "C" pocket. The C pocket is for the sprayers. These are for the people who run around the room, not establishing any real contacts, just spraying out their cards to whoever will take one. Unbelievably, they will even interrupt other people's conversations in order to give out their cards. "Hi, there! Sorry to squeeze in but here's my card! Please call me later!" Really?

They're trying to collect other people's business cards, too. There's no telling what they'll do with all of them – maybe decorate a wall in their office. Who knows?

Those are C people and they go in the "C you later" pocket. They are people with whom you will <u>*not*</u> be making any contact at all.

Sprayers need to understand they have just stuck a demerit star on their foreheads (as well as wasting the nickel). Their cards will not go into your office and will not reach your filing system. Why? Because they are of no value to you. Those cards will be going to the business card boneyard. There's simply no reason for you to waste your time and energy because, even if you do later contact them, 99% of the time they're going to be in a hurry to make a sale, not to network. You have permission (if you need it) to discard those cards on the way out the door.

If you are a sprayer, please, please remember that networking functions are not for the purpose of selling. They are for the purpose of establishing or strengthening relationships.

## RUBBER DUCKIE FOLLOW-UPS

Let's talk about what happens at the end of most networking meetings or mixers. There will have been several people who you've met. You will have a few business cards in your "A" pocket, many in your "B" pocket, and hopefully none still in your "C" pocket.

What do you do with these cards? You've met or become reacquainted with all the A and B pocket people – now what?

Follow-up! Contact the Pocket "A" people within the next day or two – literally. Either call them or send them an email. Make it personal, personable, and non-threatening. "Hey, it was good seeing you at the function last night" or "It was great getting to know what you do. I'm interested in getting more information about that." Make it something along the lines of, "Say, can we get together over lunch?" or "Thanks for your time, Friday." Let them know that they're important enough for you to follow up.

It could be they are a perfect fit for your product or services and you're sharp enough to recognize it. As we've said, networking functions are the time to sell to..., not through.... The follow-up could have several objectives. It could be purely social. This may be someone you're glad to have in your network. You would want to arrange a PIQ. The follow-up could also have opened a door to a later sales opportunity. This follow-up call or email would be the time to set an appointment to pursue that. Let them know what you have to share with them and that it will be of great value to them.

It could be you have a referral for them. That's an even better one. Don't wait until you've actually made the referral. Get clarification so you're presenting them the right way – the way they would like to be presented. The point is to reconnect with these A+ contacts.

It could be that you're personally interested in their product or services. This is the best reconnection you could make. "As I said last night, I'm interested in a new roof (or a financial investment plan, or having my hair tinted blue, or a 3-tier wedding cake in the shape of a rocket ship)."

No matter which objective you have in mind, you are essentially making a screening decision. You are deciding if this is a contact where you are going to sell to (or from) or sell through. In other words, is this a contact for a sale, or somebody who you're going to add to your network as a referral partner?

Be forthright in this communication at this point. Don't dance around the daisies. Follow-up as quickly as possible, preferably the next business day. Be confident; be bold. Don't waste their time or your time. Jump in!

Keep in mind that they have met several people, especially if it was a large event or mixer. Revert back to the conversation you had. One effective trick is to have added a placeholder in your conversation from last night. Ideally, you said something like, "Look, I know you're going to meet a lot of people today, but I'm going to contact you later. There's a risk that you won't remember me, so this is how you're going to remember me." Then say, "Yellow rubber duckie."

You'll get a quizzical look.

Then you say, "Now, if I say 'yellow rubber duckie' in our contact in the next day or two, you'll remember exactly who you were talking to." They'll probably laugh and say, "Oh, okay!" You don't have to use the yellow duckie one. That's fine. But come up with some trigger for them to remember who you are.

Turn now to your "B" pocket contacts. These are the people who you wanted to follow up with after a week or so. They are good people to know, and you want to add them to your network. There's nothing pressing, but you don't want to lose track of them.

Don't just add them to your network list and forget about them for six months to a year from now. If you don't reconnect in a week or so, they will have burned out, like a coal separated from the fire. If you try to connect after a great deal of time and have to say something like, "Remember that Acme Tool Company social the August before last August? Well, I was the third person from the left." That won't work. They won't remember you and, if they do, they may be insulted at you contacting them a year later. No, these are people who you're going to contact in the next two or three weeks.

Now to make your *first* contact. Most experienced networkers like to do this by text, although email works, too. That way, you're in and out on your own terms. The problem with an email is it is so easy to dismiss, especially when most of us get 20 to 60 a day. And, the problem with a phone call is you will likely get sucked into a long conversation. No, we recommend texting because it works well. However, the best way for you to reconnect with this contact is whatever way will make you actually do it. Say something like, "I was just remembering that mixer a couple of weeks ago where I enjoyed meeting you and shaking your hand."

Bam! That's it.

You aren't asking for anything; you aren't offering anything. And you aren't selling anything. It's a contact. It's a touch. Now, wait two more weeks after that initial touch for the <u>second</u> contact. Reconnect using the same method as the first contact, two weeks earlier (text or email). That way, they're going to get used to you connecting that way. This second contact, presumably three weeks after the networking event, is the right time to sort:

1. People who you wish to sell <u>through</u>. They will become referral partners. This is a networking growth opportunity for you
2. People who you are going to try to sell <u>to</u>. They are going to be potential customers.
3. People who have a product or service you were interested in knowing more about to possibly purchase. If your interest was deep and the need pressing, they were probably in the "A" pocket. However, if the interest was marginal and the need down the road, they are going to be potential suppliers.

If you do these simple tasks regularly, you'll find your follow-up with people will become a system for you. It will become smooth and natural.

## COUP DE GRÂCE REJECTIONS

That leaves the "C" pocket people as in, "C you later." Hopefully, you don't have any cards left in your "C" pocket but, if you do, what do you do with them?

Bottom line: nothing. Throw the cards away. Don't make any contact with those people. This may sound harsh and cold but these are people who, for whatever reason, you've already decided you don't want to connect. If you've already determined you don't need to have any contact with them, then don't keep their contact information. Just get rid of those business cards. Don't even worry about it. Of course, you don't want to hurt anyone's feelings, but 99% of the time, they won't even know, and it will be a non-issue. For the 1% who will know and who will be expecting a contact, by polite but firm. It is a rookie mistake to try to be kind and allow them to think there's something in it for them or for you. Don't lead them on. That will just confuse both of you. It may even create some strife down the road.

You may have heard the French term, "coup de grâce." It's a fencing term from the 1700s. It literally means, the "cut of kindness." The better fencer would draw blood on an arm, or a cheek – maybe cut the ear or nose. There could be a thrust through the belly tissue. The weaker opponent is humiliated, defeated, dying. The "cut of kindness" is the stab that ends the suffering of the one who is mortally wounded. Although the term comes from the 1700s, the concept is much older than that. The soldier who thrust the sword into the side of Christ on the cross was administering a "coup de grâce."

Today, the phrase has come to mean any "decisive finishing blow, act, or event" as in "The decision to cut funding is the *coup de grâce* to the governor's proposal." Many youth sporting events have "mercy rules" that end a cruel lop-sided outcome.

Be bold. This is a business; it is *your* business. You handle it. You decide who you're going to work with. If they were in your "C" pocket, move on. Your main focus is on leveraging your networking groups and functions to be as effective as possible.

In this chapter, we have discussed tips and pointers to help you leverage a BRING! meeting or other networking event in your role as a group member. In the next chapter, we will take a look at your role as a guide, teacher, and as a friend for new networkers and visitors.

# CHAPTER 16

# SERVING OTHERS AS A COMPEER

A Compeer?

What's that...?

When we first began to prepare this book, we knew we needed to address the roles people played in a BRING!-type meeting. There needed to be good coverage of the various roles members played – one of the chief among those being welcoming, nurturing, and supporting new people. This chapter will be all about how to do exactly that. But we needed a term that fits that role.

## DEFINITION OF A COMPEER

BRING! members interact with guests, visitors, and new members in a variety of ways. Hopefully, seasoned networkers always offer a warm welcome and quickly become immediate friends to new people. Since that new person is in a foreign environment, the welcoming members will typically slip automatically into also becoming guides. They may eventually serve as mentors and teachers. We needed to choose a term to refer to these friendshipping and helping/mentoring roles.

We rejected the word, "host" because of its connotations to either: 1) the person in charge of the entire event or 2) someone entertaining others, as in a moderator or emcee. A welcoming friend doesn't play either of those roles, so the term "host" just doesn't work.

"Peer" seems too weak of a word. It lacks any action. It seems restricted to merely an associate, not an engaged and helping friend. A "peer" is totally equal and, while that is true for the status of the new people, the visitor wants and needs a friendly guide, not an equal peer. So, the term "peer" doesn't fit either.

On the other hand, while the role clearly calls for a friendly guide, it is much less than a formal educator. Terms like mentor, trainer, advisor, teacher all imply too much of a status difference and emphasize too heavily the role of educator. It misses the warmth of befriending people and gently guiding them, but only as needed.

A word seldom used today is a "compeer." This is a perfectly acceptable word that is no longer in common usage. According to Merriam-Webster, this word was first used in the 13th century.[95] It is a combination of a "companion" and a "peer" (hence, "com" and "peer"). But it also includes the nuance of a subtle role difference. It's more like being a warm caretaker such as a guiding parent. So, a "compeer" implies a nuance of a parent role. Then, too, in English peerage, a peer was originally the lowest level of nobility, but it was above a commoner. Hence, a compeer is almost, but not quite, an equal. This rarely-used word seems to work perfectly.

We put all of this together and defined a "compeer" as:

*A person of essentially equal status
but who takes on the warm, companion role of
welcoming, guiding, and mentoring when needed.*

So, that's good.

## THE ROLE AND RESPONSIBILITY OF A COMPEER

No matter why or how the prospects arrive, they typically feel awkward and lost. They don't know what to do, where to go, and whose example to follow. While many of these people will be new, there will be other new people there as well. In fact, there are at least four categories of Broughts:

1. Business Prospects – Over the course of time, you will invite special clients, repeat customers, or business prospects. If you belong to a strong group, this will enhance your credibility in the eyes of your Broughts. It will also strengthen your relationship with them. These business prospects will be any of the following:

- Prospects who represent very large accounts
- Frequent and repeat customer/clients

---

[95] See: www.merriam-webster.com/dictionary/compeer

- Contacts who could provide a gateway to a large number of other prospects in an organization (a CEO or buyer for a large organization or the regional head of an organization).

2. New Novice Professionals – Broughts provide an excellent opportunity for you to serve since they typically need the most help. They are not just new to your particular networking group, they are new to business in general and to the entire concept of networking – what it is and how it works. They are usually eager to learn. They will have little to no difficulty in accepting you in a power position.

3. Seasoned Professionals – Don't make the mistake of thinking all Broughts are new to networking. Some Broughts are seasoned networkers who have just moved into your area or are looking for a new group. It's true that they will be lost as to your particular group's practices and policies, but they may know more about networking than you do. Don't make them feel discounted and forced to demonstrate their knowledge. In the case of a Brought who is an experienced networker, a compeer will need to offer friendship and mentorship …with appropriate sensitivity.

4. Broughts Invited by Others – In addition to the Broughts that you bring to BRING!, there will be other new people invited by other members. It doesn't always follow that the networker who invited them is hovering over them or is even present at the meeting. It's not unusual to see Broughts show up only to find that the one who invited them isn't there at that time. Usually there is some valid reason.

The point is for you to be on the lookout for those new people as well. The majority are in an environment that is alien and foreign for them. They need to acclimatize. They need you. You have an opportunity, perhaps even an obligation, to help and serve them as well. You can be a powerful teammate for them, helping them to understand a little bit better how to harness the power of a networking group.

Each Brought will be lost in different ways and have very different needs. However, from the perspective of all four of these categories of Broughts, you are an expert. Don't be afraid of that word. As we will explain later in this chapter, in order to be an expert, you really only have to be two or three steps ahead of them in your abilities. That's enough for them to immediately want to be where you are and do what you do. That gives you opportunities to help them grow.

Recognize any of these types of new people. Greet them with friendliness, kindness, and patience. You were once there, too. Ask what brought them to your meeting. Find out what they do. Help them find a place to sit down and feel more comfortable.

Whether you invited them, or you have befriended Broughts who were invited by others, see if there are others at the meeting who they know, or they recognize. If they don't recognize anyone, introduce them to members who you know will have instant rapport both in personality and career paths. Introduce them to every person at their table. Get them a copy of any agenda, whether published or not. That will give the Broughts an idea of what to expect during the meeting, how events will unfold, and how long each item will last. (A sample agenda was shown on page zzz.)

As a compeer, you're elevating these Broughts out of an uncomfortable situation. To have some kind soul guide them through those first steps is priceless. They only have to feel a little bit less comfortable than you do in order for them to greatly appreciate what you're doing and how you are helping them. The benefits to you are stronger connections and expanded networks.

## THE BENEFITS OF SERVING AS A COMPEER

To this point, we have emphasized that there may not be any financial return for your efforts as a compeer. And that may be true …from a monetary point of view. However, there are intangibles that are extremely valuable. Let's look at four non-monetary ways in which both your Brought, and you, each benefit from your efforts as a compeer.

### 1. INSPIRING BROUGHTS – REINVIGORATING COMPEERS

When you invite a Brought to a networking function, you energize not one, but two, individuals. You inspire the Brought, and you re-invigorate yourself. Two birds with one stone.

We are not talking about major acts of service here. Few of us have many major opportunities to serve others. However, inviting Broughts to network with you and your contacts is an easy way to offer small help. You may feel that you have merely opened a door for an individual. But you have no idea what will happen when, and if, the person walks through that door. We have all heard the analogy that says:

> *"You may be able to count the seeds*
> *in an apple, but who can count the apples in a seed?"* [96]

There is a great truth in that small saying. You have no idea what good you may have started. Your simple invitation to the networking event could change a life. By so doing, it will enrich yours. When you make a difference to someone else, you simultaneously make a difference to yourself. Someone once said:

---

[96] This quote is often attribute to Robert Schuller, but that is unlikely. To read more about this truism, visit https://quotationcelebration.wordpress.com/2018/01/29/though-you-can-easily-count-the-seeds-in-an-apple-its-impossible-to-count-the-apples-in-a-seed/

*We make a living by what we get,
we make a life by what we give.*[97]

<u>Value for the Compeer.</u> Meetings are almost always more eagerly anticipated when you have a guest. You're able to feel your Brought's excitement. Your focus on the meeting increases. Your commitment to your career grows. What was old-hat now seems new again as you see it through your Brought's eyes.

Is there value to you of bringing a Brought to a networking event and serving as a compeer? Oh, yes…. You may be privileged to see someone blossom under your hands – and all because of an opportunity that you provided. How can that fail to result in a greater commitment to your own career? You have taken a duckling under your wing, and that is always invigorating and motivating. Now, do it again for someone else. And then again, for someone else.

## 2. SERVING AS A COMPEER ENHANCES RELATIONSHIPS

Even if those you invite to the networking event do not choose to move forward with your offer, they will almost always appreciate the attention you have paid to them and the kindness and interest you have extended. People respond positively to others who reach out to them, even if it ultimately does not go further. And, if your reaching out does open doors of opportunity, how much more will they see you as a mentor and/or a friend? Building and enhancing your relationship with your Brought turns out to be good for both of you – for your Brought and for yourself.

<u>Value for the Brought.</u> Most people thrive when they have an anchor. They are more comfortable expanding their comfort zones when they know they have a home base to which they can return. As an analogy, think of a halfway house (sometimes called, a sober living house) for someone who was just discharged from a treatment facility for overcoming drug addiction or alcohol dependency. Or think of a home for someone with a criminal background who has served a sentence and is now trying to reintegrate into society. Either way, a halfway house serves as that home base.

> *They are termed, halfway houses, due to their being halfway between completely independent living on the one hand, and in-patient or correctional facilities on the other hand.… Halfway houses provide social, medical, psychiatric, educational, and other similar services.*[98]

---

[97] This is often attributed to Churchill but that is denied by those who maintain a website on him. See: https://winston-churchill.org/resources/quotes/ quotes-falsely-attributed.
[98] Definition taken from: https://en.wikipedia.org/wiki/Halfway_house

Few recovering addicts or convicts can jump right back into a society that is very different from the one they knew prior to their incarceration.

As a compeer, you serve a similar function. New Broughts are more able to extend their comfort zones if they know they have the backing of a more established professional to whom they can return for feedback, problem-solving, and moral support. As their trust in you grows, and it will, you become even more of a touchstone. A touchstone is defined as a "test or criterion for determining the quality of genuineness of a thing."[99] Another source defines it as "a basis for comparison; a reference point against which other things can be evaluated."[100] This means that your Broughts will compare their experiences with you as their gold standard. They will see how you dress, hear how much you talk and how loudly you talk, watch the intensity with which you listen, model your boldness and enthusiasm. They will compare what they find with their reference point, which will be you.

With you as their touchstone, they will be more willing to extend themselves and expand their comfort zones. They will feel safe doing this because they know that they can come back to you as their home base. That is an awesome responsibility. It is the essence of being a true professional. It is a true gift.

Keep in mind, though, some of the Broughts will prefer to just sit and watch at first. Not all swimmers enter the water by cannonballing into the deep end. Some need to hold your hand at first. Maybe they prefer toe-dipping. They carefully and very slowly acclimatize their ankles, then their calves. They build up tolerance to the cold water on their legs and tummies and work up to their chests. It is only after time that they can dip their heads. You help your Broughts much more when you take your cues from them. Do not impose your way. Respect their styles and preferences. Hold their hands in the way they need you to.

Annette Goodheart, the therapist with the priceless name, taught a similar principle. An internationally respected lecturer, Dr. Goodheart wrote a book entitled, *Laughter Therapy: How to Laugh About Everything in Your Life That Isn't Really Funny.*[101] She worked with some of the saddest people you could ever meet: victims of severe physical and sexual abuse, cancer patients, alcoholics, sufferers of MS and AIDS, those recovering from bitter divorces, and so on. Dr.

---

[99] Definition from www.merriam-webster.com/dictionary/touchstone.
[100] Definition from www.finedictionary.com/touchstone.html
[101] Goodheart, Annette, 1994, *Laughter Therapy: How to Laugh About Everything in Your Life That Isn't Really Funny.* Less Stress Press: Santa Barbara, CA.

Goodheart taught that laughter was a cathartic process that helped to rebalance the chemistry of emotions. In her mind, raucous laughter (and snotty sobbing) served as cathartic keystones of deep healing. She taught us that we must help others laugh. But she was quick to add that she would always laugh <u>with</u> people, never <u>at</u> people. She would bring people to laughter, but she would never laugh louder than they did, never laugh longer than they did. Remember this with Broughts at a networking event. Never push them out of their comfort zones. Invite, do not overwhelm.

<u>Value for the Compeer</u>. Building and enhancing your relationships with your Broughts also helps and blesses you. It does this both indirectly and directly. Relationships are the essence of life. We are social creatures and relationships make us whole. Any shared experience cements the relationship between the people who go through the experience. This works for those sharing the joy of birth, the success of a business launch, or the trauma of a horrendous accident. Captain Chesley "Sully" Sullenberger and many of the passengers of Flight 1549 celebrate the anniversary of the "Miracle on the Hudson" – his safe landing of a heavily-damaged airliner on the Hudson River. This shared trauma created bonds that will never end.

Your airliner did not land on the Hudson River in the middle of winter, but the experience of enhancing a relationship over hot chocolate at a networking event still builds a bond of friendship and shared vision. After one or two of your guests have attended an event with you, there is likely to be common ground to prime deeper sharing and joint ventures.

That isn't all. Now that you have facilitated valuable introductions between a Brought and key professionals or group leaders, you have an opportunity to follow-up on those introductions. You now have far more than a "foot in the door" with someone you hardly know. You have created a friend, with all the connection and advantages this word conveys.

It is an axiom of service that you will feel the closest to those you serve. Enhancing your relationships with your Broughts will bring you great happiness. There is an often quoted saying that runs:

> *If you want happiness for an hour, take a nap. If you want happiness for a day, go fishing. If you want happiness for a year, inherit a fortune. If you want happiness for a lifetime, help somebody.*[102]

Building a relationship with someone else through helping them will also make you feel empowered. You will feel you have provided something of value – <u>you</u> are valuable. In other words, it makes you feel validated to be a value to others. As you feel you have value, you will tend to feel

---

[102] This saying is often given as a Chinese proverb. Charles Liu questions the validity of that attribution. See "The Beijinger" at: www.thebeijinger.com/blog/2017/03/13/ mandarin-monday-inspirational-chinese-proverbs

you have some power. Feeling that you have power (feeling empowered) may bring meaning to your life and success in your profession. In fact, this was the definition of "success" for Henry Ford. In the *Ford News,* he famously said:

*To do for the world more than the world
does for you – that is success.*[103]

Since we are discussing relationships, remember a relevant referral (**RR**) *is* a type of relationship. While we have discussed non-monetary benefits of relationships, the building of a professional network is largely with an eye toward *eventual* sales, most easily to those in your top 12% (but outside of meetings). As we have said earlier, that 12% is augmented as you strengthen relationships with Broughts, and as they share their own networks with you – your "pot of gold."

That is what it means to sell *through* your network, not *to* your network. And, make no mistake, this increase in sales opportunities is real and tangible. It will bear fruit, not just for you and your referrals, but for your Broughts as well. This is the power of networking (**NP**).

Here's the best part: these are sales without pain. Any pressure of making a sale is off. The Broughts will look for others to refer to you – either as future business contacts or as future customers. Inviting a Brought to a networking event is not a cold-call on the phone. It is not a cold-knock on a door. It is a time of near one-on-one attention with your Brought in which your credibility is enhanced, your prestige is raised in their eyes, and in which a relationship is strengthened. How do you put a price-tag on that?

Value for the Brought. If your Broughts are looking for help at your BRING!-type meeting, they are likely not doing as well as they hoped and expected. They may be discouraged and close to giving up. Attending your event may be the shot in the arm that they need for their emotional health and well-being. Everyone needs a friend. In a publication by the Mayo Clinic, it was reported that having friends:

- *Increases a sense of belonging and purpose*
- *Boosts happiness and reduces stress*
- *Improves self-confidence and self-worth*
- *Helps coping with traumas, such as divorce, serious illness, job loss or the death of a loved one*
- *Encourages the avoidance of unhealthy lifestyle habits, such as excessive drinking and lack of exercise*

---

[103] From the in-house newsletter, *Ford News,* March 1, 1926, p. 2

The article goes on to point out that:

> *Friends also play a significant role in promoting overall health. Adults with a strong social support have a reduced risk of many significant health problems, including depression, high blood pressure and an unhealthy body mass index (BMI).*[104]

Attending your networking group gives Broughts motivation and helps stave off discouragement. Having you as a touchstone and friend may bring them an overall sense of well-being.

## 4. SERVING GROWS PROFESSIONAL NETWORKS

Growing professional networks is what it's all about. Inviting a Brought to a networking event is a small step that rapidly expands. Throwing a small stone into the middle of a pond is also a small thing, but the ripples spread far out into the entire pond. Just so, inviting a single Brought to your networking function seems small. However, it is in reality the bringing together of two quite different professional networks.

Imagine your network of hundreds of contacts melding with your Brought's network of another set of hundreds of contacts. What would they mean to you? What doors would that open? What sales opportunities would that create for both the compeer and the Brought? What would 12% of the other networks joining your network mean to you?

<u>Value for the Brought</u>. When your new Broughts first walk through the door into your networking event, they are not thinking of their own social or professional network. They are walking into yours. You are likely looking forward to introducing them to contacts you know who will be helpful for them. Hopefully you're anxious to introduce them to your group's leadership. These new contacts may become industry allies for your Broughts, future allies, people of influence, new friends, possibly even future clients for your Broughts.

You are sharing your closest relationships and introducing your best allies to them, free. You are providing them with new contacts, yes, but you are also giving them opportunities to grow their business. The new contacts you have provided can be leveraged by your Brought into expanding opportunities for sales. They can sell their products and services through (not to) the new network that has unfolded before them.

What a gift that is! Think about what you have given. You have shared freely what is precious to you. It is the full meaning of kindness and service! We hope your Broughts realize all of this. We

---
[104] The Mayo Clinic Handbook for Happiness: Discover 4 Simple Steps to Live a Resilient, Joy-filled Life. From: https://www.mayoclinic.org/healthy-lifestyle/adult-health/in-depth/friendships/art-20044860

hope that they appreciate your generosity on their behalf. If your guests are new to networking, we hope they will understand and appreciate what they are being given. You are showing them one way to increase their bottom line and grow their businesses and careers. This is no small thing.

<u>Value for Compeer</u>. Your Broughts have met your professional network (or a part of it). Because of this, they have received a potentially priceless gift. In most societies and cultures, gifts are reciprocated. They are either paid-back or paid-forward, or both. In the principle of reciprocity, your Broughts can be expected to open their social and professional networks to you. Through one or two Broughts, you gain entry to hundreds of new contacts and potential clients. We talked about this as your pot of gold. But, hang on! If bringing one or two Broughts can do all this, what about bringing a different Brought each month? What about being given access to not just a couple but many new professional networks? That would be many pots of gold.

True, you are not doing this for self-serving reasons. However, those Broughts know entire communities of people who you do not know. They can, and likely will, open up new and untapped networks where you may find additional Broughts.

This is BIG.

Even if this were the *only* positive result of inviting a Brought to attend a networking event with you, receiving a pay-back invitation into their network would make your invitation well worth extending. Earlier, we talked about a mindset of abundance. With networking there is enough and to spare. The possibilities spread like ripples in a pond.

And, just as we hoped your Brought appreciates your gift, we hope you appreciate this gift from your Broughts. And it is not just you who will be profiting. You've introduced your Brought to others at the meeting. Just as you gain access to new networks, so the others will be given the same access. So you are helping 3+ people:

- your Brought
- yourself
- and others at the meeting.

In fact, you may be helping every other professional at the event. How's that for a win-win ...and win situation!? It is a magnification of effort.

This chapter has discussed many of the reasons to invite, welcome, and befriend Broughts at networking events. It has been a long chapter but, we hope, a valuable one. Remember, you were a Brought once. It is time to give back.

Talking about giving back, the next chapter was written to help you decide whether giving back might include service in the leadership of your BRING!-type meeting. That is an important question.

# CHAPTER 17

# TO BE OR NOT TO BE... IN BRING! LEADERSHIP

In most professional networking groups, there comes a time when you will be invited or elected to serve as a part of your group's leadership team. This is not a token of your superiority, though it is an indication your peers believe you are doing well. It may just be a function of rotation. But you have a decision to make. You may seize it as an opportunity or let it pass by as an unwanted burden. It is your choice. However, you need to make this decision with your eyes wide open to the pros and cons of taking on what will be a significant additional load. In this chapter, we talk about some of the very real pros and cons of being a part of your BRING! leadership team.

## THE PROS AND CONS OF VISIBILITY

There is no question but that leadership brings visibility. The leaders, be it president, vice-president, treasurer, membership secretary, and so on, are most likely sitting on a raised platform at the front of the room, front and center. Does that fill you with excitement …or dread? This element, visibility, can be either a pro or a con, depending on your perspective.

Let's start with the pros of visibility, and there are many.

### PRO: VISIBILITY BRINGS CREDIBILITY AND REFERRALS

A major advantage of being on the leadership team comes simply as a function of your physical location in the front of the room. You are front-and-center. Being in front of the group is a privilege. The more people see you there:

- the more they are reminded of you
- the more context they have for you
- the more opportunities you have to leave ongoing impressions
- the more you will be a part of members' experiences.

Even if you're not the one speaking at the time and/or you are not the principle leader (or chair, or president), you are on the leaders' platform. You are part of the leadership team. You are being seen. If there are other events going on in the room, there's always a glance toward leadership. And, every time there's that look toward leadership, in any kind of event, the perception of the value and credibility of the leaders, as a group, increases. The image of you as part of the team in charge is reinforced in the minds of the members.

This perception is strengthened or weakened by how you choose to react to others, what you choose to say, even by what you choose to wear, but that image is there all-the-same. Being in front of the room reminds people of you and enhances your credibility all the time, routinely, and consistently. That's a huge advantage. When things come up for members, or they recall something, you're more likely to be a part of their recollection. Your business is more likely to be brought in front of people's minds in conversations and activities, even in ones that happen outside of the meeting.

Here's something rather striking, too. Even if you said _nothing_ and you did _nothing,_ just your mere presence on the leaders' stand at the front of the room clothes you with credibility. You can't put a dollar figure on that advantage. It is amazing! People's gaze will be continually on you. You will be imprinted on their mind in that picture.

There are several ways you can even increase this. When things happen in the room, especially things you may not be directly a part of, always react positively and with a smile. Even if it's something you happen to disagree with and you think is inappropriate, still react in a positive (just less positive) reaction. This is impactful to people's minds. You are not the enemy. You are Ms. Positive or Mr. Positive. And, if other situations happen that are more encouraging, things you enjoy, react even more positively to those. Not over the top and not in a way that's boisterous and loud, but certainly in a way that shows appreciation and engagement. Again, this will be impactful. People will take the cue from you to also be positively engaged.

There is no question but that group members will come to see you as a professional who knows how to network. If for no other reason than your presence on the leadership team, they will relate to you as someone who has been successful in networking. Like it or not, they will consider you to be an expert who they should plug into in order to learn more about networking. Further, they will follow your lead and queue off you. All will know your name.

Some people enjoy the lime-light; some do not. Some, by nature, like being center stage; some enjoy being wallflowers. Which are you? If you are in business and sales and you like to network, you are likely the former, not the latter. But If you are intimidated by being in front of your peers, rest assured that feelings of discomfort will dim over time and with experience and success.

Some people, however, have a diagnosable social phobia to a point where it paralyzes them. You may simply not be able to master your discomfort at being in front of people and addressing them. If you recognize this reaction as unreasonable, excessive, and debilitating, consider if this is a reaction for which you need professional help and/or treatment.[105]

For most people, the question of whether increased visibility is comfortable or uncomfortable is really a secondary issue. It's largely irrelevant because you will adapt, either way. And when you do, consider how good the visibility of leadership could be for your business and your networking. You will meet the most people. Every time a guest is invited to a networking function, that Brought will be introduced to you. And, every time your BRING!-type meeting interacts with the leadership of other networking groups, that will involve you as well. As one of the group's leaders, you will be facing the entire group, almost all the time. You will have multiple chances in most of your meetings to introduce yourself again and again. You will say your name and your profession. As an automatic outgrowth of all that, your professional network will explode. This means that you will have an opportunity to give the most referrals. It will also provide opportunities to receive relevant referrals (**RR**).

What could this do for your business? Truly, the possibilities are staggering. If you don't value that, you may be in the wrong career field. This is the abundant pay you will receive for your leadership. This will make the sacrifices of time, the occasional criticism, and any passing discomfort evaporate like an early-morning fog.

## CON: VISIBILITY CAN ALSO BRING HEAT

Having said this, realize there may well be occasional criticism and discomfort. It won't all be peaches and roses. Many networking groups have an online presence. If they have, your name would be prominent on that online presence. That is worth thinking about. In the United States, nobody enjoys true privacy. According to one website:

---

[105] The *Diagnostic and Statistical Manual* of the American Psychiatric Association (DSM 5) gives 5 criteria for Social Anxiety Disorder including persistent, unreasonable or excessive panic attacks resulting from performance situations in which the person is exposed to scrutiny by others.

> *A basic Google search and a run through of your public social media pages …reveal who your friends are, where you live, what you like and dislike, what you do for a living, and what your interests are.*[106]

This problem is magnified if you have a prominent presence as a business leader. You potentially have a target painted on your back. If privacy is important to you, it's already too late. However, you will minimize the attention brought upon you by laying as low as you can. The principle here is the same as what keeps people from having their cars and their homes broken into – there are hundreds available to the thieves. They have no reason to look at your specific car or home. Any professional thief can break into any car or house anytime, anywhere. Essentially you are protected because you are one of many.

It is the same idea with online presence. Your prominent role as a business person – one who is successful enough to be the leader of a professional networking group – could increase negative as well as positive attention. If this is a major concern for you, then you will need to consider carefully if you want to be a significant part of the leadership team.

## CON: BECOMING THE SCAPEGOAT AND FALL-GUY

As another possible con to think about, understand that mistakes, stumbles, and failures of your networking group, even though they may be made by the membership as a whole, will tend to become yours. You will own them. If things go south, group members could focus blame directly on you – this is human nature.

Although he did not coin the phrase, "The Buck Stops Here," President Harry S. Truman had the sign shown below with those words sitting prominently on his desk throughout his presidency. The sign meant that "he didn't 'pass the buck' to anyone else but accepted personal responsibility for the way the country was governed."[107] If a mistake was made, he owned it.

A "scapegoat," at the time of Moses, was literally a goat that was placed in the center of a massive circle made up of the Children of Israel. On the Day of Atonement (Yom Kippur), the priests would symbolically cast the sins of the people upon the goat. The animal would then be driven

---
[106] https://scramsoft.com/article/why-you-should-care-about-your-online-privacy/
[107] History of this quote from: www.phrases.org.uk/meanings/the-buck-stops-here.html

away into the desert, carrying the sins of the community with it.[108] Today, the term, scapegoat, is defined as "one who bears the blame for others."[109]

You and the leadership team could be that scapegoat if things in your group go wrong. That is unlikely to happen, but factor it into your decision. This means you will need to have thick skin – or develop it quickly. No-one likes to be criticized, but both praise and criticism may come.

Presidents of the United States, regardless of party, are increasingly attacked by media and specialty groups. And the negativity seems to be increasing exponentially. They are loved by many, but they are also hated by many. If they are in office for approval and praise, they are in trouble! This goes for all of them. The average approval ratings for recent presidents are roughly similar. Politico fact-checked and verified that Reagan, Obama and Trump all "had similar polling results ...in the second year of their presidencies."[110] All were regularly, publicly, and loudly maligned.

As bad as it gets for US presidents, it is worse in other countries. At the end of their first terms, all three U.S. presidents, including Donald Trump, enjoyed approval ratings that were at least *twice* the approval rating that French President Emmanuel Macron faced in 2019. It seems, in some cases, resentment and anger are the costly price of leadership. Clearly, political leaders must have thick skins to endure the media criticism they face every day.

Similarly, in your tenure within your group's leadership, you will experience both approval and disapproval. Hopefully, it will occur at a much smaller scale. If you are a people-pleaser, what psychologists call, externally oriented, this may be difficult for you. If you value your sleep, you had better have a happy and successful group. In other words, you had better enjoy the approval of the majority of your group's members because, if there are problems, that could cost you a few nights of *zzzz*'s.

## THE PROS AND CONS OF EXPERT STATUS

Another result of being a part of the leadership team, and this holds for any capacity, is that people will come to see you as an expert. Again, there are pros and cons for this perception.

### PRO: EXPERT STATUS OPENS DOORS

We believe your being seen as an expert is a tremendous advantage and opportunity. Accept it. Enjoy it. Remember an expert is only somebody who is just a few steps ahead of others. As we've said earlier, you may not see yourself as an expert, but you are.

---

[108] Historical definition taken from: https://en.wikipedia.org/wiki/Scapegoat
[109] Modern definition taken from: www.merriam-webster.com/dictionary/ scapegoat
[110] Fact-checking of claim that Trump tied Obama at their same point in their presidencies taken from: www.politifact.com/punditfact/statements/2018/jun/18/gateway-pundit/headline-says-trump-tied-obama-same-point-presiden/

We're all learning to do what we do better, that's a given. But they will see you from that expert perspective. When the members of the group see you as an expert they want to relate to you, have more of your time, and want to engage with you.

You will be viewed as a person who knows...

- a little bit more about business
- a little bit more about networking
- a little bit more about the people in the group
- a little bit more about that networking group specifically

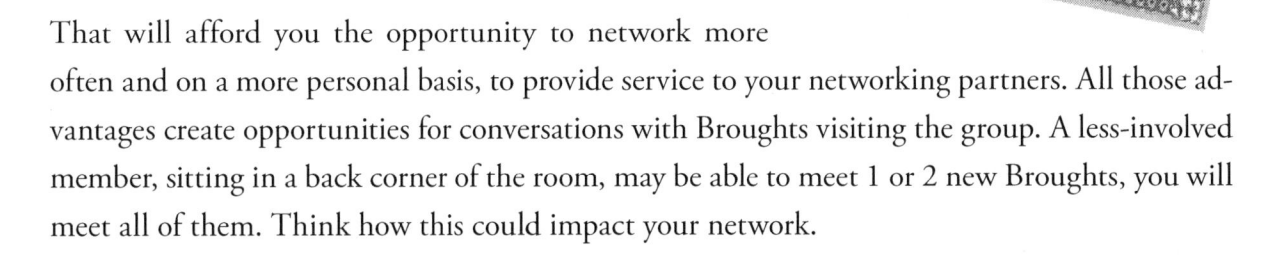

That will afford you the opportunity to network more often and on a more personal basis, to provide service to your networking partners. All those advantages create opportunities for conversations with Broughts visiting the group. A less-involved member, sitting in a back corner of the room, may be able to meet 1 or 2 new Broughts, you will meet all of them. Think how this could impact your network.

## CON: EXPERT STATUS FEELS AWKWARD

On the other hand, some people will see the perception of being an expert as a disadvantage. The opposite of being criticized too much may be being praised too much. Despite our efforts to normalize the word, expert, few of us are comfortable with being referred to this way. We live in a culture of humility (although some may argue this may be changing rapidly). For most of us, the term, expert, fits awkwardly, if at all. If you are just starting out, you may really feel overwhelmed with this perception. You may even think of yourself as inferior to your BRING! peers. You may doubt your ability to help members along their paths of professional networking. You may question your ability to lead meetings and make decisions that affect the group. If you feel this way, this could be a distinct con for you.

These feelings need to be, and will be, overcome with experience. You will settle into the role and be accepted as competent. In fact, many new leaders are shocked to see the degree to which many group members hang on their every word. It's as if, after a simple election, your words suddenly come from the most seasoned expert in the room. Some group members act as if your every opinion is absolute truth and total fact.

Keep in mind this perception comes from them, not you. But it is still heady stuff, and counterintuitive is the fact you will become accustomed to this status. In fact, you may grow to like it (too much). Some leaders get used to this intoxicating rush and rock-star status very quickly.

Many grow to like it – even need it! This can create a situation somewhat akin to a little boy playing with his father's gun – it can go off at any time. There is truth in Sir John Acton's 1887 comment "Power tends to corrupt, and absolute power corrupts absolutely."[111]

Weigh the pros and cons of the perception of you as an expert carefully in your decision. We hope you will decide it is more of an advantage than a disadvantage.

## THE PROS AND CONS OF EXTRA INVOLVEMENT

Carefully consider the time commitment of being in a leadership role. No matter what level of leadership you take on, there will always be something you need to do outside of the regular BRING! meetings. Expect it will cut into some of the other parts of your life. Will you be adequately compensated for this extra involvement? Well, this depends on what you see as compensation.

### CON: THE LACK OF MONETARY COMPENSATION

If you are looking for financial compensation for your time …no, you won't find it. On the pro side, there will be some perks, gifts, and price breaks, but it will not equal your worth. Among the few financial rewards you can expect, there will often be a reduction or elimination of group dues, but this will be far less than what a leader's salary would be. If your group charges high membership dues, a reduced membership fee is a nice token. If you meet in a coffee shop or restaurant meeting room, your meal may be included. Some members who arrive will bring gifts, samples, and coupons for their products and services. They may give those to you. That's nice. If you are traveling on behalf of the group, possibly to national networking events, part or all of your travel and accommodations may be covered.

These may or may not be sufficient advantages in your mind. But if you are looking for anything resembling a per-hour rate of return, you will not find it.

The compensation for most leadership roles comes in the form of opportunities to grow your network. So, a required commitment of non-compensated time could be a con for you. If the group is running well, the amount of time required should be minimal. However, in start-up BRING! networking groups or groups that rely heavily on leadership, this time commitment and effort could be quite significant. It could easily involve multiple hours per week. This time will not usually be compensated – at least in income revenue.

---

[111] See https://en.wikipedia.org/wiki/John_Dalberg-Acton,_1st_Baron_Acton

## PRO: THE MANY NON-MONETARY COMPENSATIONS

On the other hand, you will be richly and generously rewarded in non-monetary compensation. This will occur in many ways and in many forms. Let's talk about just four of those very real pros – but they are a big deal.

<u>Pro 1: Being on the Inside of a Close-Knit Team</u>. A major advantage of being selected or elected as a leader is you will become an insider in an important and close-knit team. Anytime you are a part of any team, you are able to build close bonds with the other power players. Remember, leadership teams typically meet together outside of the regular group time. They set goals, discuss policies, and make progress forward. This creates a team energy and forges bonds that last a lifetime.

The advantages to this is you see other leader's strengths in a working situation, and they see your strengths. The other group members do as well. Both the members and the other leaders see the things you bring to the table and they have more of a desire to make you part of other aspects of their lives also. Because they see the things you're able to do – not in theory, but in practice – you become a resource for them. You are validated and your contributions multiply as a result. Besides, it's fun to be on the inside of a dynamic growing organization and, if your BRING!-type meeting is not that, then something is wrong.

<u>Pro 2: You Will be a Decision Influencer</u>. Another advantage of being a part of the leadership team is you have the opportunity to help chart the course of the group. You get to help decide what direction the group will be taking in both large, and in seemingly insignificant, ways. Even if the group as a whole is the entity that votes on the decisions, you have a subtle yet profound influence on those decisions. Other members may raise their hands and offer 1 or 2 comments; you will offer 10 or 20. We are not suggesting you will become a dictator ramming through your ideas. It's that you are at the center of that discussion and have more influence than other group members. Examples of such decision areas might include:

- The decision to host an event in addition to the standard weekly meeting
- Support for an outside event sponsored by a group member
- The decision to cancel a meeting for a holiday or a funeral, and so on.

You can influence the promotion or avoidance of activities and help steer directions because of your role on the leadership team. This holds true even in groups that have a really tight structure in what they're doing. Even in such highly structured groups, members have a tendency to take on the personality of the leadership team. When you are a part of that leadership team, even in less visible positions like treasurer or membership secretary, your personality will be reflected in the course of the group.

Where before, you may have been frustrated with how some things were done, you now have direct input into changes and a host of improvements. As an effective leader, you will, of course, welcome the sharing of ideas, group discussions, and majority decisions. However, now your ideas will definitely be heard and felt. You have the potential to guide and sway decisions in directions that make sense to you both professionally and personally.

<u>Pro 3: Building Stronger Relationships with Members</u>. Another advantage to being in any leadership role is that you will have the ability to learn very quickly other members' names, as well as their habits. You will build stronger relationships with all of the members. As you sit in front of the room, observing week after week, you will see people click together, or even avoid each other, and you'll see professions that interact together. Those are all normal things, but to sit and watch this happen allows you to offer better referrals to the people in the group. Remember relevant referrals (**RR**) are the multiplicative part of the formula. The **RR**s supercharge your network power (**NP**). You're able to give higher quality referrals because you've been observing those people. This distinctly and directly impacts your networking power (**NP**), not just in that arena and in that meeting, but in all sorts of areas.

Watching people and learning who they are in personality and strengths and even weaknesses should significantly impact the type of referrals you give and to whom you choose to give them. For example, there may be several financial advisors, and you're not sure which person to give a referral to. Having observed them acting in the group, you are able to make a better referral. You can base your referral not on who you like the most, but on who would be the stronger fit. That is better for them and better for you.

In addition, because you are in a leadership role, people will gravitate towards you. They will want to be a part of you. They will work to nurture their relationship with you. In addition, it makes them feel more comfortable giving you referrals. This is always a good thing.

Another advantage is all Broughts will normally be introduced to the leadership team. If you're part of this team, you are privileged to meet more Broughts than most members. These are people who have contacts who you wouldn't normally have access to. Conversely you have contacts they don't have access to. So, by being introduced routinely to as many new people as possible, you are creating many new contacts (**CC**). Can't be better than that! This is the whole goal of networking.

Your leadership role is also a plus for the Broughts. In the past, when you, yourself, attended a new group or a new event, it has felt much better to know those in the leadership role. It felt as if you had an "in." Right? The same thing holds for other Broughts with you on the leadership team. Those Broughts want to feel like they have an "in," too. They want to know whoever it is who can help them navigate their transition into the group.

You are that person.

People who feel awkward, even after having attended a few times, are now a part of your network. When they keep coming to you to ask how to do this or that, they are moving closer to your 12%. They are asking you to nurture your network (**NN**), which in this case is them. Even better, they are the ones setting it up for you. Again, how great is this?

Pro 4: Learning and Growing as a Networker. When you are on the leadership team, you cannot help but enhance and hone your networking skills. It will happen as an automatic consequence of your service. Your time in leadership will force you to learn more about networking. If you weren't the expert the group takes you to be at the beginning of your leadership tenure, you will be by the end. Your service will force you to grow, learn, and develop your networking skills. It will enhance your ability to communicate with others to a greater degree than you ever thought possible. You will have earned an advanced degree in both networking and in leadership – a double major.

Another way of saying this is it will force you to be in a learning mode and not just in a participation mode. You become networkers – not just net-attenders. Attending a meeting, by itself, is not networking. You are not there to observe or to sell, you are there to network. So, you need to work the meeting. Being part of the leadership will help you accomplish this.

More than the opportunity to learn, though, is the opportunity for service. Being in a leadership role in your group, especially if you are called on to provide any kind of training, will help you to understand the importance of putting other people first. You will develop an interest in being able to help them. You will feel a greater willingness to understand them and overlook their idiosyncrasies. The bottom line is you will more keenly see the importance of them growing and succeeding in their businesses. As we have quoted two other times: "celebrate the success of others" because the rising tide of their successes will "float all ships" including yours.[112]

There are distinct advantages and disadvantages to serving in your group's leadership. Weigh each of these pros and cons carefully before you agree to serve. Only you and your loved ones can decide if the scale falls out on the positive or negative side. All we can say is that you need to understand the commitment it takes – but understand, too, how that commitment will heap benefits upon you.

The bottom line, though, is this: Make your decision based on sound logic and reasoning. Please don't reject this golden opportunity based solely on a lack of confidence. Confidence can, and will, be built. A lack of confidence can, and will, be overcome. Don't live below your potential simply because you were afraid to seize it.

---

[112] Quote from Phillips, Susan Elizabeth, 2001, in *Romance Writer's Report*; see: http://quotationsbywomen.com/authorq/52222/

# CHAPTER 18
# A FEW FINAL THOUGHTS

**Beyond Networking – Investing in Yourself**

Networking is about more than transactions or opportunities; it's about relationships that shape who we are and who we become. Benjamin Disraeli said it best: *"Nurture your mind with great thoughts, for you will never go any higher than you think."* Your professional network is a powerful tool for nurturing your mind, challenging your assumptions, and helping you grow. By surrounding yourself with individuals who inspire and uplift, you create a network that not only supports your career but also enriches your life.

**Networking as a Path to Personal Growth**

Networking teaches us fundamental lessons about human connection—listening, empathy, collaboration, and trust. These are the same qualities that enrich our personal relationships. When we approach networking with authenticity and a mindset of service, we practice the very skills that strengthen bonds with family, friends, and community.

Think about the essence of a referral: one person introducing another to help them achieve their goals. Isn't this the foundation of all meaningful relationships? Helping others, sharing opportunities, and creating connections are acts that transcend professional boundaries. They remind us that relationships are at the heart of a fulfilling life.

**Investing in Yourself Through Lifelong Learning**

One of the most powerful takeaways from this book is the realization that we don't know what we don't know. Every person we meet, every new group we join, and every experience we embrace is an opportunity to learn something new. Networking isn't just about expanding your circle; it's about expanding your mind.

By stepping out of your comfort zone and engaging with others, you expose yourself to ideas, perspectives, and knowledge you might never encounter otherwise. This commitment to lifelong learning is the ultimate investment in yourself. It ensures you're always growing, always improving, and always moving closer to your goals—both personal and professional.

**Networking as a Lifestyle**

At its core, networking is more than a skill; it's a mindset and a way of life. It's about showing up for others, being curious, and seeking ways to serve. It's about adopting a lifestyle of connection, contribution, and continuous improvement.

When you approach networking as an investment in yourself, you stop seeing it as a transactional activity and start seeing it as a path to transformation. The relationships you build, the lessons you learn, and the opportunities you create ripple out into every aspect of your life.

**THE Final Thought**

This book is just the beginning of your networking journey. The tools, strategies, and philosophies we've shared are meant to inspire you to take action, to embrace growth, and to make connections that enrich your life. But ultimately, the power lies with you.

Your professional network is an asset, but so is your personal growth. Investing in your ability to connect with others is one of the most valuable things you can do—not just for your career, but for your relationships, your community, and your sense of purpose.

So, as you move forward, remember this: Networking isn't just something you do. It's a reflection of who you are and who you're becoming. Make the most of it.

# GLOSSARY

**Top 12%ers** – *Relates to Rule of 12; the portion of people (approximately 12%) who you meet who will love you immediately and unconditionally just as there is another 12% who will reject you out-of-hand and for no particular reason and will never want to work with you as a contact*

**101-level Networking** – *Introductory understanding of networking typical of those who do not yet fully understand how powerful networking can be.*

**212-level Networking** – *An understanding of networking typical of those who are seasoned and fully understand that networking is about relationships and begins with giving, not getting. They understand the formula: **NP** = (**CC**+**NN**) x **RR**.*

**7-7-7** – *The principle that from 7 in the morning till 7 in the evening, 7 days a week, business professionals encounter opportunities to network that occur all the time and all around; they must be recognized, appreciated, and put to work.*

**A B C Pockets** – *A system for using designated jacket pockets to rank the relative value and then house the many business cards that are received at networking functions. A is for the most valuable "A+" cards, B means they'll "B for another time," and C is for the least valuable and destined to be thrown away; it means, "C you later!"*

**BOTTOM 12%ers** – *Relates to Rule of 12; the portion of people (approximately 12%) who reject you out-of-hand and for no particular reason and will never want to work with you as a contact.*

**BROUGHT** – *A person invited to a BRING! networking group as: 1) a prospect or client, 2) a novice networker, 3) or a seasoned networker in order to either: 1) strengthen a relationship, 2) establish credibility, or 3) display a sample group meeting.*

**BRING!** – **B**usiness **R**eferrals (and) **I**nteractive **N**etworking *This is not a suggested <u>name</u> for anyone's group but is a term, or synonym, for a <u>category</u> of networking groups: i.e. formal groups that are based on the BRING! philosophy.*

**BRING! Philosophy** – *The philosophy that groups exist for two primary and related purposes: 1. to facilitate relevant referrals among professionals who are bonded to each other based on strong relationships and 2) to encourage professional networking activities to be shared and interactive. The basic elements of the philosophy form the acronym: Business Referrals (and) Interactive Networking Group! (! to indicate importance).*

**Compeer** – *A person of essentially equal status but who takes on the warm companion role of welcoming, guiding, and mentoring.*

**Confidence-Enhancing Humor** – *Building others up in a constructive manner that compliments and enhances them, all delivered as humor.*

**Curse of Knowledge** – *When people forget that they didn't always know what they now know. It is most often revealed when they use terminology (jargon) or references that are specific to their company or industry or known only to a select few within their cadré or circle.*

**Get-Acquainted PIQ Session** – *One type of Personal Information and Question session, also known as a PIQ, is similar to what some networkers call a simple one-on-one. However, it is deeper and more intimate, usually involving an hour in a quiet place without interruptions. It is designed to get to know a contact, client, or colleague in depth including interests, history, family, and business and career aspirations.*

**Elevator Speech** – *A way to share your expertise and credentials quickly and effectively with people who don't know you. Designed to spark interest and open doors for further conversation. It is named an elevator speech to indicate that the length of the speech must be no longer than the time it takes to ride an elevator several stores with a stranger.*

**Informational PIQ Session** – *One type of Personal Information and Question session, also known as a PIQ, is an informal training or mentoring session, usually involving an hour in a quiet place without interruptions. It is designed to give aid to someone, usually a new networker, related to concepts or actions required for 212-level professional networking. It can also involve mentoring in non-business-related areas.*

**Interactive Networking** – *One type of Personal Information and Question session, also known as a PIQ, is an informal training or mentNetworking that emphasizes mutual engagement, active listening, and reciprocity to build trust and meaningful relationships.*

**Memory Hooks** – *Device or tool that is usually a part of a professional commercial or an elevator speech and is designed to make commercials "sticky" (unique and memorable); they can be verbal, visual, or involve give-away products or souvenirs.*

**Memory Taglines** – *Device or tool that is usually a part of a professional commercial or an elevator speech and is a catchy slogan, ditty, or 3- or 4-word label that encapsulate the brand of your product or services in just a few words and that a listener comes to associate with a presenter.*

**Networking Layers** – *The idea of categorizing contacts into close, intermediate, and outer layers based on the strength and frequency of interaction.*

**Networking Power (NP)** – *The outcome of effective networking, based on the Power Formula: NP = (CC + NN) × RR. It represents the strength and influence of your professional relationships.*

**Networking Return on Investment (NROI)** – *The measurable benefit gained from time, energy, and resources invested in networking activities, such as referrals, opportunities, or partnerships.*

**Professional Brand** – *The perception others have of your professional image, values, and skills, cultivated intentionally through consistent messaging and behavior.*

**Referral Partner** – *A trusted connection who actively refers clients, opportunities, or contacts to you, and whom you reciprocate with referrals.*

**Relevant Referral (RR)** – *An introduction to, or between, people in a professional network for the purpose of solving a problem or filling a need that one party feels. The problem may be solved via the product or services that one party represents or, in the case of a non-business-related problem, may be a general problem that is solved with no monetary return for either party.*

**Rule of 12** – *A principle that states that there is a portion of people (approximately 12%) who you meet who will love you immediately and unconditionally just as there is another 12% who will reject you out-of-hand and for no particular reason and will never want to work with you as a contact. The remaining 76%ers are people who are willing to listen to what you have to say, evaluate what you have to offer, and possibly purchase your product or services but they are not your core and your base.*

**Sticky Networking Commercial** – *A 30- to 60-second opportunity provided as a part of a formal networking meeting, for group members to communicate information to be recalled when a referral opportunity presents itself in the day-to-day life of each listener. They are "sticky" when they are memorable and remain in our heads long after the meeting is over.*

**Top 12%ers** – *Relates to Rule of 12; the portion of people (approximately 12%) who you meet who will love you immediately and unconditionally and want to do business with you and share referrals with you.*

# INDEX

| | |
|---|---|
| 101-level networkers | 218 |
| 212-level networkers | 142 |
| | |
| ABC pockets | 93 |
| Abundance Mindset | 68 |
| Active Listening | 93 |
| Additive Networking Elements | 180 |
| Additive v. Multiplicative Networking | 201 |
| Agenda, Importance of | 94 |
| Asking for Testimonials | 75 |
| Audience-Centric Presentation Style | 205 |
| Authenticity in Networking | 139 |
| | |
| Barriers to Confidence | 114 |
| Brianna's Story of Woe | 57 |
| BRING! Philosophy | 19, 89 |
| Building Rapport | 69 |
| Building Trust Through Referrals | 17 |
| Business Cards, Effective use of | 36 |
| Business Etiquette | 175 |
| | |
| Career Advancement Through Networking | 82 |
| Casual Social Networks | 153 |
| Client as Advocate | 31 |
| Cold Contacts v. Warm Leads | 167 |
| Collaboration in Networks | 40 |
| Collaborative Networking | 28 |
| Communication Nuances | 92 |
| Compeer | 203 |
| Confidence-Building Exercises | 191 |
| Confidence-Enhancing Humor | 66 |
| Consistent Follow-Up | 136 |
| Cooperation Over Competition | 109 |
| Coup de Grâce Rejections | 2 |
| Creating Contacts (CC) | 36, 73 |
| Creating Memorable Impressions | 17 |
| Cross-Pollination of Networks | 189 |
| Cultural Sensitivity in Networking | 108 |
| | |
| Decisive Actions in Networking | 208 |
| Difference Between Selling v. Networking | 132 |
| Digital Tools for Networking | 145 |
| Digital v. Analog Networking | 222 |
| Dottie's Lesson | 29 |
| Dress and Speech as Networking Tools | 58 |
| Dress for Impact | 81 |
| | |
| Effective Questioning in PIQs | 104 |
| Elevator Speech | 120 |
| Emotional Intelligence in Networking | 55, 131 |
| Encouragement, Power of | 85 |
| Engagement in Networking Events | 83 |
| Escalating to the Prez | 144 |
| Ethical Considerations in Networking | 50 |
| Expanding Professional Reach | 162 |
| | |
| Face-to-Face Networking | 209 |
| Family as a Network | 18 |
| Feedback Loops in Networking | 178 |
| First Impressions | 123 |
| Follow-Up Strategies | 88 |
| Following Through on Promises | 206 |
| Formal Networking Groups | 126 |

Friend Referrals  126

Generosity in Networking  212
Geographical
    Considerations  133
Giving Referrals as Strength  152
Giving v. Taking
    in Networking  195
Gratitude as Networking
    Power  158
Gratitude in Professional
    Relationships  177
Group Tone  104

Handshake, Professional  25
Humility in Networking  115
Humor  132
Impactful Introductions  128
In-Person v.
    Digital Networking  149
Industry Jargon
    and Accessibility  100
Influence of Mindset  15
Informal Networking  115, 216
Integrity in Networking  90
Intentional Relationship
    Building  35
Interpersonal Relationships  37
Invisible People
    in Networks  137

Leveraging Existing
    Networks  54
Leveraging Opportunities  170
Life-Long Learning
    in Networking  212
Limiting Beliefs
    in Networking  39
Listening More, Talking Less  81

Marc Evans Effect  68
Mastermind Group  80
Maximizing Networking ROI  38
Memorable Taglines  143
Memory Hooks
    in Commercials  198
Mentoring Relationships  119
Mindset Shifts for
    Networking Success  113
Mindsets for Success  219

Miracle of the Ripple Effect  224
Multiplicative Power
    of Referrals  7
Mutual Support
    in Networking  153

Networking
    7-7-7 Principle  66, 137
Networking Agenda  214
Networking as a
    Service Model  20
Networking as
    Emotional Currency  176
Networking as
    Emotional Support  24
Networking Challenges
    and Solutions  148
Networking Events
    as Lifestyle  204
Networking Events,
    Leveraging  192
Networking Groups,
    Logistics of  126
Networking Lifestyle  173
Networking Power (NP)  7, 221
Networking Power Formula  221
Networking Tiers,
    First and Second  87
Networking Tips
    for Introverts  72
Networking with Abundance,
    Not Scarcity  149
Non-Monetary Costs
    of Networking  201
Nurturing Your
    Network (NN)  153

Obstacles to Networking
    Success  21
Opportunities for Growth  177
Overcoming Networking
    Fatigue  8
Overcoming
    Past Programming  169

Park-n-Ride Fiasco  123
Peer-to-Peer Networking  203
Perceived Value Barometer  44
Personal Branding
    Through Networking  22

Personal Connections 90
Personal Growth
    Through Networking 96
PIQs (Professional Interview
    and Questions) 166
Power Formula for Networking
    NP=(CC+NN) x RR 37
Power of Personal Stories 136
Power of Referrals 20
Practice and Preparation 100
Presentation Skills 101
Proactive Networking
    Strategies 191
Professional Attire 135
Professional Growth
    Through Networking 146
Professional Handshake 10, 152
Professional Networking
    Toolkit 169
Professional Relationships 47

Rebuilding
    Broken Networks 148
Reciprocity in Networking 58
Referral Etiquette 220
Reframing Challenges 47
Relationship-Building 130
Relevant Referrals (RR) 18, 53, 139
Relevant v. Irrelevant
    Referrals 134
Ripple Effect in Networking 89
Role of Gratitude
    in Networking 166
Rubber Duckie Follow-Ups 67
Rule of 12 94, 184

Scaling Networking Efforts 217
Scarcity Mindset 44
Self-Awareness
    in Networking 106
Sell Through, Not To 7, 203
Service as a Mindset 122
Service Through Sales 140
Service Oriented 203
Sharing Contact
    Information Tactically 98

Sharing Testimonials 185
Short-Term v. Long-Term
    Networking 169
Social Media Networking 204
Social Proof
    Through Networking 145
Soft Skills for Networking 29
Speaking with Impact 61
Sticky Commercials 117, 156
Strengthening Connections 210
Strengths, Identifying 165
Structured Networking
    Presentation 124
Support Within a Network 90
Systematic Networking
    Strategies 112

Team Collaboration 115
Testimonial Stories 162
The Art of Testimonials 201
The BRING! Meeting
    as a Prototype 150
The Curse of Knowledge 96
The Family Network 117
The Value of Social Proof 178
Time Management
    in Networking 17, 165
Trust-Building 1
Types of Networking Groups 90

Value of Networking 101
Verbal Memory Hooks 46
Visibility Brings Credibility 188
Visibility in Leadership 224

Weekly Presentations 105
Why Networking Matters 38
Work-Life Integration
    in Networking 9
Written Testimonials 48

Your First Network 182, 204

Zap Collars and
    Pachyderm Strings 211

Zig Ziglar 5

Made in the USA
Columbia, SC
18 January 2025

ba40bed1-2a35-429b-b8dc-38e428ec8fe6R01